VULNERABILITY AND YOUNG PEOPLE

PEOPLE

Care and social control in policy and practice

Kate Brown

First published in Great Britain in 2017 by

Policy Press
University of Bristol
1-9 Old Park Hill
Bristol
BS2 8BB
UK
t: +44 (0)117 954 5940
pp-info@bristol.ac.uk
www.policypress.co.uk

North America office:
Policy Press
c/o The University of Chicago Press
1427 East 60th Street
Chicago, IL 60637, USA
t: +1 773 702 7700
f: +1 773-702-9756
sales@press.uchicago.edu
www.press.uchicago.edu

© Policy Press 2017

British Library Cataloguing in Publication Data
A catalogue record for this book is available from the British Library

Library of Congress Cataloging-in-Publication Data
A catalog record for this book has been requested

ISBN 978-1-4473-1818-7 paperback
ISBN 978-1-4473-1817-0 hardcover
ISBN 978-1-4473-1822-4 ePub
ISBN 978-1-4473-1821-7 Mobi
ISBN 978-1-4473-1819-4 ePdf

Cover design and image: Kenn Goodall
Printed and bound in Great Britain by CPI Group (UK) Ltd, Croydon, CR0 4YY
Policy Press uses environmentally responsible print partners

MIX
Paper from
responsible sources
FSC
www.fsc.org   FSC® C013604

Contents

List of tables and figures

Tables

Figures

Acknowledgements

I am lucky to have had support from lots of people to produce this book. I am deeply grateful to Malcolm Harrison, who nurtured my interest in vulnerability and whose expertise and generous engagement with my work was extremely formative. John Hudson's guidance and mentorship have been invaluable, especially in writing stages. Teela Sanders encouraged me from the beginning and helped keep momentum going. I am also very fortunate that colleagues in the Department of Social Policy and Social Work at the University of York have supported me in other areas of academic work, which has been so important, thank you in particular to Lisa O'Malley, Sharon Grace and Peter Dwyer.

The research study was funded by Leeds University's School of Sociology and Social Policy, and staff and students there provided valuable intellectual and practical input. Contemplating vulnerability with a range of people contributed to the development of ideas, at conferences and events, and via comments on earlier work. John Flint, Nick Emmel, Jo Phoenix, Kathryn Ecclestone, Carol-Ann Hooper and Rachael Dobson deserve special mention but thank you to others who shared thoughts and suggested improvements. Valued support has come from the publishers. I am also grateful to Matthew Bell for help with editing and historical research, and to Kenn Goodall for his excellent cover design.

Special thanks go to the young people who participated in the study. The experiences they shared were not always easy to discuss, and I hope that the way their voices appear in the book does justice to the openness, tenacity, goodwill and humour with which they told their stories. The research would not have been possible without the dedication and support of colleagues involved in local services, who allowed me to work alongside them at a time of significant struggles with resources. I do not include names for reasons of confidentiality but really appreciate their assistance and interest in the research. Thank you also to key informants who shared their time and expertise so willingly.

Friends and family helped me to go the distance. Ruth Patrick always helped make sense of things. For good times and troubles shared along the way, thanks to Scott Brown, Kate Jones, Anna Shemeld, Naomi Hersey, the Sharkeys, and friends in Leeds. For their never-faltering care and concern, thank you to my parents, Liz and David Brown. Finally, a massive thank you is due to Chris Sharkey, for his patience, encouragement and partnership in the struggles and adventures of producing things.

ONE

The vulnerability zeitgeist

When Chris was 10 years old, he was taken to Pakistan by his family, where he was regularly beaten by his uncle for a period of six years. He returned to England to live with his parents and shortly afterwards became homeless after fleeing from his abusive father who had threatened to kill him. At age 17, he had recently secured the keys to his own social housing tenancy in a large inner-city housing estate and was being supported by a voluntary sector service for 'vulnerable' children. When asked about his vulnerability he responded:

> People have even more difficulties than me. This might not be such a big thing. I've seen other people have more difficulties even worser than these. Yeah it's difficult, but not difficult difficult, I'd say.

Alicia had become involved in heroin use and selling sex at the age of 14, through an older boyfriend. When she was 15 she slept in a tent for a month after running away from her care home because of bullying. She had been prosecuted criminally a number of times, for various offences that included stealing tanning wipes from a chemist. Alicia no longer took heroin or sold sex but still used other drugs sometimes, and explained her vulnerability as follows:

> If my mates are doing like M-CAT [mephedrone] or something like that, I'm easily persuaded to take it, if they're going 'oh come on, take it'. But then I think in my head that's my decision, everyone makes decisions like that every day, but it doesn't mean you're vulnerable, it just means that you've made a decision to do something like that.

While 'vulnerability' would seem appealing as a 'common-sense' concept to help make sense of these stories and accounts, a number of tensions and policy matters are raised by the young people's experiences and views. Those who are supposedly vulnerable may be resistant to being classified in this way. At the same time as being seen as vulnerable, they may be transgressive or criminal, raising the thorny issue of whether support or discipline is the most appropriate response. Attention to vulnerability opens up difficult questions about deservingness, human agency, care and social control. This book addresses and unpicks some of these complexities. It takes the idea of vulnerability as a starting point to explore what it means to be vulnerable, what the conceptual dimensions of vulnerability might be and the implications of the notion as a governance mechanism in contemporary society.

Speaking to narratives of empathy and inclusion, policies and practices that seek to help those who are considered to be vulnerable have strong moral overtones. At first glance, such initiatives seem to support the pursuit of social justice and the protection of those who need it most, but closer attention to the prioritisation and exceptional treatment of vulnerable citizens reveals a more complicated picture. A shadow concept of 'risk', vulnerability is frequently drawn on across policy, practice and research and in everyday life, yet has received relatively little scrutiny. This lack of critical attention seems surprising given that ideas about vulnerability shape justifications of state intervention in citizens' lives, influence allocations of resources and play a role in defining social obligations.

Deployment of vulnerability in policy arenas such as housing, criminal justice, provision for disabled people, welfare and child protection has largely remained un-interrogated, despite complexities such as those raised by Chris's and Alicia's stories and accounts. Attention to such matters would seem especially important given that systems that aim to support or protect 'vulnerable' people affect those whom it is generally considered we have special moral obligations or duties to assist and protect.

Building on the small body of work that has developed insights into the concept, this book analyses theories, mechanisms and realities of vulnerability, taking young people as a case study group through which to explore the implications of the notion on the ground. Official understandings of vulnerability are reviewed, academic ideas about the concept are summarised and investigated, and the book also draws on in-depth case study research into how vulnerability was operationalised in services for 'vulnerable' young people in a large northern city in England. At the heart of the book is a concern with exploring 'lived experiences' of vulnerability alongside how these might relate to 'official' accounts and wider welfare and disciplinary developments. There is a particular focus on vulnerability as a conceptual instrument in processes of inclusion and exclusion. As well as examining care and support processes, matters of social control are also addressed, with attention given to how vulnerability in certain contexts can function simultaneously as a tool for assistance but also as a subtle disciplinary mechanism.

Although vulnerability is used frequently across the social science literatures, its meaning remains an elusive matter and taken-for-granted assumptions about the concept are common. As Wiles (2011: 579) argues, vulnerability is a 'vexed subject'. In terms of etymology, both 'vulnerable' and 'vulnerability' are words derived from the Latin term '*vuln*', which means 'wound' or 'to wound'. Also noted as significant in the origins of the word is the quality of 'weakness' (circa 1300). These meanings and associations have shared connotations of fragility, defencelessness and deficiency, framing those who are vulnerable as being different or 'other'. Such resonances endure in contemporary and normative uses of the term, where to be vulnerable is often construed as some kind of failure. As Harrison (2008: 427) notes, vulnerability can be seen as the antithesis of positive capacity or power, or what he calls an 'un-power'.

Yet the meaning of vulnerability would appear to be shaped by the historical, political, socioeconomic and disciplinary context in which it is used. Almost every commentary that considers vulnerability notes a problem of definition (see for example Chambers, 1989; Appleton, 1999; Levine et al, 2004; Fineman, 2013; Mackenzie et al, 2014). Increasingly, the term seems to be used less in its relational sense (where someone is vulnerable to something specific, such as illness or violence) and more as a stand-alone term. Although definitions have been proposed, wide divergences in understandings become apparent when these are reviewed together. Some scholars have argued that this fluidity and amorphousness make vulnerability well suited to facilitating understandings of the diversity and depth of human experiences of adversity (Misztal, 2011; Wallbank and Herring, 2013). Others have questioned whether the term is useful at all (see Fawcett, 2009; Daniel, 2010). Whether or not vulnerability is too vague a notion to be valuable and the issue of how it can be defined are key questions that the book returns to.

Bringing academic views of vulnerability into focus reveals a kaleidoscope of perspectives. The concept has been advanced almost evangelically as being able to offer a unique platform for the realisation of social justice (Goodin, 1985; Beckett, 2006; Turner, 2006; Fineman, 2013), criticised for its damaging and potentially stigmatising effects (Wishart, 2003; Hasler, 2004), noted as tied to behavioural or 'psychoemotional' understandings of social problems (Ecclestone and Goodley, 2014; Ecclestone and Lewis, 2014) and condemned for problematic paternalism (Dunn et al, 2008; Furedi, 2008).

A slippery idea loaded with moral and ethical connotations about deservingness and entitlement, vulnerability is an under-researched and highly relevant concept in debates about citizenship and the relationships between individuals and the state. Distinguishing people as vulnerable implies something about a person's degree of choice or human agency in their circumstances, carrying inferences about the responsibility and duty of the state to assist them. Vulnerability therefore occupies a surprisingly uncharted position at the forefront of fractious and long-running debates about the 'deserving' and 'undeserving' in society.

Vulnerability is also a prominent term in everyday language and in media discourses on social problems, and there are some indications of public interest in the notion. According to a Google book search, the incidence of the term increased by around 650% from 1950 to 2000.[1] In 2010, Brené Brown – a psychologist and social work academic in the United States – delivered a TED talk entitled 'The power of vulnerability',[2] which at the time of writing was one of the most-watched TED talks, having been viewed by over 18 million people and translated into more than 38 languages. Brown's (2012) book *Daring Greatly: How the Courage to Be Vulnerable Transforms the Way We Live, Love, Parent and Lead* has had similar success. The rising popularity of the use of the term 'vulnerability' has been a focus of concern for some, who see this as part of moves towards citizens' notions of themselves as fragile and having 'suffered trauma' (McLaughlin, 2012: 98), bolstering the advancement of 'therapy culture' (Ecclestone and Goodley, 2014; Ecclestone and Lewis, 2014) and the encroaching authority of the state (Furedi, 2007, 2008; Waiton, 2008; McLaughlin, 2012). When these competing ideas are seen together, a rather murky picture becomes evident, with 'vulnerability' emerging as a concept that seems useful for naming emotional difficulties and previously normalised injustices, but also a potential buttress for a troubling problematisation of adversity.

This opening chapter sets out the importance of the concept of vulnerability in society, exploring its relevance in policy and practice. The idea is advanced that vulnerability appears to be something of a conceptual zeitgeist or 'spirit of the time' in contemporary social policy; a notion that is intellectually fashionable, reflecting and influencing welfare and disciplinary processes in a range of ways (see also Brown, 2014a, 2014b). The following section explains how I became interested in the concept as a practitioner and manager in services for vulnerable groups. An overview is then given of how the notion appears and is contested in literature, policy and practice, with a particular focus on vulnerability and youth. The relevance of vulnerability at a time when the behavioural regulation of marginalised populations is intensifying (Dwyer, 2004; Wacquant, 2009; Harrison and Sanders, 2014) is also highlighted. A summary of the theoretical orientation of the book follows, and the research methods used in the empirical study are outlined in brief. Finally, the chapter gives an overview of book's key messages about the concept of vulnerability as a mechanism of care and social control in contemporary policy and practice.

Researching vulnerability: motivations and aims

My interest in vulnerability developed gradually, through a mixture of experiences working in voluntary sector services for 'vulnerable' people, and later through returning to university to learn more about social approaches to 'problem' groups. In early employment as a support worker for sex workers and sexually exploited children, I often invoked the term 'vulnerable' when advocating for those I considered to be experiencing a particularly difficult set of circumstances. Later, in management roles, I would make the case to funding bodies and local authority commissioners that they should finance my particular agency because we were involved in supporting some of the 'most vulnerable' in society. Research has shown that taking this approach to describing and classifying service users is not uncommon (Appleton, 1999; Mulcahy, 2004; Warner, 2008). Despite my continued reliance on the notion of vulnerability, I grew increasingly uneasy about this.

Work with sexually exploited young women had highlighted divergences in opinions about vulnerability. Young people I had worked with were sometimes resistant or apparently unresponsive to attempts to support them, and could be volatile in their responses to certain interventions or practitioners. Yet policy and guidance in this area paid little attention to such challenges, focusing instead on the 'vulnerability' of the young people (see DH and Home Office, 2000). Although in some ways this seemed a sensible strategy to 'protect' young people, it also struck me that some professionals seemed to perceive the more 'difficult' young people as less vulnerable and more in control of (and culpable for) their actions. As one young woman with a history of heroin use and selling sex since the age of 12 explained to me: 'Some kids get left out of being seen as victims. They don't seem vulnerable, but just because they don't seem vulnerable, doesn't mean they aren't' (Brown, 2004: 19). Her comment resonated with my concerns at the time; vulnerability appeared to some extent to be conditional on 'appropriate' behaviour.

Notions of 'deservingness' continued to intrigue me and university studies sensitised me to the subtle ways in which support services could also be part of systems that might regulate the behaviours of people who are considered problematic. After conducting some small-scale empirical research on young people's experiences of Anti-Social Behaviour Orders (ASBOs) (Brown, K., 2011a), it struck me that although young people served with ASBOs had much in common with sexually exploited young women, 'official' views of their vulnerability were very different. While the 'antisocial' young men were generally seen as deviant and rebellious, the young women were most often positioned as 'vulnerable victims' (officially, at least). The apparently gendered implications of vulnerability interested me. Initial investigations revealed that academic work on the concept was scarce and that the majority of the literature seemed to relate to 'vulnerable adults' (see Hasler, 2004; Beckett, 2006; Dunn et al, 2008; Hollomotz, 2011). This crystallised my interest in vulnerability and its implications for young people, and a research project in this area followed.

The research conducted for the book aimed to investigate the concept of vulnerability and its use in the care and control of young people, and research questions that orientated the study were as follows:

- How is the concept of vulnerability constructed in selected policy domains where it appears as highly significant?
- What can a case study tell us about lived experiences of vulnerability and how far do young people defined as vulnerable share practitioners' and policy makers' understandings of vulnerability?
- How are the concept of vulnerability and its practical effects received and perceived by young people, and what are their responses to vulnerability-based notions/interventions?
- Where young people are deemed vulnerable but also as needing to be socially controlled, how does this affect interventions and inform understandings?

As the work developed, tensions between young people's perceived vulnerability and their potential to also be transgressive seemed increasingly significant. How such complexities played out on a daily basis in service interventions came to be an area of particular interest. A more general concern related to preoccupations with young people as a 'social problem' (Kelly, 2003; Squires and Stephen, 2005; France, 2007). Although there is nothing new about public perceptions of moral decline related to youth (Cohen, 1972; Pearson, 1983, 2009; Hendrick, 2006), the idea of young people's 'dangerousness' remains a pervasive influence on social policy developments, as reactions to rioting in towns and cities across England in August 2011 highlighted (see Flint and Powell, 2012). Young people's voices are often side-lined in debates about the threats they pose, so a broader aim was that the study might contribute something to understanding the social worlds of young people who are seen as problematic.

'Vulnerability' and 'youth': contested territories of care and control

Academic interest in the concept of vulnerability seems to be burgeoning, although it remains an underexplored notion in social policy and sociological research, certainly in comparison to other ideas such as risk. Writers from different disciplines in the social sciences have variously been critical of how notions of vulnerability play out in society. That vulnerable people's own opinions about their care are sometimes overridden by decision makers on the basis of their vulnerability has been a particular focus for concern, especially from disability writers (see Hasler, 2004; Dunn et al, 2008) and for those interested in solidarity based on entitlement and 'new social movements' (McLaughlin, 2012). Criticisms of the concept's use in welfare systems often draw attention to the way in which presumed 'inherent' vulnerability can function as an excuse for failing to tackle overarching structures and systems of marginalisation (see Lansdown, 1994; Hollomotz, 2011), foregrounding personal experience in the difficulties experienced by individuals (Wishart, 2003) and serving to legitimise justifications for the narrowing of provision (Lévy-Vroelant, 2010). Focusing resources selectively on those who are most 'in need' is unlikely to run into political opposition in a context of economic austerity, but arguably this strategy can detract attention from a broader view of how resources should be distributed in society.

Alongside such critiques, a small but growing number of commentaries emanating particularly from moral philosophy and critical-legal studies have argued that vulnerability offers a conceptual basis on which to reorganise society in a more 'just' way. Interest in vulnerability in this field stems from the moral weight and emphasis on social obligations that the notion carries (Goodin, 1985; Turner, 2006; Mackenzie, 2009; Mackenzie et al, 2014). Focusing on human interdependence, writers who have advanced the concept in academic work see the state of vulnerability as something that all humans share; a potentially unifying and transformative notion that is able to offer a powerful model for a reorganisation of the relationships between

7

citizens and the state (Kittay, 1999; Butler, 2004; Beckett, 2006; Turner, 2006; Fineman, 2008). In the United States, Martha Fineman has been at the forefront of developing this work via the 'Vulnerability and the Human Condition Initiative',[3] a critical-legal studies research centre that advances the 'vulnerability thesis' as the starting point for meaningful social change. The website for the centre proposes that vulnerability is 'the characteristic that positions us in relation to each other as human beings and also suggests a relationship of responsibility between the state and its institutions and the individual'. In academic writings, Fineman (2013: 13) explains that the 'vulnerability thesis' represents 'a stealthily disguised human rights discourse, fashioned for an American audience'. Such ideas have been formative in the development of similar work in the UK (see Beckett, 2006; Wallbank and Herring, 2013) and also in Europe (see Peroni and Timmer, 2013).

The emotive ethical connotations attached to vulnerability would seem especially prominent when referring to children. According to normative understandings of childhood, children tend to be positioned as innately vulnerable and largely unaccountable for their lives and actions. Longstanding and widely held 'lifecourse' understandings of childhood assume that children are inherently and inevitably vulnerable due to their incomplete 'stage' in the developmental process, rendering them at risk from disruptions to a 'successful' or 'normal' transition to adulthood (see Bynner, 2001; Malin et al, 2002). However, representations of children as passive, incompetent and incomplete also compete and overlap with the idea that children are active agents in the social process (see James and Prout, 1997). Critics influenced by social constructionist ideas have called developmental accounts of childhood into question (see James and Prout, 1997; Mayall, 2002; Moran-Ellis, 2010), highlighting the structural nature of differences experienced by children and young people. Despite these 'new sociology of childhood' ideas, understandings are still heavily influenced by assumptions that children are among the 'most vulnerable' in society, but for young people, vulnerability is a more complicated matter. The subjective nature of 'youth' is well documented (Muncie, 1999; Lee, 2001) and there are varying ideas of where youth begins and ends, with young people seemingly occupying a kind of developmental limbo in terms of accountability, autonomy and citizenship responsibilities.

Commonly held perceptions about the apparently deteriorating behaviour of 'deviant youth' seem to complicate matters further (see Kelly, 2003; Brown, 2005; Squires and Stephen, 2005). A classic example of the ambiguities that underpin attitudes towards children and young people's deviance, vulnerability, agency and accountability is perhaps the case of Robert Thompson and Jon Venables who in 1993, at the age of 10, killed two-year-old James Bulger in Liverpool (see Fionda, 1998). While the *Daily Star* responded to the guilty verdicts with the headline 'How Do You Feel Now You Little Bastards' (25 November 1993), many felt that the boys should have been afforded special allowances within the criminal process due to their age, 'competency' and status as children. When young people behave problematically, questions inevitably arise about their responsibility for their actions and the ways in which their circumstances (or vulnerabilities) determine their accountability for their transgressions. While all young people seem to be classified as vulnerable in relation their age, there also appear to be certain young people who are seen as especially vulnerable in various ways, leading to debates about when exceptionalism is required and what balance of care and social control might be most appropriate as a response. Considering the complexities that underpin considerations of the rights and responsibilities of younger citizens, McLeod (2012: 12) notes that vulnerable young people can be seen to represent the 'antithesis of proper citizenship'. Focusing on young people who are seen as especially vulnerable thus provides rich and fertile ground for exploring the key dimensions of 'vulnerability' as a concept.

Vulnerability in policy and practice

Vulnerability has rarely been brought to centre stage in analysis of policy developments, yet has now become a significant mechanism in the processing and management of certain individuals and groups. While focusing mainly on contemporary developments, it is important to note that vulnerability discourses have been operating in UK policy for some time. For example, in 1957, the Wolfenden Report on 'prostitution and homosexual offences' made reference to the need to provide safeguards to those who were 'specially vulnerable because they are young, weak in body or mind, inexperienced, or in a state of special physical, official or economic dependence' (Wolfenden, 1957: 9-10). The concept appears to have been particularly significant before 1997 in arenas such as nursing (see Appleton, 1999) and housing (Carr and Hunter, 2008), but literature and legislation archive searches on vulnerability would indicate that it took on a new significance in policy during the New Labour era and endured in popularity under the Conservative–Liberal Democrat coalition government, elected in 2010 (see also Brown, 2014b).

Vulnerability is now used as a classifier for exceptional treatment in a wide range of welfare and disciplinary arrangements. For example:

- those deemed as vulnerable are legally entitled to 'priority need' in social housing allocations (see Carr and Hunter, 2008);
- vulnerable witnesses are treated differently in court (see Hall, 2009);
- vulnerable victims of crime are seen as requiring a special response in the criminal justice system (see Roulstone et al, 2011; Roulstone and Sadique, 2013; Campbell, 2014); and
- vulnerable adults are responded to in different ways under the law both in the UK (Dunn et al, 2008) and in Europe (Peroni and Timmer, 2013; Timmer, 2013).

Beyond the UK, the notion increasingly features in framings of European and global problems such as poverty, natural disasters, armed conflict, financial crises, unemployment and environmental changes (see Adger, 2006; Furedi, 2008; Ranci, 2009; Bradshaw, 2013; OECD, 2013; UNDP, 2014). Although primarily focusing on the concept as it operates in a predominantly English context, this book also draws on selected international examples and references where these are useful to compliment analyses.

In relation to young people, the concept of vulnerability plays a particular role in the child protection system, especially since being heavily utilised in the New Labour government's landmark policy guidance on children and young people, *Every Child Matters* (DfES, 2003), an initiative that still continues to inform the governance and delivery of welfare services for those under the age of 18. Those governed by such policies include young people who are 'difficult', 'non-compliant' or criminal (see Goldson, 2002a), raising the thorny issue of how 'transgressive' young citizens should be treated in terms of support and discipline. A particularly pertinent example of divergences and ambiguities about transgression and vulnerability in policy and practice is the case of several young women who were sexually exploited in Rochdale, which received widespread media attention in September 2012 and which has been a source of much public concern since. Social workers judged that the young women (some of whom were considered to be highly problematic to agencies) had been 'making their own choices' and 'engaging in consensual sexual activity' with older men, yet the local safeguarding board returned a verdict that perpetrators of abuse had exploited 'vulnerable victims' (Rochdale Borough Safeguarding Children Board, 2012: 9). Governance arrangements for 'vulnerable' people generally – but especially for vulnerable young people – bring into focus fault lines and tensions over appropriate balances of support and discipline, which are particularly pertinent in the case of those who might be considered 'deviant' in some way.

Vulnerability in a context of economic liberalism and behavioural regulation

It has been widely chronicled that in high-income liberal democracies, substantial changes in the nature of governance have taken place in recent decades, remodelling relationships between citizens and the state based on notions of the 'active' and self-regulating human subject (Rose, 1999; Clarke, 2005; Flint, 2006a; Raco, 2009). Such moves have been associated with the rise of economic liberal or 'neoliberal' ideas and discourses in social policy, which have a long history but which have become especially influential since the 1970s when they were advanced by Margaret Thatcher in the UK and Ronald Reagan in the United States, spreading internationally since. Economic liberal agendas link with distinctive policy preoccupations, which include: freely functioning financial markets and free trade; strong individual property rights; prioritisation of individual 'freedoms'; the limiting of public ownership of goods and services in favour of privatisation; and limiting (or attempting to limit) the role of the state in citizens' lives as far as possible to areas where they are unable to make their own provisions (Harvey, 2005: 64-5).

Although ostensibly centred on economic arrangements, such governance strategies also penetrate and cultivate a range of social, cultural, legal, ideological and discursive practices (Bell, 2011: 7). Economic liberal discourses tend to emphasise individual resilience and self-reliance, with citizens largely imagined as free, rational actors who are able to 'succeed' in life despite structural constraints, which means they have important implications for how 'problem' behaviours and vulnerability are understood.

Where individuals are imagined as free, rational actors, it follows that they must also be responsible for instances of transgression (see Squires, 2008a). Such understandings have cultivated and informed the development of what has been called a 'new governance of conduct' in contemporary society (Flint, 2006a) or a 'new behaviourism' (Harrison with Hemingway, 2014: 25-6), with politicians and professionals exercising 'powerful supervisory, surveillance or therapeutic emphases where behaviour and lifestyles are at issue' (Harrison and Sanders, 2014: 26). Although using welfare as a means of regulating the behaviours of 'problematic' populations is by no means new (see Squires, 1990; Welshman, 2013), this form of governmental regulation has arguably intensified over recent decades (Wacquant, 2009; Harrison with Hemingway, 2014). In the UK, certain 'problem' groups have found themselves subject to increasingly punitive sanctions where they have failed to conform to acceptable notions of the 'active' and self-regulating citizen. Such trends have been reported extensively across various social policy arenas, including: housing (Fitzpatrick and Jones, 2005; Flint, 2006a, 2009); antisocial behaviour (Flint and Nixon, 2006; Squires, 2008b); unemployment (Wright, 2009; Dwyer, 2010); drug use (Monaghan, 2011); sex work (Phoenix and Oerton, 2005; Scoular and O'Neill, 2007; Phoenix, 2008); and criminal justice (Garland, 2001; Crawford, 2003; Rodger, 2008; Bell, 2011).

Forms of governance that position individuals as responsible for their own actions and self-management (Rose, 1999) have been accompanied by the rise of conditionality in social welfare (Dwyer, 2004, 2008, 2010). Conditional approaches to welfare centre on the idea of a contract between the state and the individual, where in order to draw down their social rights, citizens must fulfil certain responsibilities (Dwyer, 2004, 2010; Deacon and Patrick, 2011). According to such approaches, conduct is heavily linked with entitlement. Although balances of rights and responsibilities are in many ways an enduring feature of governance arrangements, conditionality in welfare and disciplinary policy was utilised especially heavily by the Conservatives in the 1980s, is generally understood to have become further embedded during the New Labour era (Dwyer, 2004, 2008; Clarke, 2005) and is being extended further still under the coalition government (see Harrison and Sanders, 2014). Since 1997 especially, governments have invested in programmes that are deemed to 'support' certain 'problem' groups on the basis that where those who are targeted fail to respond in the 'appropriate' way, stronger persuasions or disciplinary mechanisms should follow. Commentary on welfare conditionality often emphasises potential for further marginalising populations who are already facing considerable difficulties (Squires, 2008b; Patrick, 2011, 2014). Yet despite being delivered within a context of coercion, for some welfare recipients, the intensive support that can accompany more conditional interventions can be experienced as beneficial (see Flint, 2012). Flint (2009: 252) highlights that agency and resistance are still present within coercive contexts, albeit in '(limited) spaces of manoeuvre'. Balances of care and control have become increasingly significant as the policy landscape has changed and developed over recent decades and as welfare systems have become more selective. Thus, a complex interplay of welfare support and coercive sanctions now dominates much of contemporary social welfare (see Harrison and Sanders, 2006; Phoenix, 2008; Flint, 2009, 2012).

Such context provides an important backdrop for the investigation of vulnerability. In contemporary Western societies, by and large vulnerability is heavily lined with deficiency. Rather than being seen as a bodily inevitability, it is construed as 'an empirical trait which must be solved, overcome and thus eliminated' (Harrison, 2008: 436). Many groups subject to increased behavioural sanctions via coercive welfare strategies are those often positioned as vulnerable (see Harrison and Sanders, 2006, 2014), meaning that vulnerable groups invariably seem to constitute some kind of 'problem' to be solved. However, vulnerability discourses are also associated with moves to look beyond blaming a particular individual for their problems (see Goodin, 1985), leaving unanswered questions about how far 'vulnerable' people might be subject to or exempt from conditional welfare arrangements. Where people are assumed to be vulnerable, there would appear to be implications in terms of how far they are able to achieve 'active citizenship' (see Campbell, 1991), opening up difficult questions about how far this might affect their entitlements. Furthermore, if we understand there to be 'spaces' for resistance to and/or acceptance of conditionality among welfare recipients, how vulnerability might inform such dynamics seems an area worthy of investigation.

It is generally argued that wider policy developments related to economic liberalism have had particular ramifications for young people, linking with a 'punitive turn' in youth (and especially youth justice) policy (Goldson, 2000, 2002b; Goldson and Muncie, 2006; Muncie, 2006; Hopkins Burke, 2008). Welfare arrangements for young people arguably intensified during the New Labour period, with the then government issuing a raft of new policies designed to address child poverty and disadvantage and to prevent problems occurring later in childhood (Parton, 2006, 2007; Lloyd, 2008). However, at the same time, increasingly punitive policies characterised responses to youth crime, informed by moves towards 'responsibilisation' (Goldson, 2000, 2002b; Goldson and Muncie, 2006; Muncie, 2006). This was perhaps most obvious in the *No More Excuses* agenda (Home Office, 1997), which advised that stricter punishments were the most appropriate way to 'tackle' the issue of 'problematic' young people. Critics of the punitive turn thesis have emphasised that processes did not necessarily all move in one direction (Matthews, 2005). Indeed, implementation of youth justice policy might better be seen as an intricate interplay of mixed messages and contradictory practices, where welfare and disciplinary responses mesh together with complex outcomes (Muncie, 2006; Bateman, 2012a).

More recent developments are less easy to judge. Child imprisonment rates have declined in recent years, for reasons that seem unclear and contested (Bateman, 2012a). The coalition government seemed to push to increase the discretionary powers of frontline professionals within the youth justice system (Ministry of Justice, 2010; Bateman, 2012b), which may be significant in terms of how judgements about vulnerability influence policy and practice for young offenders. Overall trends remain difficult to discern but seen in a context as far back as the 1970s, contemporary youth policy is in many respects considerably more punitive, with a significant reversal of this trend seeming unlikely (Bateman, 2011, 2012a).

Wider developments in youth policy and more general policy trends have produced inevitable tensions between child welfare and criminal justice (Muncie, 2006), which Goldson (2002a, 2004) suggests has resulted in a 'deserving–undeserving schism' in provision for children and young people. It has been noted by youth justice writers that where disadvantaged children behave in ways that disturb moral sensibilities, the structural context in which they are viewed arguably shifts from one of poverty and inequality to one of agency and individual responsibility (Goldson, 2002a). At the policy level, young people tend to be constructed either as 'vulnerable victims' or as 'dangerous wrong-doers' with full responsibilities in situations where they transgress behavioural norms (Goldson, 2002a, 2004; Fionda, 2005; Such and Walker, 2005). How far practitioners share such dichotomised understandings is less clear, and there are indications that official systems are starting to take a more nuanced view of the relationship between young people's 'vulnerability' and 'offending'. For example, a recent parliamentary committee review of the child protection system indicated concern over the safety and wellbeing of 'older children' (House of Commons Education Committee, 2012), noting that the reason for the enhanced 'vulnerability' of teenagers related to 'behavioural issues':

> Older children in need often present as 'badly behaved'; whether in trouble with the criminal justice system, abusing drugs or alcohol, going missing, truanting, self-harming, or in other ways [...] this can *mask their vulnerability*, and lead professionals to 'blame' or judge children. (House of Commons Education Committee, 2012: 34, emphasis added)

Configurations of vulnerability and 'bad behaviour' seem to be appearing on the policy horizon, yet little attention has been given to this interrelationship in the academic literature.

One in a constellation of concepts

'Vulnerability' is one of a number of prominent concepts commonly used by researchers, practitioners and policy makers to refer to lower-income, disadvantaged or less well-off groups. Similar notions include: risk (see Culpitt, 1999; Lupton, 1999; Taylor-Gooby, 2000; Sarewitz et al, 2003); resilience (see Harrison, 2013; Ecclestone and Lewis, 2014; Runswick-Cole and Goodley, 2014; Slater, 2014); need (priority need in the case of housing); and adversity (see Daniel, 2010).

Risk has perhaps received the most sociological attention. A further prominent policy idea within the same constellation is that of 'troubled families', which merges notions of 'troubled' and 'troublesome' (Levitas, 2012; Ribbens McCarthy et al, 2013). Just as is the case with vulnerability, all of these notions can prove difficult to define and have nebulous conceptual boundaries. Similarly to 'risk' and terms such as 'troubled families', vulnerability serves a dual purpose in discourses related to precariousness. It not only highlights that the person or population requires help; the implication is also that they also pose some kind of risk to others or to society as a whole (Warner, 2008). Preoccupations with vulnerability can be seen as a contemporary manifestation or expression of broader long-running debates about those populations who might be considered as 'problematic', 'excluded' or socially marginalised; Standing's (2011) 'precariat'; Tyler's (2013) 'revolting subjects'; or Murray's (1984) more pejorative 'underclass' perhaps. Concerns with vulnerability are therefore unlikely to abate in a context of cuts in public expenditure, debates about low pay and the 'cost of living' and the extension and amplification of conditionality across a range of policy domains.

Speaking to a sense of insecurity and powerlessness, vulnerability is a close conceptual cousin to risk and, unsurprisingly, the 'risk society' thesis (referring to Beck, 1992) is often drawn on to explain the prominence of ideas about vulnerability. Indeed, Beck (2009: 178) himself has stated that 'vulnerability and risk are two sides of the same coin'. How far vulnerability and risk overlap is a theme that is returned to over the course of this book. The boundaries between the two terms appear decidedly indistinct. Similarly to risk, vulnerability has been noted as being particularly well suited to the measurement, auditing and assessment of individuals against neoliberal citizen ideals that elevate the independent, rational, capable individual (see Campbell, 1991; Lupton, 1999). However, vulnerability also appears to speak to a sense of social inclusion, empathy and sympathy in a way that risk does not, meaning that there are important differences that deserve attention. For some time now, risk has consistently been at the forefront of analysis of the processes by which people are classified, appraised and regulated, with vulnerability fading into the background in such critiques. This book makes the case that attention to vulnerability should be brought to centre stage in contemporary analyses of regulatory welfare, and that the notion should no longer be in the shadow of its conceptual cousins. It will advance that alongside other similar notions that frame the construction of contemporary social problems, vulnerability now fundamentally influences the ways that interventions are designed, delivered and received.

Theoretical orientations

From the outset of the research, my gaze was inclined towards structural factors associated with vulnerability, while also wanting to consider more individual 'responses' to situations of precariousness and classifications of vulnerability. The approach to the research was thus orientated towards socially rather than biologically or 'innately' constituted vulnerability. 'Care' was chosen for inclusion in the subtitle of the book as policies and interventions that seek to address vulnerability often include broader emotional or practical 'support' than might be indicated by a focus on 'welfare' (see also Wallbank and Herring, 2013), but the scope of the book remains orientated towards institutions and their role in the provision of 'supportive' services rather than towards interpersonal caring relationships. Social structures as well as social events were seen as forming social reality. Borrowing from Harrison with Davis (2001), the term 'structure' is used here and throughout the book to denote the institutional factors and forces that shape the choices, views and lives of individuals and which persist over time, but which can be modified by human action. Seen in this way, structure is linked to political, economic, cultural or ideological power, while still acknowledging the 'possibilities of change' through individual agency (Harrison with Davis, 2001: 4).

A number of constructs recur in the book, reflecting a certain theoretical emphasis. Ideas about social control, governance and the regulation of behaviour appear frequently. Such concerns stem from a view that social policy is increasingly used as a tool for monitoring and reviewing people's actions as well as supporting and assisting those who are 'in need', a trend sometimes referred to as 'behaviourism' (Harrison, 2010; Harrison and Sanders, 2014). The idea that contemporary society can be characterised by a 'culture of control' was one that informed the development of the ideas and the research for the study (Garland, 2001) and 'resistance' and how this might occur within a context of regulation and power (see Foucault, 1980) is also a theme. I have found various works useful that have drawn on Foucault's (1980: 142) view that 'there are no relations of power without resistances'; and Foucault's theories about 'governmentality' also proved useful as a framework for considering vulnerability as a mechanism in care and social control processes. Foucault's (1980) notion of governmentality is generally used to describe the nuanced and far-reaching nature and rationalities of state power and social control whereby power is dispersed across society via the social practices of a variety of governing authorities and through systems of thought. There is no assumption made in the book that controlling mechanisms in social policy are necessarily problematic and unacceptable in principle, and indeed it may be considered that constraining or disciplining indefensible transgressions is an important and necessary element of social policy and practice. It is acknowledged that there may be instances where persuasions or compulsions that entail normative elements are desirable in seeking to shape people's actions positively, perhaps especially in relation to younger citizens. However, as advanced by Harrison and Sanders (2014), a view is taken that due to relationships of power, tendencies to impose particular moral standpoints can be problematic, especially if framed within situations of inequality and discrimination.

As well as institutions being seen as fundamental to 'structures', the approach was taken that in order to make sense of public policy it is necessary to appreciate the ways in which policies and daily practices are shaped and mediated by those who deliver and receive them. Assumptions are made that human agents 'interpret and re-interpret' policy according to their particular 'values, identities and commitments' (Barnes and Prior, 2009: 1) and throughout the book, 'processed' is used as a summarising term to refer to the ways in which people are managed and classified in dynamic ways. Social practices were seen as having a semiotic element, with language playing a role in shaping processes of change within society, and the book explores vulnerability as both an empirical reality and a way of producing meaning. Discourses of vulnerability are taken to be important on the basis that the ways in which the idea or word 'vulnerability' is configured in texts and language can provide clues as to prevailing social practices and resistances against these. My understanding of 'discourse' was influenced by definitions provided by Fairclough (2003: 123-4; see also Fairclough, 2001) who sees it as the 'rules' that 'govern' groups of statements or 'bodies of texts'.[4]

As the book takes young people as a case study group through which to explore notions of vulnerability, it is useful to outline the understanding of 'childhood' and 'youth' that underpinned the study. Rather than using developmental psychology traditions, which position those under the age of 18 as in a state of continuous progression towards eventual adulthood and 'full competency', a standpoint known as the 'new sociology of childhood' informed the approach taken (Jenks, 1982, 2004; Mayall, 1994; James and Prout, 1997; Moran-Ellis, 2010). Being guided by this perspective means seeking to value children and young people's social worlds as having meaning in their own right, rather than as trivial or partial imitations of the adult state of being. Such a standpoint also emphasises that in order to understand how childhood and youth might be experienced, attention must be given to the ways in which children and young people are marginalised within socioeconomic structures and systems. Views of children and young people as competent in a different way from adults have raised questions about they should be treated as a distinct group in research (Harden et al, 2000; Punch, 2002). I opted for an approach that positioned young people as 'fragile' and marginalised in some ways, but which also appreciated them as potentially skilled social actors who would be able to communicate more readily with me if I was capable of finding ways to 'tap into' their competencies.

Research methods and the case study investigation

Research for the book employed a mixture of qualitative methods (see Brown, 2013, for detailed consideration). The three interlinked components of the investigation were:

- a literature review of academic writings on vulnerability in the social sciences;
- a general review of national policy trends related to 'vulnerability' and thematic documentary analysis of arenas where vulnerability seemed significant in policy and practice;
- a geographically based case study of providers and users of services for 'vulnerable' young people, which included exploration of complexities arising where individuals are seen as vulnerable and also 'troublesome'.

The empirical research utilised qualitative methods including interviews with 25 'vulnerable' young people aged 12–18, 15 interviews with practitioners and policy makers involved in services supporting this group, and more informal ethnographic immersion in practitioner worlds through meetings, conversations and interactions.

The case study was informed by 'post-positivist' ideas, which advance that research provides one view of a particular phenomenon, which may be subject to multiple interpretations and perspectives (Holstein and Gubrium, 1995; Denzin and Lincoln; 2005). A view was taken that although validity of knowledge cannot be assessed with certainty, phenomena do exist independently of our claims concerning them and our assumptions can appropriate them in some way (see Hammersley, 1992). The different strands of the research carried out for the book – including a literature review, documentary analysis and various case study methods – were not employed with the intention of 'proving' one 'truth'; the approach was more to collect and seek to understand various perspectives on vulnerability. As the case study research relied on interviews, this could be seen as raising questions about the validity of interviewees' accounts. I took the position that the purpose of the interviews was to accept, report and analyse the interviewees' perspectives, on the basis that seeking to appreciate the way in which both key informants and young people made sense of 'vulnerability' would offer valuable insights when viewed alongside other research.

Sampling and access

The city in which the empirical case study took place is among the largest in England, with a population of around 750,000 people. It has a sizable local authority and varied infrastructure aimed at supporting vulnerable children and young people, in that certain commissioning arrangements, services and interventions are explicitly targeted at this particular group. The decision was taken to focus on this city with the aim of developing rich insights into how vulnerability is operationalised in services for young people, rather than a positivist approach to 'representativeness' being taken. Young people were accessed through six 'gatekeeper' agencies:

- a service for young carers;
- a locality-based antisocial behaviour project;
- a young people's drugs service;
- a sexual exploitation project;

- a private education provider for young people having problems at school; and
- a service for vulnerable children (which supported homeless young people, runaways and refugees/asylum seekers).

Access through gatekeepers has well-documented benefits and disadvantages when working with vulnerable groups (Lee, 2001; Miller and Bell, 2002; Emmel et al, 2007). In the present study, working through gatekeepers was central to answering the research questions about how vulnerability was operationalised, and therefore formed a key part of the research strategy. There were also substantial ethical advantages, which are discussed below. In order to engage in the most detailed way possible with vulnerable young people's views and experiences, the decision was taken not to include the perspectives of parents/carers, although this group would certainly seem worthy of attention in future investigations.

For interviews undertaken with professionals or 'key informants' involved in the delivery of services for vulnerable young people in the city, participants were selected using the rationale that the sample needed to include roughly equal numbers of frontline workers, operational managers, commissioners and strategists, in order to give an adequate mix of positions of responsibility. Furthermore, reasonable coverage of agencies involved with vulnerable (and also 'transgressive') groups of young people was also required. The sample of key informants consisted of five frontline workers, three commissioners and seven managers (some of whom also had commissioning and service user-facing duties). Interviewees worked across a range of settings, some providing interventions that were more 'compulsory' in nature (the youth offending service, social care and a family intervention project, for example), while others worked for services that might be considered more 'supportive', such as third-sector youth projects working with young people who were 'in need' or 'at risk'. Informants were asked about how they made use of the concept or idea of vulnerability in their work, their understandings of the notion and how they measured and classified vulnerability. These interviews were complemented by informal data gathering through participation in various meetings, conversations and correspondence. Such ethnographically based approaches were especially useful in generating insights into how professionals perceived and managed young people's vulnerability.

Ethical considerations and researching vulnerable young people's lives

Ethical considerations were of paramount concern in the design and implementation of the fieldwork for the study, especially in interviews conducted with young people. In line with standard child protection practice, young people were offered confidentiality except for in instances where risk of significant harm might be indicated, an eventuality that did not arise. Throughout the book, the names of young people have been changed for confidentiality reasons and the names that appear are pseudonyms, chosen by the interviewees. Support workers were enlisted in the process of informed consent in order to ensure that every effort was made to fully explain the nature of the research and its potential uses to all interviewees and their parents where appropriate.[5] Working through agencies meant that young people had workers who could pick up on any emotional or practical issues that young people might encounter as a result of the interview process, and post-interview support for young people could be implemented where required. Working through access projects also reduced risk to my personal safety, linking me with a professional body and enforcing mutually protective boundaries between researcher and participant. In many cases, agencies provided a safe location from which to conduct the interviews and provided valuable information to help me assess and manage risks.

'Child-friendly' methods are often advocated as an effective way of addressing power differentials arising where adults are involved in research with those under the age of 18. Research techniques are seen as more child friendly where they enable communication between the conceptual outlooks of children and young people on one hand, and those of adult researchers on the other (see Fraser et al, 2004). The logic behind such techniques is that by using certain activities during communication, this enables the researcher to assess and respond to a particular child or young person's competencies during the interview process. In my study, rather than viewing child-friendly methods as necessarily bridging the gap between adult communicator and young person, I took the approach advocated by Connolly (2003) that although certain methods can help to reduce power differentials, these can never be overcome and must be reflected on and dealt with through a reflexive approach. Interviews with young people made use of distinctive 'task-based' techniques (see Conolly, 2008; Bagnoli, 2009), where interviewees undertook a series of semi-structured activities along with me, talking as the tasks were completed. The aim of using this method was to elicit richer data from a group who are sometimes considered to be 'difficult to reach' or 'hard to engage'. The tools were developed in the light of previous experiences, which had taught me that 'vulnerable' young people could often be shy or tentative in interview situations (see Brown, K., 2011a).

Using life-mapping activities (see Figures 1.1 and 1.2), young people were asked about their past experiences, hopes for the future and previous/future vulnerabilities. The idea of vulnerability was introduced by discussion of short video vignette clips of other 'vulnerable' young people telling their stories. Interviewees watched two young people speaking about their lives and situations: a 17-year-old pregnant young woman who lived in care and had come to the UK as an unaccompanied minor; and a young man who had been excluded from school and who was heavily involved in offending, drug use and the sale of drugs. After watching these clips with me, interviewees were asked about the 'vulnerability' of the young people in the clips, which provided a springboard for conversations about interviewees' views of their own vulnerability. A 'mutual language dilemma' (Punch, 2002: 328) is faced by youth researchers, in that children and young people's vocabulary and frame of comprehension are usually different from adults', and vice versa, creating potential problems in shared understanding in discussions. Talking about the concept of vulnerability

Figure 1.1: Example of a past life map, co-produced by researcher and young person

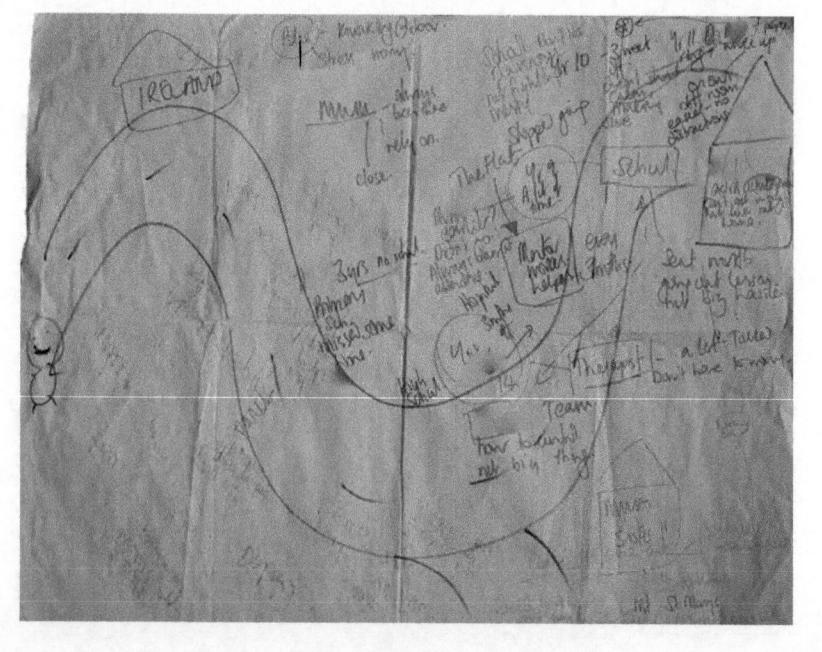

Figure 1.2: Example of a future life map, co-produced by researcher and young person

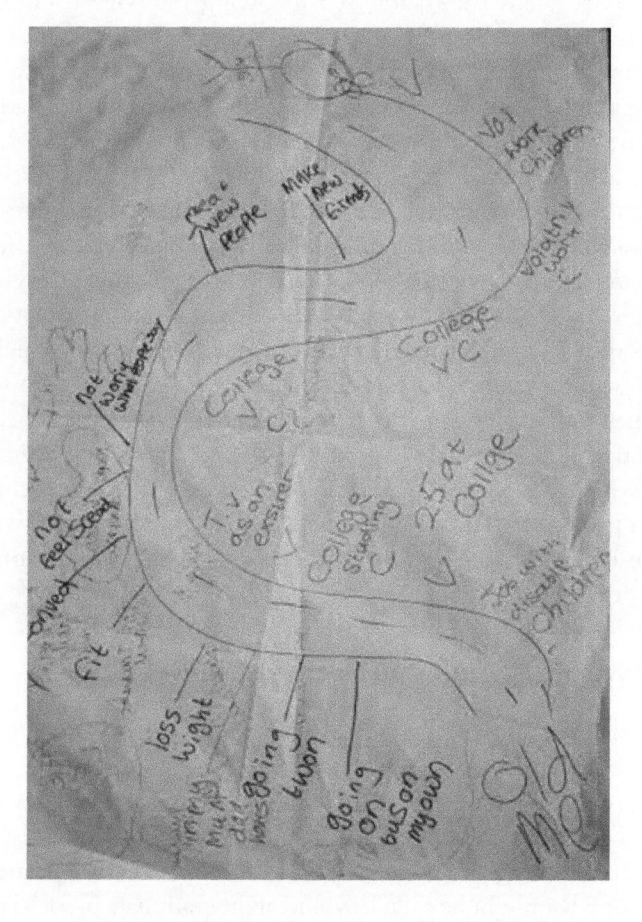

with young people posed challenges in this respect, and sometimes various proxies were used such as 'difficulties', 'difficult lives', 'things that were hard' or 'risks', with the notion and term 'vulnerability' then introduced directly wherever possible. Through the video vignette technique, most of the young people connected with and discussed 'vulnerability' explicitly, although in a small number of instances (especially where young people spoke English as a second language) interviewees were very unfamiliar with the word and I stuck to using the various proxies.

As quotations in later chapters demonstrate, sensitive issues were raised in discussions of vulnerability. Young people often shared things that were concerning to hear and which they indicated had been distressing or upsetting for them at the time when they had occurred. During these situations I made every effort to respond with empathy and understanding, and worked closely with support workers to ensure that support needs were addressed following interviews. Given the particularly 'intimate' sphere that discussions about someone's sense of their own vulnerability involved, I felt that, as well as having a role as data gatherer, I had an ethical responsibility to make every attempt to ensure that interview interactions helped young people to feel positive about themselves (see Birch and Miller, 2000), so discussion of topics that were sensitive but not directly relevant for the research were avoided. In efforts to maximise the chances of interviewees feeling valued and appreciated, I would make a point of offering interviewees some feedback about what had been useful about information or insights they had given. Young people also received a £10 voucher as a thank you for taking part and sharing their time, which also served as a small acknowledgement of the value of their experience and knowledge. The interview conversations offered rare insights into the social worlds of supposedly vulnerable young people and later chapters contain powerful accounts of lived experiences of vulnerability. They provide especially rich grounds for analysis when viewed alongside policy developments and academic accounts of the concept.

Structure of the book and key messages

Earlier chapters of the book explore broader vulnerability trends and ideas. Chapter Two focuses on 'vulnerability' as a concept in social policy. It charts the influence of the notion in the principal policy arenas where it has been most influential, such as children's services, adult social care, housing and criminal justice. Some of the implications of the rise of what might be called a vulnerability rationale in social policy are considered, and attention is given to the effects of constructing policies that prioritise particular vulnerable groups or individuals. Academic accounts of vulnerability are then set out in Chapter Three, which seeks tentatively to theorise the dimensions of the concept and 'make sense' of some of the key ways in which it can be understood.

Chapter Four is the first of four chapters to report from the qualitative case study investigation. It draws on the interviews with key informants working with vulnerable young people, highlighting the importance of vulnerability in welfare and disciplinary systems and examining the main practical applications of the concept. In particular, it explores the relationship that vulnerability has with ideas about deservingness and 'appropriate' behaviour. Gender also emerges as a key theme in the operationalisation of the notion, a matter that is returned to in subsequent chapters.

Chapter Five moves on to consider the life stories of 'vulnerable' young people, revealing interviewees as having encountered a range of substantive difficulties and challenges in their lives. It explores how young people 'imagined' their futures, offering distinctive insights into their social worlds and perspectives.

Chapter Six considers how young people viewed 'vulnerability', as well as their responses to being classified in this way, with Chapter Seven then exploring the factors and interventions that young people considered to have augmented or reduced their levels of vulnerability, considering not only immediate family contexts but also young people's experiences and perceptions of interventions, processes and broader structures.

Finally, Chapter Eight draws together themes and findings that emerged from the various strands of the research, reflecting on the importance of vulnerability in care and control processes. Disjunctures between official views and lived experiences of vulnerability are reflected on, the key dimensions of 'vulnerability' as a concept are reviewed, and its significance as a tool in 21st-century governmentalities is highlighted.

The central contention of the book is that in a context of economic liberalism and welfare retrenchment, the rise of vulnerability in policy and practice can serve to further marginalise those who might be considered the 'most vulnerable'. In an age when care and control processes are tightly knitted together to manage and contour the behaviours of 'problem' groups, interventions organised on the basis of vulnerability contribute to broader trends where those with conformist or 'compliant' behaviours are most likely to benefit. Due to its connotations of frailty and deservingness, it seems that there is a tendency for those with more 'troublesome' attitudes or behaviours – who might arguably be considered some of the 'most vulnerable' – to be excluded from vulnerability classifications. As well as being a tool in the support and care of disadvantaged citizens, the book demonstrates that vulnerability rationales also function as a subtle social control mechanism. Furthermore, classifying people as vulnerable may well help to 'protect' certain individuals and groups, but this can also have implications for those citizens' entitlements and rights to autonomy over their own lives. Although it has gained momentum largely without attracting attention, the book makes the case that the vulnerability zeitgeist represents a significant development in social policy and practice, subtly but pervasively influencing how a range of interventions with 'problem' groups are designed, delivered and received.

Notes

[1] See Google's 'Ngram' tool, which counts the number of times a term is used in a selection of Google's digitised books: www.books.google.com/ngrams/

[2] TED is a non-profit organisation devoted to spreading ideas and making them accessible. The talk can be viewed at www.ted.com/talks/brene_brown_on_ vulnerability

[3] http://web.gs.emory.edu/vulnerability/

[4] Fairclough's understandings of discourse are heavily influenced by Foucault (1972, 1984).

[5] Obtaining verbal parental or guardian consent was explored as a matter of good practice, although the majority of young people were over the age of 13, and so participation was possible without parental/guardian consent due to the Gillick competency principle or Fraser Guidelines generally applying to those aged 13 and above. These guidelines refer to a landmark legal case in 1985, where Lord Fraser ruled that a doctor could give contraceptive advice or treatment to a young person without parental consent provided (a) the young person understood the intervention and (b) they may be harmed if they did not access it. The Gillick principle is now widely used in policy and practice and governs the majority of the support work with young people in the UK that is carried out without parental consent.

TWO

Making sense of vulnerability

Introduction

The idea of vulnerability has come to feature prominently in academic debates concerning situations where people might suffer harm, injustice or precariousness. Yet despite powerful ethical connotations and prevalence in research, vulnerability is a concept most often characterised by vagueness and plurality of meaning (Hurst, 2008; Fawcett, 2009; Misztal, 2011; Wallbank and Herring, 2013; Mackenzie et al, 2014). Texts that deploy the notion in a specified, theorised or defined way are relatively few. Attention to vulnerability often appears alongside research and ideas concerned with risk – one of the most theorised terms in the social sciences – yet vulnerability remains firmly in the shadow of its conceptual cousin. Often it carries normative implications and implies a duty for action to be taken. Given the influence of post-modern approaches, which have emphasised how concepts or ideas shape the social world when they are 'operationalised' or put into practice, this lack of critical attention seems surprising.

By way of an overview of key clusters of vulnerability writings, there is a substantial literature in the human sciences that refers to vulnerability in relation to environmental hazards (Blackie et al, 1994; Schiller et al, 2001; Bankoff et al, 2004; Adger, 2006), global poverty, famine and 'natural' disasters (Chambers, 1989; Downing, 1991; Watts and Bohle, 1993; Lindley et al, 2011; Bradshaw, 2013). The notion has also attracted attention in health literature (Peterson and Wilkinson, 2008: 3; Heaslip and Ryden, 2013) and in psychology (see Glendening and Carter, 2013; Willoughby, 2013). In ethics and philosophy, a number of writers have advanced the potential of vulnerability as an idea that could form an ontological foundation for social justice and a fairer society (Goodin, 1985; Butler, 2004; Turner, 2006). The concept has also been given attention in the fields of social research (see Beckett, 2006; Warner, 2008; Emmel and Hughes, 2010, 2014; Hollomotz, 2011) and law (Fineman, 2008; Fineman and Grear, 2013; Wallbank and Herring, 2013) and in policy-based commentaries (see Furedi, 2008; Daniel, 2010; McLaughlin, 2012; Ecclestone and Lewis, 2014). Many texts use vulnerability as an entry point for discussing inequalities or adversities of some kind, with the concept used to anchor consideration of a range of issues connected with relative disadvantage, 'resilience' or unmet need.

This chapter charts the key contours of vulnerability as a notion in the academic literature. Predominantly focusing on social sciences research, the chapter takes 'vulnerability' as a thread and follows it through various disciplines and territories, exploring commonalities and differences in the way the term has been used. Particular attention is given to instances where vulnerability relates to children and young people and to ideas about behavioural regulation and social control.

Scrutiny of the academic literature reveals five different, if overlapping, themes as the principal manifestations of vulnerability:

- 'natural' or 'innate' vulnerability, determined by physical and/or personal factors that are often associated with certain points of the lifecourse such as childhood and older age;
- 'situational' vulnerability, referring to biographical circumstances, situational difficulties or transgressions – this can include the input of a third party or structural force, and can also involve human agency (often to a contested extent);
- vulnerability as related to social disadvantage, the environment and/ or geographical spaces;
- universal vulnerability, where vulnerability is seen as a state shared by all citizens, but which is socially or politically constituted to varying extents; and
- vulnerability as a concept closely related to risk.

These are considered and reviewed in turn. Association with risk is given specific attention in the chapter due to the close alignment of vulnerability with risk in the literature. This is not to say that that other concepts have not been significant in how they have appeared alongside vulnerability, but rather that the substantial body of literature on risk provides particularly useful insights.

As well as mapping some of the key ways in which vulnerability is drawn on in the social sciences literature, the chapter draws out some of the more developed thinking on the dimensions of the concept. It will be highlighted that attempts to theorise vulnerability are usually contingent on the historical, political and disciplinary context in which it is being utilised. Diverse configurations of vulnerability are shown to map onto various notions of citizenship and particular constructions of disadvantage (see Chapter Three; also Brown, 2011b, 2012). When vulnerability is framed as a natural or 'individual' state, it carries very different implications from when it is imagined as socially or politically constituted. The various uses and understandings of vulnerability reveal the profound ethical implications of the concept, and over the course of the chapter it becomes evident that any attempt to make sense of vulnerability also brings into focus the nature of the connections between institutions, social practices, individuals and the state.

Natural or innate vulnerability and child development

'Natural' or 'innate' vulnerability theories tend to position individuals as 'at risk' in a way that can be modified by action, but where some risk will always remain. Notions of innate vulnerability are often connected with childhood, but can also be associated with other aspects of the lifecourse, most notably the states of older age, physical or sensory impairment and mental health difficulties (see for example Palmer et al, 1988; Pinsker et al, 2010). The concept is also used to refer to temporary biological states associated with elevated fragility and which inspire protective responses, such as acute illness or pregnancy. Innate vulnerability has long been associated with childhood. Writing in 1792, Rousseau reasoned: 'Is there anything so weak and wretched as a child, anything so utterly at the mercy of those about it, so dependent on their pity, their care, and their affection?' (translated by Foxley, 1974: 52). More recently, since the emergence of childhood studies in the 1990s, there has been a growing academic interest in children's vulnerability to harm (James and Prout, 1997; James and James, 2008: 139) or lack of ability to protect themselves (Malin et al, 2002), and children's vulnerability is a key concept in developmental childhood studies (see Brotherton and Cronin, 2013) where it is held that because children are not fully mature they are vulnerable to adverse influences that may disrupt the 'normal' completion of the developmental process.

The influence of these developmental ideas has been far reaching, particularly in normative understandings of youth vulnerability. According to lifecourse perspectives, youth is seen as a period of conflicting personal identity and 'crisis' (see Erikson, 1968). Generally speaking, young people are taken to be at a more advanced 'stage' within childhood, meaning that the vulnerability of this group within the developmental lifecourse approach is, as McLeod (2012: 13) notes, 'intriguing' and unresolved. As well as being assumed to have universal innate vulnerabilities, there are particular children and young people who are seen as having additional vulnerabilities that mark them out as 'other' in some way. Differentiations in wider and narrower uses of the concept of children and young people's vulnerability tend to be tacit or implied rather than specified (Daniel, 2010). So-called vulnerable young people are positioned simultaneously as innately fragile due to biological and social immaturity and also as 'at risk' in some way due to particular adversities, often in relation to others. As McLeod (2012) notes, their capacity, competence and associated vulnerabilities are usually configured in terms of personal difficulties, possibly extending to 'community' and family matters but rarely to wider social or transnational processes.

Offering a counterweight to developmental and behaviourist approaches, the emergence of the new sociology of childhood has called into question understandings of children as innately vulnerable. According to these theories, representations of childhood vary over time (Pearson, 1983; James and Prout, 1997; Lee, 2001) and notions of children's innate vulnerability change along with these variations. Such variances are closely associated with shifting understandings of what constitutes 'risk' and the need for 'protection'. James and James (2008: 138) cite differing attitudes to child labour as an example, highlighting that children can be seen either as important economic contributors in society or as 'at risk' due to working from too early an age. Although innate vulnerability remains a central theme in normative understandings of childhood, representations of children as natural, passive, incompetent and incomplete now contend and co-exist with notions of children as agents in, as well as products of, the 'social process' (James and Prout, 1997). Nygard (2009) highlights the paradox inherent in dominant discourses that give emphasis to children's rights on the one hand, while also implying a need for stricter demands on the public and adult control of children on the other. How human agency is imagined where children are positioned as inherently vulnerable is particularly contested and complex (Piper, 2008).

That some adults are innately vulnerable is central to prominent accounts of disability. However, the concept of vulnerability seems to have divided disability theorists and writers and the implications of the notion in approaches to disability has been given substantive attention (see Wishart, 2003; Hasler, 2004; Beckett, 2006; Dunn et al, 2008; Hollomotz, 2009, 2011). Some writers have been highly critical of understandings that advance disabled people as innately vulnerable, arguing that such a construction is disempowering and patronising, undermining the position and rights of disabled citizens and diminishing attention to the responsibility of society in the creation of their 'vulnerability' (see Wishart, 2003; Hasler, 2004; Hollomotz, 2009). In critiques of innate approaches to vulnerability, certain scholars have argued for a 'social construction of vulnerability' (see Wishart, 2003; also Hollomotz, 2009), broadly in alignment with the highly influential 'social model of disability' (Barnes and Mercer, 1996). Other disability writers have regarded the identification of vulnerability as an important means of obtaining external protection (see McLaughlin, 2012, for a useful account of social movements based on vulnerability). Beckett (2006) uses disability as a case study to highlight understandings associated with the experience of impairment, arguing that vulnerability can offer a basis for the advancement of disabled people's rights provided that it is seen as a state that we all share due to the 'fragile and contingent nature of personhood' (2006: 3). As well as alerting us to the concept's disempowering connotations, Beckett (2006) sees vulnerability as potentially emancipatory due to its potential to unite people in a shared understanding of their relationships to others in society (see also Ecclestone and Goodley, 2014). This work demonstrates that there is a particular view of innate vulnerability that emphasises connectedness to others and uniform shared precariousness, highlighting that views of vulnerability as innate are not necessarily tied to ideas about developmental accounts.

Situational vulnerability and 'deservingness'

A further key manifestation of vulnerability draws attention to the situation of people who find themselves at elevated fragility or 'risk of harm' due to particular circumstances or transgressions, or what I have previously termed 'situational vulnerability' (Brown, 2013). Generally speaking, this tends to be associated with the active input of a human third party or a structural force, but is also imagined to contain elements of individual agency or choice. This configuration of vulnerability is often aligned with the notion of 'vulnerable groups' (see Chapter Three), where certain groups or individuals are seen to have experienced a degree of misfortune that generates special social or statutory duties towards them. Narratives that highlight the particular or situational vulnerabilities of certain groups have links with increasingly popular ideas about 'victimhood' and the particular obligations that society is assumed to owe to those classified as 'victims' (see Garland, 2001; Waiton, 2008; Hall, 2009; Bottoms and Roberts, 2010). Examples of situationally vulnerable people might include: homeless people; women involved in prostitution; asylum seekers and refugees; Roma people; women experiencing domestic violence; drug users; poorer people; and prisoners (especially women).

They can also include more general groups such as women, or black and minority ethnic people (see Peroni and Timmer, 2013).

Such configurations have close links with ideas about 'deservingness' and normative ideas about transgression, bringing into focus a more behavioural dimension to the concept. Warner's (2008) empirical study on community care settings found that social workers sought to contest the construction of their clients as a social risk by emphasising their personal biographies and by positioning them as vulnerable. This suggests that due to the moral potency of the terminology, constructing individuals or groups as situationally vulnerable can circumvent them being seen as 'to blame' for their problems, or can at least appeal against the impulse to condemn them for their actions or lifestyles. Goodin (1985: 129) notes that because of its link to moral duty, vulnerability status can transcend how much people are thought to 'have themselves to blame' for their circumstances. For him, this is why using vulnerability as the starting point for ethics and social justice is so powerful. According to Goodin (1985: 129), at the point where an individual's opportunities of self-help have passed and the situation is beyond their control, this is when they are 'uniquely and most' vulnerable, as it is precisely when others possess the most power to take action to avert harm to the vulnerable person. Elsewhere, I have argued that in this sense, vulnerability seems to function in ethics as a 'get out of jail free card' (Brown, 2011b: 318). In other words, responsibilities generated from situational vulnerabilities would appear to act as a powerful appeal against the idea that people 'deserve' their problematic circumstances or difficulties.

While situational vulnerability certainly has a strong conceptual connection with ideas about 'deservingness', the nature of this link is complex. As noted elsewhere in this book (see Chapters One and Three), those who are seen as situationally vulnerable (and usually by implication as 'deserving') may also be constructed simultaneously as a 'problem'. Writing on mental health service provision, Moon (2000: 241) notes a 'juxtaposition of threat and vulnerability' in constructions of mental health service users. Sex work is another prominent example (see Phoenix and Oerton, 2005; Scoular and O'Neill, 2007; Carline, 2011), and also those who are seen as potential terrorists (Richards, 2011; Coppock and McGovern, 2014). In certain contexts, vulnerability seems to imply risk and danger to others from those individuals labelled as vulnerable, as well as an ethical duty to respond to the problematic situation of those who are 'in need'. In her work on mental health service users, Warner (2008: 32) describes a 'vulnerability/dangerousness axis', where 'vulnerability' is used to indicate the risk posed *by* certain individuals as well as *to* them. This is an especially useful idea when considering situational vulnerability. It would seem that as well as highlighting some sort of risk of adversity, vulnerability classifications are also used to indicate that attention is required so that a person or group does not disrupt the social order (see Harrison and Sanders, 2006). Thus, in instances where individuals or groups are delineated as situationally vulnerable, this can imply not only that they *deserve extra support* and assistance but also that they *require extra control* in order that they meet tacit standards associated with behavioural norms.

The behavioural dimensions of situational vulnerability would seem to have important implications in matters of 'difference'. Scholars have noted gendered aspects to classifications of vulnerability in housing allocations, with women more firmly located within 'vulnerability' classifications due to their being more inclined to behave with deference and accept dependence (Passaro, 1996, reporting from New York; Cramer, 2005). Warner (2008) and Fawcett (2009) argue that young black men have been ill-served by mental health service provision due to vulnerability constructions operating to exclude this group. They argue that black men have been configured as a threat and are therefore by default seen as less deserving and less vulnerable. Situational vulnerability classifications might therefore potentially be problematic in terms of how they take account of notions of difference, a theme that will be returned to in later chapters.

Social disadvantage and spaces of vulnerability

A significant body of academic work has utilised the concept of vulnerability in terms of social exposure to natural or environmental hazards, or more broadly as a way of bringing social and economic disadvantage and 'coping capacity' into focus. As Bradshaw (2013: 1) notes, vulnerability 'has emerged as a key concept to help explain how and why natural events have severe negative socio–economic outcomes or become "disasters" for some groups of people and not others'. Rashed and Weeks (2003: 547) similarly flag that it is an 'essential concept' in 'hazards' research. Originating from the disciplines of geography and environment studies, these ideas have more recently migrated into and merged with social science work. Social–ecological vulnerability studies have a relatively longer tradition in comparison with considerations of vulnerability in other disciplines and Adger (2006) offers a particularly useful overview of antecedent and successor scholarship in this vulnerability research tradition (see especially p 275).

Sen's (1981) work on poverty and famines and Chambers' (1989) analysis of systems that give rise to vulnerability seem to have had a substantial influence on this tradition. Studies in this arena sometimes involve quantitative metrics to develop social vulnerability indices according to key variables (see Hewitt, 1997; Ebert et al, 2009) and usually have a spatially focused approach (see Cutter, 1996; Bolin and Stanford, 1998; Bankoff et al, 2004), which can be explicitly focused on cities or urban spaces (see Burton et al, 1978; Mitchell et al, 1989). More recently, the concept has also been of interest to climate change scholars (see Castro et al, 2012; Lindley et al, 2011). Attention to vulnerability in this arena seems often to appear alongside increasing attention to 'resilience' (see Pugh, 2014, for resilience as a buzzword in policy) or 'georisk', orientated towards social and environmental systems rather than the circumstances of particular individuals. According to Chandler (2014) and Pugh (2014), the growing popularity of 'resilience' as a notion in international development literature seems broadly to reflect moves towards engagement with new complexities of 'reality', but critics have noted its emphasis on 'responsibilising risk away from the state and on to individuals and institutions' (Welsh, 2013: 15), a debate that has distinct parallels with ideas about vulnerability.

As is the case in more sociologically orientated research, writers on social and environmental vulnerability have noted a lack of precision in how the concept is used. Chambers (1989: 33) argued some time ago that although being 'vulnerable' has become a common idea in the lexicon of international development, the usage is often vague and interchangeable with 'poverty' in this context. Similarly, Watts and Bohle (1993: 45) noted that vulnerability is omni-present in the literature on geographical adversity; as a theoretically ill-defined notion that delineates those who are at risk of ongoing lack of access to food and risk of starvation. Despite the fact that vulnerability seems to be seen as an underdeveloped concept in this arena, some of the more advanced theorising on the notion can be found in this ecological or geo-vulnerability literature. Chambers (1989: 33) sees vulnerability as related to defencelessness, defining it as referring to 'exposure to contingencies and stress, and difficulty coping with them'. He goes on: 'Vulnerability thus has two sides: an external side of risks, shocks and stress to which an individual or household is subject; and an internal side which is defencelessness, meaning a lack of means to cope without damaging loss (1989: 33). Such accounts of vulnerability as related to the likelihood of hazard and the risk of a negative outcome are extremely common in geographically orientated hazards research.

Developing this definition, Watts and Bohle (1993) use the notion of vulnerability to help map an account of locally and historically specific configurations of poverty, hunger and famine. They outline three 'coordinates' of vulnerability (1993: 45) that can be simplified as follows:

- the risk of exposure to crises, stress and shocks;
- the risk of inadequate capacities to cope with these; and
- the risk of severe consequences arising in these instances.

Watts and Bohle (1993: 46) explore 'choice' and 'constraint'; or 'degrees of freedom', which determine exposure, coping capacity and potentiality. They use the idea of causal structures of vulnerability, which link with entitlement and institutions of access and control, and they label these 'spaces of vulnerability'. These spaces revolve around three axes – potentiality, exposure and capacity (meaning the capacity to deal with adversity) – ideas that underpin many of the studies of spatial vulnerability. More recently, in environmental research published by the Joseph Rowntree Foundation, similar approaches to vulnerability have been used to assess the social justice implications arising from climate change in the UK (Lindley et al, 2011), with vulnerability defined simply as 'characterised by the degree to which an external event converts into losses in their well-being' (2011: 2).

More heavily focused on institutional and environmental structures than on the spaces where human agency operates, this approach develops a socially and potentially politically orientated account of vulnerability. More recent work has drawn on these ideas to highlight the gendered dimensions of vulnerability (Bradshaw, 2013). Spatial or environmental theories of vulnerability alert us to the concept's link with 'assets' or ability to cope with adversity, and to the capacity of institutional practices to 'cushion' the effects of negative events. Used in a socioeconomic sense, such ideas have been utilised to explore nuanced and 'textured' understandings of lived experiences of deprivation (Emmel and Hughes, 2014). Working on social exclusion, Emmel and Hughes (2010: 171) adapt Watts and Bohle's ideas to theorise a longitudinal 'social space of vulnerability', which can be viewed as 'multiple deprivation, limited resilience and (in) appropriate service provision', with coordinates that relate to:

- material shortages in households, characterised by 'making do' with limited resources for basic everyday needs;
- a lack of capacity to address needs in the present and plan for the future; and
- an uncertain reliance on welfare services acting to address crises when they happen.

Central to Emmel and Hughes' hypothesis is the idea that vulnerability involves individuals and households living with a fear of future events tipping them into further difficulties or crises. In this respect, the unrealised element of vulnerability is crucial to how marginalisation is manifest in the social world.

In later work focusing on intergenerational patterns of disadvantage, Emmel and Hughes (2014) further develop a 'temporal dimension' to how they conceptualise vulnerability, calling this their 'Toblerone model'. According to this model, the three coordinates are the 'face' of the triangular vulnerability prism and the length is a fourth dimension: time (for temporal accounts, see also Archer Copp, 1986; Bankoff et al, 2004). The model aims to draw attention to structures that operate through health and social care provision and to highlight social marginalisation processes through time and generations, showing how the concept of vulnerability can usefully facilitate understandings of social disadvantage. While such social science accounts of vulnerability are very different from more ecological or environmental accounts in certain respects, they share a concern with vulnerability as a tool for understanding socio-material realities and the structures that underpin them. These writings raise the possibility that vulnerability can be 'designed out' (Sanders and Campbell, 2007). In a somewhat separate strand of vulnerability scholarship, other more philosophically inclined scholars have sought to do something similar.

Universal vulnerability and the vulnerability thesis writers

Over the last decade especially there has been a small but growing number of academics across the ethics, philosophy and critical legal studies literatures who have been extremely interested in the notion of vulnerability, with certain writers from across these fields advancing that the concept is able to function as a basis for achieving equality, autonomy and freedom in society (Goodin, 1985; Butler, 2004; Turner, 2006; Fineman, 2008; Fineman and Grear, 2013). These writers see vulnerability as a concept that can alert us to the universal precariousness of human existence, and one that can act as a unifying theoretical catalyst through which society could potentially be transformed. The vulnerability thesis writers share a conception of vulnerability as biological and permanent, but also connected to the personal, economic, social and cultural circumstances within which individuals find themselves at different points in their lives. According to this view, the state of vulnerability is a fundamental feature of humanity (see Beckett, 2006) and a powerful conceptual building block in relation to ethics and social justice (Goodin, 1985; Turner, 2006; Dodds, 2007; Ramsay, 2008; Anderson and Honneth, 2009; Fineman, 2008, 2013).

This vulnerability-focused ontology is advanced on the basis that the concept appeals to tenderness and compassion. Turner (2006: 35), for example, argues that the sympathy that vulnerability elicits can be cultivated to forge a stronger civil society: 'The experience of vulnerability provides a norm for the assertion of a human bond across generations and culture.' Similarly, in moral philosophy writing, Goodin (1985: 42) argues that the relational vulnerability of citizens should be the grounds for how moral responsibilities (both individual and group) should be generated. At the heart of the universal vulnerability thesis is a focus on interdependency, dependency and interconnectedness (Campbell, 1991; Kittay, 1999; Dodds, 2007; Ramsay, 2008; Anderson and Honneth, 2009). Many of the writers draw on vulnerability as a concept that can challenge and offer a counterweight to what Fineman and Grear (2013: 2) describe as the 'myth' of the autonomous and independent subject of liberal and neoliberal theory (see also Fineman, 2008).

A prominent theme in 'universal vulnerability' approaches is the idea that as humans we share an ontological and bodily insecurity that can unite us with others in society and which can be a motivator for more careful consideration and treatment of others (Goodin, 1985; Butler, 2004; Turner, 2006; Ramsay, 2008). Anderson and Honneth (2009: 137) see recognising vulnerability and threats to our 'self-trust, self-respect and self-esteem' as the starting point for individuals to be truly autonomous, rather than having the right to act without constraint. They advance 'theories of vulnerable autonomy' as a basis for an alternative version of liberalism; one focused less on individualism and more on the fragility of human existence. The authors argue that at the centre of every individual's ability to lead a worthwhile life is the intersubjective process of 'mutual recognition' of each other's worth, wherein lies the innate vulnerability of all human existence (2009: 137).

Campbell (1991) advances that a fundamental problem with liberalism is that our attitudes to vulnerable people are shaped by popular desires to be rational independent beings, and by a dislike of 'dependency'. He implies that it is the citizenship model in economic liberal democracies that renders vulnerability patronising, rather than this being a problem with the concept itself. According to Campbell (1991: 10), if citizens were to accept that vulnerability is universal, 'doing one's best' for others would no longer be patronising but would in fact foster autonomy.

Similarly, in work on the September 11 terrorism attacks in 2001, Butler (2004: 31, 44) draws on the idea of a 'common human vulnerability', which is bodily and inescapable, but also constituted politically and according to 'norms of recognition' (see also Butler, 2009). She argues that the vulnerability of some goes unrecognised because of the lack of value placed on the lives of certain citizens. For Mackenzie et al (2014), Butler's work on vulnerability has similarities with other writings on precarity (Standing, 2011), emphasising economic vulnerabilities experienced by certain social groups as a result of recent financial changes and the advancement of economic liberal ideas and policy pursuits. Kittay (1999) and Dodds (2007) use theories of universal vulnerability to examine the role of carers, with particular reference to feminist theories and the role and status of women within society. Such feminist writings foreground vulnerability as a mechanism for understanding and placing importance on the role of caring for dependants within society. Writing on vulnerability in bioethics and feminist philosophy, Mackenzie et al (2014) note that while 'universal' models of vulnerability can be criticised for being too broad and ill-defined, they are also useful in respect of drawing out shared precariousness and human experiences of adversity. The authors advance a 'taxonomy of vulnerability' (Mackenzie et al, 2014: 7-9), which encompasses both inherent (or universal) and 'context-specific' forms of vulnerability.

How far such aspirational universal vulnerability ideas might be of assistance in halting or reversing the advancement of more individualised constructions of disadvantage is open to debate. The vulnerability thesis writers argue that the concept is able to emphasise structurally constituted aspects of people's varying degrees of fragility and need, engendering a society-wide and blame-avoiding rationing of resources. Yet questions remain about how far this approach confers ideas about human powerlessness. Concerns include enhanced state intervention (Furedi, 2008), as well as appeals to behaviourist social policy approaches and the potential implication that increasing numbers of 'mainstream' people require therapeutic and 'expert' psychological interventions (see McLaughlin, 2012; Ecclestone and Lewis, 2013). As one example of this thesis being used to argue in favour of social control mechanisms, in political philosophy work, Ramsay (2008) defends the use of Civil Protection Orders such as Anti-Social Behaviour Orders on the basis of 'theories of vulnerable autonomy'. He advances that because 'autonomy related vulnerabilities' (2008: 15) are deeply rooted across the spectrum of mainstream political theories (the Third Way, communitarianism, neoliberalism), when individuals fail to reassure one another that they will not affect someone else's pursuit of wellbeing and security, this should be taken very seriously and intensive social control interventions should be triggered. According to Ramsay, political systems need to offer protections from the vulnerabilities and risks we experience as citizens. This raises the question of how vulnerability connects and maps onto ideas about risk in contemporary society.

Vulnerability and risk: similarities and differences

Since the 1990s, the concept of risk has attracted significant sociological attention. Something of a consensus has emerged about the pervasiveness of the notion, its link to institutional power and the importance of its deployment in processes by which official authorities appraise and regulate people (O'Malley, 2000; Mythen, 2004). Theories related to such developments are sometimes referred to as the 'risk society' thesis (referring to Beck, 1992). Pioneers of risk society ideas such as Beck (1992), Giddens (1991) and Bauman (2000) have argued that modernisation processes and technological developments have resulted in fundamental changes to 'late-modern' societies. A rapid quickening of the pace of change and an apparent loosening of the structural ties that bind and constrain the lives and lifecourses of individuals, they argue, have resulted in citizens feeling less in control of their lives. According to risk society ideas, increased feelings of insecurity intrinsic to 'late-modern' societies have fuelled an insatiable effort across society to seek to control that which apparently threatens security. Scholars have used the risk society thesis to explain a growing preoccupation with risk in everyday life, especially the risk of hazards associated with crime and disorder (Garland, 2001; Burney, 2005; Zedner, 2006).

In criminology, the ascendance of the concept of risk has been noted as a conduit in moves away from 'transformative' interventions with offenders towards accepting and 'managing' problem behaviour (see Feeley and Simon, 1992). In social policy and practice, risk has gained prominence and credence as a concept, with similar trends noted (Culpitt, 1999; Lupton, 1999; Mitchell and Glendinning, 2007). A growing body of empirical work has developed about the significance of risk in health, social care and welfare (see Alaszewski et al, 1998; Kemshall, 2002; Parton, 2007). In analysis of concepts utilised in the child protection process, Daniel (2010: 233) notes that 'risk' denotes the 'chances of adversity translating into actual negative outcomes for children' and also that risk has a certain predictive element as it plays a role in determining 'likelihood'. Waugh (2008: 113) notes a 'narrow' and 'broad' definition to notions of risk, arguing that narrow definitions emphasise individual events and risk of harm, whereas broader definitions are based on a more comprehensive assessment from 'ecological and feminist' perspectives.

The risk society thesis has obvious overlap and explanatory power in terms of relevance to vulnerability, which has been reviewed elsewhere (see Misztal, 2011; Potter and Brotherton, 2013). Indeed, as noted in Chapter One, Beck (2009: 178) himself has stated that the concepts are 'two sides of the same coin'. Taylor-Gooby (2000: 6) positions the notions as heavily intertwined, arguing that there has been an 'explosion of concern about risk, vulnerability and social need' within contemporary society. In terms of comparisons between the two notions, vulnerability discourses can similarly be seen as associated with ontological concerns about insecurity and powerlessness. Risk society ideas have been used by a number of scholars to argue that vulnerability has become a pervasive and problematic defining feature of the state's relationship to the individual (see Kemshall, 2002; Furedi, 2006, Waiton, 2008; McLaughlin, 2012). McLaughlin (2012: 113) argues that there has been an 'expansion of the concept of vulnerability' to the extent that it has become central to understandings of the concept of the self in contemporary society. For McLaughlin, vulnerability is now such a pervasive notion in society that it occupies a position at the forefront of individuals' relationships with social structures, a development that he sees as directly linked with a decline in the power of collective social movements and political activism.

Writing about the political environment in which the notion of antisocial behaviour came to be significant in contemporary society, Waiton (2008: 45) asserts that a 'politics of vulnerability' has now emerged. He uses this term to describe New Labour's approach to order maintenance; one centred on the individualised sense of insecurity and the 'defence of the anxious and chronically vulnerable' individual (2008: 48). As specific interest groups (mainly, he says, women, poor living in poverty and people from black and minority ethnic backgrounds) came to be seen as in need of protection, vulnerability 'increasingly became a term used for ever more groups in society and ultimately the population as a whole' (2008: 78).

Furedi (2003) has linked vulnerability to a 'culture of fear', where contemporary society's emphasis on the notion has led to an etiquette where anxieties about risk taking have become central to experiences of everyday life, and where 'safety' is enshrined as one of the main virtues of society. In later work, Furedi (2007, 2008) condemns the way that the concept of vulnerability has 'effortlessly migrated' into the social sciences literature and has become a condition that, he argues, is now intrinsic to existence rather than an expression of an individuals' experiences. Across this work concerned with the paternal implications of vulnerability, problematic preoccupations with 'risk' are a notable theme.

Policy commentaries have argued that risk occupies a central role in the way that individuals are monitored and managed by governments in the context of attaining neoliberal goals (see Lupton, 1999). The proliferation of intervention and information that promotes risk-avoiding behaviour by citizens (pregnancy-related health advice is one example given by Lupton) is argued to be a moral enterprise that can be understood within a context of moves to 'responsibilise' individuals (Culpitt, 1999; Lupton, 1999). Kemshall's (2002) analysis asserts that vulnerability functions in a similar way, with the rise of vulnerability within social care settings linked with the ascent of Thatcherite agendas of reducing welfare. As 'personal social services' became increasingly preoccupied with the auditing and assessment of individuals and with bureaucratic systems of 'risk management', she argues, so the concept of vulnerability was taken on by local authorities to further enable the implementation of 'top-down' welfare reduction priorities (2002: 78): 'Gatekeeping was considerably simplified by replacing the inclusive, ambiguous concept of need with the exclusive and managerially defined concept of "vulnerability" in which clearer positions could be set' (2002: 28). According to this analysis, in the state's struggle to meet the 'needs' of citizens, vulnerability has been an essential tool in moves to frame welfare provision in terms of more 'selective' ideas and practices.

While similarities between risk and vulnerability have received some attention from certain scholars, the concepts are often used interchangeably (Appleton, 1999) and differences have received very little attention. Authors interested in notions of vulnerability have been critical of the relative obscurity of vulnerability when compared with risk, with Sarewitz et al (2003: 810) arguing that: 'Too often vulnerability lies in the shadow of risk, or worse still, the concepts are integrated with a net result of losing focus on vulnerability.' Generally speaking, a lack of clarity exists about how far risk and vulnerability are the same or different, perhaps exacerbated by the somewhat porous and ill-defined dimensions of both concepts. Attempts to draw a precise distinction between indicators for risk and vulnerability will always be prone to oversimplification, but there would appear to be three key facets of vulnerability that could be tentatively advanced as marking it out as conceptually distinct from risk.

First, vulnerability would appear to have even more pronounced ethical connotations than risk, with particularly potent overtones of the duty of care. This is especially evident in normative understandings of vulnerability. The concept has a special moral weight due to its links with compassion and responsibility, as is highlighted in works by the vulnerability thesis writers and in the ethics literature (especially Goodin, 1985). This may be important when it comes to designing and implementing interventions that seek to address vulnerability. Discussing teenage parents and social policy arrangements, Van Loon (2008: 59) uses Foucault's (1980) theories on the dispersed and subtle nature of state power to argue that vulnerability has a 'cloak of concern', which means that it can be used to justify stronger controlling mechanisms. This idea is something that will be returned to in later chapters. Vulnerability has a deep connection in discourse with connotations of empathy and tenderness, apparently aligning it with therapeutic and supportive approaches that help those in need but which may also serve social control functions (see Harrison and Sanders, 2006). While risk is undoubtedly enormously significant in the social control apparatus, what is distinctive about vulnerability is that the controlling undertones of vulnerability would appear to be perhaps more *hidden from view or camouflaged* than in the case of risk.

Second, vulnerability could be argued to have potentially further-reaching implications, as vulnerability can denote something more remote in terms of potential harm, as well as the actuality of something negative happening (see Mackenzie et al, 2014). Highlighting difference with risk in the field of the human sciences, Sarewitz et al (2003: 805) argue that vulnerability refers to the wider 'characteristics of a system that create the potential for harm', whereas risk is the 'risk of occurrence' or the probability of a particular outcome. According to this approach, there can be potential for harm present (vulnerability) without a high chance of a certain hazard occurring (risk). Such accounts indicate that vulnerability is perhaps more *contingent* than risk. In other words, vulnerability often denotes the presence of a *possibility* of a negative outcome as well as a fairly advanced *likelihood* of a negative outcome. This means that as a net-widening mechanism, vulnerability could extend further than risk.

The third key way in which vulnerability is distinct from risk would appear to be in its particular behavioural associations. Given that vulnerability involves 'difference' from accepted norms of personhood and 'proper' citizenship, it has stronger links with deservingness than risk. Unlike risk, vulnerability is intrinsically linked to ideas about weakness and frailty, raising questions as to how far vulnerability classifications might be influenced by normative assumptions that vulnerable people should display or *'perform' weakness and frailty in some way*. Despite growing attention to vulnerability more recently, this behavioural aspect of the concept remains underexplored. In later chapters, it becomes apparent that this dimension is one of the most significant aspects of the concept of vulnerability when it is operationalised in welfare and disciplinary interventions with 'vulnerable' young people (see especially Chapter Four).

Chapter summary

Although popularly drawn on in the academic literature, the concept of vulnerability seems to have received relatively little critical attention, especially in comparison with similar notions such as risk. In the main, vulnerability lacks accepted indicators and methods of measurement. It varies enormously in its conceptual dimensions depending on the disciplinary contexts and theoretical underpinnings that shape how it appears and is deployed. Different constructions of vulnerability evidently have a diverse range of trajectories with manifold implications. There are a variety of definitions that have been advanced and reviewed here, with some of the key ones drawn together and summarised in Table 2.1. For Misztal (2011) and Wallbank and Herring (2013), the indistinct boundaries of the concept are what make it well suited to reflect the diversity of human experiences of adversity; for others, this imprecision and vagueness is problematic, perhaps especially when it is drawn on in more 'applied' settings (see Hurst, 2008; Fawcett, 2009).

Attention to how vulnerability appears in the academic literature revealed five particularly prominent configurations of the notion, which are imprecise and overlapping. Firstly, innate vulnerability describes where the condition of being vulnerable is presented as associated with particular aspects of the lifecourse or with 'biological' factors. Such an approach to vulnerability appears to have particular resonance for children and young people due to dominant developmental ideas, which imagine children as in some way incomplete, not fully developed and dependent on adults. Innate vulnerability helps to draw attention to points in the lifecourse where people may require extra support or attention in order to be healthy and safe. Such innate understandings of vulnerability have also been applied to disabled people, which certain writers influenced by the social model of disability have been critical of, arguing that to see disable people as inherently vulnerability is patronising and oppressive and obscures the role of society in the construction of disabled people's lived experiences of vulnerability.

Table 2.1: Examples of vulnerability definitions

Author	Disciplinary orientation	Definition
Sarewitz et al (2003)	Environmental and human sciences	The 'characteristics of a system that create the potential for harm' (p 805)
Watts and Bohle (2003)	Environmental and human sciences	Three coordinates of vulnerability (p 45): • risk of exposure to crises, stress and shocks • risk of inadequate capacities to cope with these • risk of severe consequences arising in these instances
Goodin (1985)	Philosophy	Relational definition: social responsibilities generated by one person's vulnerability in relation to another's capability
Mackenzie et al (2014)	Philosophy/feminist theory	Taxonomy of vulnerability (pp 7-9). Vulnerability 'types' are not mutually exclusive and include: • inherent /intrinsic • situational: context-dependent, may be temporary or enduring • potential or actual (which the authors call 'dispositional' or 'occurring') • 'pathogenic': generated by interpersonal relationships as well as institutional structures
Butler (2004)	Philosophy/feminist theory	Bodily 'human vulnerability' is inescapable and innate, but 'vulnerability' is also constituted politically and according to 'norms of recognition' (p 44)
Fineman (2013)	Critical legal theory/ ethics	Connected to 'human embodiment' and the 'imminent or ever-present possibility of harm' and may be compounded by possibilities of 'accompanying economic and institutional harms and disruption of existing social, economic or family relationships' (p 20)
Misztal (2011)	Sociology	Important, inevitable aspect of the human condition, socially and politically constituted; we are 'biologically frail' and 'socially vulnerable' (p 221)
Emmel and Hughes (2014)	Sociology	Toblerone model with four dimensions: material shortages in households, characterised by: (a) 'making do' with limited resources for basic everyday needs; (b) a lack of capacity to address needs in the present and plan for the future (c) an uncertain reliance on welfare services to act to address crises when they happen (d) dynamic and changing realities of (a-c) as experienced through time

Second, vulnerability may be tied to particular adverse experiences or circumstances, a configuration that might usefully be termed situational vulnerability. Pertinent literature on this aspect of vulnerability includes writings that emphasise the particular vulnerabilities of those who are 'in need' or who are likely to come to experience particular dangers or harms. Here, vulnerability has close links with deservingness and victimhood, and is drawn on in efforts to circumvent disadvantaged groups being 'blamed' for their problems. Claims to deservingness for situationally vulnerable people are often tacit or implied, with vulnerability used as a signifier to indicate a 'sympathetic' approach. Close attention to situational vulnerability highlights that so-called vulnerable individuals or groups are also 'transgressive' in some instances, opening up questions about how far 'victimhood' status might be conferred on such populations.

Third, vulnerability has been utilised in attempts to understand and explain material and social disadvantage, drawing attention to the structures that shape and constrain individual circumstances. This spatially orientated vulnerability literature seems to draw attention not only to the particular problems or 'adversities' that vulnerable people might face, but also to the role of social and political systems in shaping how effectively people can respond to these (see Watts and Bohle, 1993). Social researchers have usefully borrowed from this tradition in order to highlight how lived experiences of vulnerability are shaped and mediated by social systems as well as by agency and more personal and individual factors. In these works, a temporal dimension to vulnerability becomes evident, with certain academic work highlighting that vulnerability can be a notion that manages to capture something of precariousness over time as well as in the present (Archer Copp, 1986; Emmel and Hughes, 2010, 2014).

The fourth configuration is the notion of universal vulnerability, which has attracted significant attention in ethics and philosophy and has more recently been used across a number of other fields within the social sciences and humanities. While this approach to vulnerability is necessarily broad in scope and perhaps open to the criticism of being ill-defined, it emphasises the interconnectedness of human existence and gives weight to commonly held precarities that are relational in nature, and socially constituted. This could be seen as especially valuable to those interested in citizenship models that offer a counterweight to the hegemonic ideal of the independent, autonomous and capable agent, which is fundamental to governance in economic liberal societies. For some advocates of the vulnerability thesis, universal vulnerability represents a concept that is able to emphasise compassion and interdependency in ways that might have a broad enough appeal to become meaningful as a new way of seeing the relationship between citizens and the state.

Finally, vulnerability can be seen as aligned with risk and ideas about the 'risk society' (Beck, 1992). Both notions are bound up with ontological concerns about insecurity and an increased desire to control apparent hazards and threats. The risk society thesis is undoubtedly powerful and relevant in attempts to make sense of the concept of vulnerability, yet there are also key distinctions that might usefully be drawn between the two notions. It has been argued here that vulnerability is more contingent than risk, has more intense ethical and moral connotations (especially in normative accounts) and is also perhaps more deeply imbued with heavily camouflaged assumptions about deservingness and 'appropriate' behaviour. Classifications of vulnerability are used to indicate not only that an individual is at risk, but also that they may pose a risk to others and need to be controlled. This vulnerability–transgression nexus is significant in terms of informing how people are managed and appraised, and in shaping which individuals and groups are included and excluded when interventions are organised on the basis of vulnerability (see Chapter Three).

Analysis of how vulnerability can be understood shows that it is a concept that can be utilised in the pursuit of universal social systems, but that it can also be one that is tied heavily to paternalism and individualism. Underpinning alternative uses of the notion is a tension between broader and narrower ways of understanding vulnerability. The concept can be seen as one that is patronising and stigmatising, or as one that has a unique, unifying and socially transformative quality that can be utilised to foster autonomy and social justice. Frictions between these two views of vulnerability reveal that far from being neutral or benign, the concept is deeply imbued with ethical and practical implications in terms of how resources and sanctions might be distributed, and how far the state is seen as responsible for lived experiences of vulnerability. In making sense of vulnerability, we are forced to examine mechanisms that frame and re-frame adversity, agency and entitlement, raising a range of questions about how the concept is applied in policy and practice. It is to these more applied matters that the book now turns.

THREE

The rise of vulnerability in social policy

Introduction

Somewhat by stealth, the delineation of vulnerability has come to be a key dividing line across a wide range of welfare and criminal justice policy domains, shaping and informing both day-to-day and strategic priorities. That 'vulnerable' people deserve and require special assistance is an increasingly prominent idea in public policy, with vulnerability-based policy mechanisms often operating to form an additional 'net' for those who might fall through the gaps in a broader 'safety net'. The rise of vulnerability in policy reconfigures and reworks welfare and disciplinary provisions in a range of ways, yet seems largely to have escaped scrutiny. Vulnerability is one of the factors that qualifies someone for 'priority need' in state social housing allocations. In the criminal justice system, exceptions are made to standard processes on the basis of 'vulnerability', for both offenders and victims of crime. In social care arenas, procedures for safeguarding 'vulnerable' adults can override service user confidentiality or restrict the behaviours of those who receive services, and in child protection and education arenas, vulnerability now shapes an array of practices and routines. On the surface, such developments might seem to support the pursuit of social justice and the protection of those who need it most, but closer inspection reveals a more complicated picture. Differential treatment on the basis of vulnerability opens up important questions about how the notion is understood, who is included and excluded from 'support' on the basis of vulnerability, and what appropriate balances between individual rights and state powers might be in instances where people are 'vulnerable'.

Shortly before the 2010 General Election in the UK, David Cameron pledged that the 'test of a good society' is how it looks after 'the vulnerable' (BBC, 2010). Mahatma Ghandi is widely attributed to having said something similar, and this would seem a compassionate and 'morally appropriate' starting point for philosophies of state intervention and power. Yet in a context of economic liberal governance systems, the practicalities of supporting vulnerable people can look rather different. In a later speech on welfare reform, Cameron as Prime Minister outlined that support for vulnerable people should be conditional on certain behaviours and responsibilities: 'If you are vulnerable and in need, we will look after you. And if you hit hard times, we'll give unprecedented support. But in return, we expect you to do your bit' (Cameron, 2011). When vulnerability is deployed in the context of highly conditional welfare systems (Dywer, 2004, 2008), difficult questions open up regarding what an appropriate response is where vulnerable people are *not* able to 'correctly' meet their assigned responsibilities, and how far vulnerable groups are entitled to 'full' citizenship rights (see also Brown, 2014b).

Such questions have relevance beyond UK social policy developments. Vulnerability classifications now play an important role in decision making and case law in the European Court of Human Rights (Peroni and Timmer, 2013), developments described by legal scholars as a 'quiet revolution' (Timmer, 2013), and vulnerability appears increasingly frequently in public policy initiatives aimed at addressing a wide range of international social policy matters such as global poverty, natural disasters, armed conflict, financial crises, unemployment and environmental changes (OECD, 2013; UNDP, 2014). In times of financial austerity and welfare retrenchment, the targeting of particular groups on the basis of vulnerability could be considered to take on even further significance (see Brown, 2014b). As well as appealing to moral sensibilities, preoccupations with vulnerability seem aligned with growing contemporary concerns with fragility and precariousness (Furedi, 2007, 2008) or notions of structural crisis (Ecclestone and Goodley, 2014).

This chapter considers how vulnerability appears and operates as a notion in welfare and disciplinary policy and practice. The review focuses mainly on developments since 1997, as research into statutory instruments reveals that the deployment of vulnerability rationales seems to have gained particular momentum under the New Labour and the Conservative–Liberal Democrat coalition governments. The next section outlines how the concept of vulnerability has been used in four policy domains where it has been drawn on heavily: housing; adult social care; criminal justice arrangements; and children's services.

The review centres on policies in England, but there are selected references to Scottish and international developments where these serve as useful illustrative examples. Consideration is then given to the idea of 'vulnerable groups' and some of the implications of this motif in policy and practice are explored. Finally, how vulnerability classifications operate in relation to governmental power, professional discretion, the distribution of resources and conceptions of citizenship are discussed. It will be highlighted that vulnerability discourses can advance a more 'inclusive' or sympathetic approach to those who are less well-off. At the same time, however, within certain political contexts, focusing attention and resources on 'vulnerable' people can act as a mechanism that obscures the politically and economically constituted nature of social problems, which can contribute to the maintenance of social pathologies of groups who are seen as 'troublesome'.

Mapping vulnerability in policy and practice

By way of a brief overview of historical patterns related to the rise of vulnerability, although appearing in policy occasionally from as early as the 1950s in responses to prostitution and 'homosexual offences' (see Wolfenden, 1957; also Chapter One), 'vulnerability' surfaced fairly infrequently in UK statutory instruments until the 21st century. In the 1970s and 1980s, there were sporadic references to the notion, growing to 25 mentions in the 1990s and then to around 170 mentions in the first five years of the 2000s.[1] However, it is from the mid-2000s that we see its use on the statute books increase substantially. In 2007, there were 139 legal provisions that contained a reference to vulnerability, with its deployment then steadily rising year on year until 2012, which was the busiest year yet for vulnerability in statutory instruments.

Some of the most well-established and long-running classifications and appraisals of vulnerability developed in the field of housing policy, where legal delineations formalised the housing entitlements of 'vulnerable' people in the 1970s. This was followed by developments in the field of social care, where vulnerability was classified in relation to those who were seen to lack the capacity to protect themselves (particularly older and disabled people), moves that developed momentum after 1997 and especially during the course of the 2000s (see Dunn et al, 2008; Hasler, 2004). Safeguarding 'vulnerable' adults initiatives then seem to have been followed by a more rapid spread of vulnerability rationales into various other policy arenas such as criminal justice processes and children's services. While special protections have been focused on children for some time (see Chapter Two), under New Labour, vulnerability seemed to take root in more formal policy and processing mechanisms for those under the age of 18. Here, rather than attempting to catalogue all of the policies where vulnerability appears, attention is focused on the ways in which vulnerability rationales operate in selected arenas where they seem highly significant.

Housing policy and designating 'priority need'

'Vulnerability' was one of the three defined predicaments that triggered 'priority need' under the Housing (Homeless Persons) Act 1977, which made 'the vulnerable' among those classified as needing special fast tracking and prioritisation in UK social housing applications and allocation processes.[2] Initial statutory definitions of what constituted 'vulnerability' in this arena were set out in the Act, which referred to old age, 'mental illness', 'handicap or physical disability' or 'other special reason', leaving scope for wide interpretations of meaning. Since this statute was passed, what does and does not 'count' as vulnerability has become one of the key dividing lines in the provision of social housing resources, and one that has been particularly contentious and heavily litigated (Robson and Watchman, 1981).

In the absence of specific legislative direction, decisions about vulnerability status have been heavily informed by precedents in case law. For example, *R v Waveney DC, ex p Bowers* (1983) overturned a local council decision that 59-year-old Mr Bowers – a street homeless person who had been hospitalised for periods due to his heavy alcohol use – was not vulnerable. This case was to establish precedent that to be classified as vulnerable meant being 'less able to fend for oneself so that injury or detriment will result', but contingent on the likelihood of this happening in relation to someone else who is homeless (Carr and Hunter, 2008). In other words, vulnerability was not assessed merely as the risk a person may be exposed to as a result of being homeless, but the risk of harm in comparison with someone else who is also homeless (see also Meers, 2015: forthcoming). In the Homeless (Priority Need for Accommodation) (England) Order 2002, vulnerability status was extended to former members of armed forces, former prisoners and those fleeing violence. After the Conservative–Liberal Democrat coalition government came to power in 2010 there were radical changes to housing services and allocations of social housing, but priority need based on vulnerability endured as a key determinant of provision in England. This is not the case for Scotland, where priority need was scrapped as a policy and practice tool in 2012.

Vulnerability has been seen as particularly important in terms of the more informal ways in which people are processed within the housing system (Cramer, 2005), with judgements about the notion representing an interplay between 'the social, the political and the technical' (Carr and Hunter, 2008). Legal developments in relation to vulnerability have given rise to what is sometimes referred to as the 'vulnerability test' or the 'Pereira test' (see Meers, 2012, 2015: forthcoming), a judicial guide that offers some parameters for decision making but which still leaves wide scope for discretionary judgements about whether a housing applicant is 'vulnerable' or not (see Niner, 1989: 96; Lidstone, 1994; Meers, 2015: forthcoming). Medical evidence has become important in such delineations, especially in relation to 'mental illness' (Carr and Hunter, 2008). Companies now offer services where councils are able to purchase 'vulnerability tests' on particular claimants in order to ensure speedy undertaking of determining eligibility.[3] While Loveland (1995) argued that flexibility offered by vulnerability classifications could be lenient and favourable, others have drawn attention to the issue of gatekeeping (Lidstone, 1994) and 'downward drag' (Meers, 2015: forthcoming) and it is interesting that 'rates' of vulnerability have fallen in recent years (see Meers, 2014). Scholars have noted that allocating housing according to vulnerability can exclude groups who some may consider among the 'most vulnerable', with young single homeless people and childless couples being among those least well served (Carr and Hunter, 2008).

Behavioural factors would appear to be highly significant in the operation of vulnerability classifications in housing. Under New Labour, the Supporting People programme was explicitly aimed at homeless 'vulnerable' individuals and families, with those using services attached to this funding stream subject to certain behavioural conditionalities. Often, however, behavioural conditionalities have operated through vulnerability classifications in more subtle ways. Lowe (1997: 26) argues that the close links that housing vulnerability classifications have with ideas about deservingness connects them to Victorian Poor Laws, which distinguished between 'deserving' and 'undeserving' people. He notes that ex-offenders have often not been treated as vulnerable by some local authorities despite their official categorisation as a vulnerable group. In certain examples, scholars have noted a gendered dimension to assumed vulnerability in housing allocations, with women more firmly located within 'vulnerability' classifications due to their being more inclined to behave with deference and accept dependence (Passaro, 1996, reporting from New York; Cramer, 2005).

Further afield, Lévy-Vroelant (2010) notes the expansion of the designation of vulnerable groups in European housing policy, arguing that this has led to the treatment of homeless people becoming increasingly specialised and resulting in placing people and groups into competition for rare state resources. Other European housing policy academics have viewed a focus on vulnerability as a potentially progressive development. Vonk (2014) makes the case for a European

Union standard for the protection of vulnerable people 'in extreme need', which he argues would be instigated as a human rights platform and common minimum requirement for member states' responsibilities to homeless people who reside in their countries. Both in Europe and in the UK, in relation to housing the concept of vulnerability is closely linked with legal duties to protect citizens who do not have anywhere to live. It appears to operate primarily as a means of a quasi-official prioritisation mechanism, or indeed as a gatekeeping tool within the potentially expansive and broad boundaries of 'need' (see also Kemshall, 2002: 28), with subtle behavioural conditionalities attached. In housing, vulnerability is a concept closely connected to how people are managed and appraised as well as supported and assisted.

Adult social care and the governance of disability

Over recent decades, vulnerability has come to play a fundamental role in the governance of provision for adults who are seen to 'lack the capacity' to protect themselves. The *No Secrets* guidance issued in 2000 was central in such developments as it had 'the protection of vulnerable adults' (sometimes abbreviated to 'POVA') at its core (DH, 2000). Initiated after a series of high-profile cases of exploitation in residential homes, the guidance addressed older people and disabled people under the same banner of 'vulnerable adults'. While definitions of what constituted a 'vulnerable adult' were not straightforward, the most commonly used definition referred to that given in a consultation paper from the Lord Chancellor's Department (1997: 68), which was as follows: 'Someone over the age of 18 who is or may be in need of community care services by reason of mental health or other disability, age or illness and who is or may be unable to take care of him/herself or unable to protect him/herself against significant harm or exploitation'. This definition was drawn on in the *No Secrets* guidance and has in turn informed an array of different interventions in efforts to assure suitable 'protections' for disabled people. According to this definition, 'vulnerability' centres on an individual's inherent characteristics and/or circumstances, given which that person might be denied 'free choice' due to a malign third party influence or a structural force. Vulnerabilities such as older age and learning difficulties are presented as natural or innate (see Chapter Two).

This policy guidance enshrined vulnerability as one of the key criteria in the assessment of which adults qualify for various state interventions and safety procedures (Dunn et al, 2008; Fawcett, 2009; Hollomotz, 2011). *Safeguarding Adults* (ADSS, 2005) and other more recent initiatives such as the Care Act 2014 have revised the language used in policy making, but the legacy of the idea of vulnerability endures in legislation and the *No Secrets* definition is still widely used in practice (Hollomotz, 2009, 2011; McLaughlin, 2012). Alongside *No Secrets*, various other initiatives developed under New Labour, which addressed the presumed vulnerabilities of disabled people. Having won the right to receive 'direct payments' in 1996, disabled people were entitled to arrange some of their own services and buy the help they wanted. New Labour then later altered initial plans for the direct payments scheme, designing in exceptions for 'vulnerable' disabled people, who were deemed incapable of making these choices (Hasler, 2004). Extensions of the High Court's power to make declarations about interventions into the lives of 'vulnerable' instead of simply 'mentally incapacitated' adults were also granted in the first decade of the new millennium (see Dunn et al, 2008).

Turning to matters of public protection, New Labour passed the Safeguarding of Vulnerable Groups Act in 2006, which legislated for a 'Vetting and Barring Scheme' that would instigate extra checks for people who work or volunteer to support vulnerable adults and children. As has been the case in certain other areas, vulnerable adults were deemed as requiring a similar approach to children under this initiative. This followed the Bichard inquiry's investigation of the 2002 'Soham murders' of school children Holly Wells and Jessica Chapman in Cambridgeshire, who were killed by the caretaker of their school (Bichard, 2004). Under the Act, a national database of the details of workers/volunteers who were in contact with 'vulnerable' people was legislated for. For small government advocates, this policy was alarming and disproportionately far-reaching in scope in relation to the risks posed to vulnerable groups by individuals who sought to harm them. McLaughlin (2012: 113) argues that the policy was a classic example of a governmental presumption of citizens' inherent vulnerability, with 'caring' relationships 'recast as ones of potential harm and abuse', resulting in overbearing and paternalistic policy. The coalition government made significant changes to the plans for the Vetting and Barring Scheme after it came to power (see DfE, 2011). The Protection of Freedoms Act 2012 has more recently been passed, which introduced a scaled-back employment vetting scheme and reform of the criminal records checks system for those working with vulnerable groups. A more cautious approach perhaps, but a discourse of vulnerability nonetheless remains institutionalised within this policy domain, just as is the case in wider governance arrangements for disabled people.

Crime and antisocial behaviour: victims and offenders

Special exceptions on the basis of vulnerability have come to be seen as an important means of ensuring fairness within the criminal justice system. Such moves might be viewed as part of broader processes in the governance of crime and disorder whereby the 'victim' is located as centrally important in the administration of justice (see Garland, 2001; Hall, 2009; Bottoms and Roberts, 2010) and the effects of crime on 'vulnerable' populations such as children and women are given special consideration (Rock, 2002). Some academics have argued that a 'politics of vulnerability' now underpins contemporary approaches to order maintenance and systems of social control, operating alongside a new and disproportionate focus on the effects of crime and antisocial behaviour (Waiton, 2008: 45). One illustrative example of vulnerability rationales operating in criminal justice arenas was when in 2014 the Chief Constable of Greater Manchester Police called for enhanced police powers in order to protect vulnerable people, arguing that the police should have access to medical records without consent in cases of vulnerability (Dodd, 2014).

At various points in the criminal justice system, special provisions are now made where people are seen as 'vulnerable', perhaps most prominently in the policing of hate crimes (see Roulstone and Sadique, 2013). Obligations to 'vulnerable victims' (as opposed to victims generally) and those 'least able to protect themselves' seem to be taking on further significance (see Home Office, 2011: 1). While this has been associated with important safety gains for highly victimised groups (see for example Campbell, 2014), such developments might also be considered problematic. In an important case in Leicestershire, Fiona Pilkington and her disabled daughter Francecca Hardwick repeatedly reported violent and threatening incidents committed against them to the police, over a number of years. Fiona then went on to kill both herself and her daughter (see Independent Police Complaints Commission, 2011). In the incidents leading up to Fiona's death, police believed these to be related to her extreme vulnerability, meaning that the targeted hate crimes and abuse from perpetrators were arguably not policed in a way that was commensurate with full judicial rights (Roulstone et al, 2011; Roulstone and Sadique, 2013). Following the inquest into Pilkington and Hardwick's deaths, the protection of 'vulnerable' adults seems increasingly to be used as one of the justifications for the continuation of strong control mechanisms to deal with those seen as perpetrating 'antisocial behaviour' (see Home Office, 2011).

Turning to the courts, exceptions are made in the case of 'vulnerable' witnesses, who in the context of the legal system are those witnesses under the age of 17, or people deemed to have mental health problems or physical disabilities (see Home Office, 2002; Ministry of Justice, 2011). This strategy has been guided by attempts to limit the considerable emotional stress that giving evidence can entail within an adversarial system, and in practice has particularly applied to witnesses in cases connected with gendered crimes such as rape and domestic violence (see Hall, 2009). Such developments have broadly been received as a progressive, although some scholars argue that feminist anti-violence vulnerability discourses can also serve the creeping legal regulation of relatively 'normal' behaviours that should not be governed by the state and the courts (see Reece, 2009).

Particular groups of offenders have also been positioned as especially 'vulnerable', with special interventions and initiatives triggered as a result. The Corston Report highlighted the particular vulnerability of women in the criminal justice system, showing how vulnerability classifications can be applied broadly to highlight how social groups might be poorly served in more 'mainstream' provision (Corston, 2007). Vulnerability also became central to the governance of prostitution under New Labour, with women who sold sex increasingly configured as 'vulnerable' rather than 'criminal', while at the same time being treated in highly punitive ways (Phoenix and Oerton, 2005; Carline, 2011; Phoenix, 2012a). The antisocial behaviour agenda tends to now be couched in terms of 'tackling troubled families' (DCLG, 2011) or 'problematic populations' (Flint, 2006b), but a cluster of other terms are also often used to describe those governed by this agenda, among which 'vulnerable families' often features (see Centre for Social Justice, 2010; Morris, 2013). As Flint (2006b) has argued, this discourse highlights the problematic behaviour of particular individuals or households, distinguishes the actions of these populations from the behaviour of 'ordinary' people, and reflects tendencies to locate the causes of and solutions to 'problem behaviour' within local communities rather than within society as a whole.

Vulnerability can also be found to be drawn on heavily in terrorism policy, both in the UK and internationally. Richards (2011) notes that in the updated version of the government's strategy document on terrorism (HM Government, 2009), the words 'vulnerable' and 'vulnerability' were used a total of 32 times (in reference to people who are vulnerable to committing terrorism). This use of vulnerability in relation to 'extremists' functions to imply 'diminished capacity for rational behaviour' (Richards, 2011: 51), demonstrating how the concept might be associated with the advancement of particular ideological views. Terrorism prevention work in schools now targets those children and young people who are 'vulnerable' (meaning vulnerable to extremism), a contentious strategy in that this could be seen as the state assuming responsibility for 'protecting' supposedly vulnerable potential 'extremists' from their own arguably political preferences, amounting to ideological positions being advanced on the grounds of 'vulnerability' (see Coppock and McGovern, 2014). Vulnerability discourses in relation to terrorism would seem to serve to underline that people who disagree with mainstream ideas are not of 'sound mind', highlighting how vulnerability connects with normative assumptions about 'acceptability'.

Children and young people's services

Contemporary intervention in family life is legitimated on the premise that children are innately vulnerable and dependent, and that it cannot be taken for granted that parents will offer them appropriate protection (Daniel, 2010). Under New Labour, however, a more 'official' discourse on vulnerability seemed to creep into many of the governing policies and documents that were concerned with child protection and wider 'safeguarding' agendas. By way of an overview, a selection of policy documents that provide insights into how children and young people's vulnerability appears at the 'official' level are reviewed and summarised in Table 3.1. The most important of these was arguably New Labour's landmark *Every Child Matters* government guidance (DfES, 2003), which informed the Children Act 2004 and underpinned much of New Labour's approach to children's services. This document drew on theoretical notions of all children as positioned along a spectrum of vulnerability. According to *Every Child Matters*, while all children were vulnerable, some were more vulnerable than others, with special or enhanced vulnerabilities configured as primarily relating to (a) 'harm' as encountered in the child protection system or (b) particular behaviours or victimisations that may lead to a poor future for a children or young person.

Various other New Labour initiatives targeted resources at specific groups of children seen to be at elevated vulnerability because of their adverse circumstances. The Common Assessment Framework (CAF) initiative was designed to standardise the assessment of children's 'additional needs', which connected with the idea of all children being on a vulnerability spectrum. Targeted Youth Support was also launched under New Labour in 2007, a multi-agency working initiative aimed

Table 3.1: Examples of policy approaches to children and young people's vulnerability

Document/ initiative	Policy domain	Vulnerability and vulnerable groups identified
Every Child Matters (DfES, 2003)	Children's services	'Most vulnerable' children are those most at risk of significant harm and 'vulnerable' children are those at risk from poor outcomes. Vulnerability is associated with all children, but particular groups needing extra attention are listed according to factors associated with poor outcomes.
Think Family (Social Exclusion Task Force, 2007, 2008)	Antisocial behaviour and family policy	'Most vulnerable' and 'disadvantaged' are discussed throughout. Policy targets 'families at risk' and 'vulnerable families'. Alerts reader to same population 'caught' by various interventions at different points in their lives.
Department for Education report on outcomes for vulnerable young people (Walker and Donaldson, 2011)	Education policy	Vulnerability factors (p 8): truancy/school exclusion, behavioural problems, poor coping skills, poor mental health, learning difficulties, specific disabilities, low aspirations or low self-esteem, poor family support or problems in the family, friends/ family members involved in antisocial or criminal behaviours, deprivation/poverty, family instability, drug or alcohol misuse, not being in education.
Interventions to reduce young people's substance use (NICE, 2007)	Drugs policy	Those whose family members misuse substances, children/young people with behavioural or mental health problems, excludees and truants, young offenders, 'looked-after' children/young people, those who are homeless, those involved in sex work, those from some minority ethnic groups. Young people are classified as those aged under 25.
Asset guidance (Youth Justice Board, 2006)	Youth offending	Mental and physical health needs; behaviours such as 'acting out' and 'inappropriate responses to stress'; risk from others including bullying, abuse, neglect, exploitation; life events such as poverty, bereavement, insecure housing (see also Phoenix, 2013).
Operating Framework, City Council Vulnerable Groups Commissioning Partnership Board (2009)[1]	Children's services – local arrangements	Young people who offend, children who misuse substances and alcohol, teenage parents and those at risk of conceiving, children with mental health problems and 'behavioural difficulties', disabled children and those with complex needs, 'looked-after' children and those 'on the edge of care'.
Service user involvement (National Institute for Health Research, 2001)	Public health and social care	Notes that the term means different things to each of us. Lists 28 groups as example vulnerable groups (p 2) including: 'children in general', children in care, young carers, asylum seekers and refugees, people whose 'voices cannot be heard', people who cannot read or write English, people who need (but are not receiving) health or social care services.

[1] A local document used in the city of the empirical case study. A full reference is not given for reasons of anonymity.

at supporting 'vulnerable' young people in order to prevent them from reaching the thresholds for statutory 'child protection' interventions (DfES, 2007). While undoubtedly a powerful tool in highlighting potential risks beyond those related to the previously narrower focus on 'significant harm', Daniel (2010) sees such a conceptualisation of vulnerability as connected with an expansion of the child protection system under New Labour. She argues that the popularity of the concept might usefully be seen as linked to the 'problematisation' of childhood (2010: 236). Such concerns are congruent with other commentaries that have raised the possibility that 'overprotection' of children and 'risk avoidance' can be damaging, leading to potential impairment of competency development and poor coping skills (Waiton, 2001; Newman and Blackburn, 2002; Gill, 2007).

In the field of education policy, special funding programmes were instigated that were designed to help vulnerable children in the education system. The Vulnerable Children Grant, introduced in 2003, intended to improve access to education for 'vulnerable' children, encouraging local authorities to develop their 'strategic approach' to dealing with this group (Kendall et al, 2004a). This funding replaced previous 'ring-fenced' sums for predefined groups of pupils (such as looked-after children or Gypsy and Traveller children) and enabled local authorities to be more flexible about which children and young people received additional educational support (Kendall et al, 2004b: i). More recently, under the coalition government, the coalition's first Education Minister Michael Gove centred his defence of the new bursary scheme for 16- to 19-year-olds in education on the premise that the Educational Maintenance Allowance (EMA) would be replaced by a fund that 'targeted' the 'most vulnerable' in full-time education (Gove, 2011). However, Gove quite tightly defined his 'most vulnerable' children as those in care, care leavers and those on income support,[4] indicating a possible narrowing of entitlement in relation to children's vulnerability status in this domain.

Direct behavioural interventions have also been targeted at 'vulnerable' young people within the education system, such as the Promoting Alternative Thinking Strategies Programme (see Ecclestone and Lewis, 2014). While offering an important trigger for enhanced support within universal systems that may overlook the particular needs of disadvantaged or 'troubled' children, such vulnerability-based interventions can also be deemed problematic. As Ecclestone and Lewis (2014) highlight, attention to the vulnerability of children and young people in educational settings is often closely aligned with programmes that aim to develop 'resilience' and 'wellbeing', focusing interventions on behaviours and psychological approaches rather than broader political matters associated with educational problems. While clearly having the potential to improve the 'responsiveness' of the education system to certain children, there is a tendency for such initiatives to facilitate a revival of 'character building' (Ecclestone and Lewis, 2014: 196) and incline developments towards prioritisations on the basis of 'emotional need' rather than structural disadvantage.

Within youth justice policy and practice, the assessment of vulnerability has come to play an important role in determining interventions for young offenders. For some years now, assessing and managing vulnerability has been a key part of Youth Offending Service tools for measuring and addressing 'risk' (see Youth Justice Board, 2006), which in this context mainly relates to the risk of reoffending. The national Youth Justice Board screening tool, *Asset*, has a detailed section that addresses vulnerability (see Phoenix, 2013), with this defined broadly as the risk of a young person being harmed due to a variety of factors: mental and physical health needs; behaviours (such as 'acting out' and 'inappropriate responses to stress'); risk from others (including bullying, abuse, neglect and exploitation); and life events (such as poverty, bereavement and insecure housing).

In the newer assessment and planning interventions framework (*AssetPlus*; see Youth Justice Board, 2014) being introduced at the time of writing, the focus on vulnerability remains. The vulnerability status of a young person is deemed 'highly relevant' when determining 'a suitable response' to young people's actions, especially where a young person might face a custodial sentence (Youth Justice Board, 2006: appendix 12: 7). Phoenix (2013: 364) argues that the assessment of vulnerability in youth justice represents a point at which a contradiction emerges between protection and punishment, with risk and vulnerability conflated in a way that brings 'individually centred criminogenic risks' to the foreground.

The particular relevance of vulnerability classifications as they apply to young people involved with the justice system is a matter given further consideration in later chapters (see especially Chapter Four). Overall, attention to how vulnerability classifications operate in various policy domains reveals a rather complicated picture where, often, tensions between care and the regulation of 'problem' behaviours appear to be particularly pronounced. Requirements to balance the needs of 'vulnerable' individuals with resulting restrictions on individual freedoms emerge as a thorny issue, as does the issue of which groups of people might be likely to be classified as vulnerable and what might happen as a result.

Vulnerable groups and vulnerable identities

The designation of 'vulnerable groups' has come to be a common motif in policy and practice. Generally speaking, such designations seem to serve to reaffirm and/or challenge the dominant conceptions of individuals' or groups' requirement for special care and attention and/or a duty of care that might be over and above that required in relation to 'non-vulnerable' people. In some cases, examples of vulnerable groups are detailed in official documentation; in others, definition is left open to interpretation. Even whole nations can be seen as vulnerable (Bradshaw, 2013: 7), and vulnerability to a specific adversity often merges with general 'vulnerability' as a stand-alone state or a noun. Which populations are framed within categorisations of particular 'vulnerable groups' varies widely, but it is also possible to discern broader patterns and themes. According to Fineman (2013: 16) vulnerable groups can be either 'identity based' (related to factors such as gender and ethnicity for example) and/or 'status based' (related to circumstances or situations). As highlighted above in relation to children and young people (see Table 3.1), although designated 'vulnerable groups' tend to vary, there are also some that are commonly occurring (such as children in care or young drug users), indicating a certain shared tacit understanding of what constitutes a 'vulnerable group'.

Just as it is popular everyday language, the phrase or idea of 'the most vulnerable' appears often alongside policy and practice, but perhaps especially in relation to children and young people. The opening of the executive summary of *Every Child Matters* (DfES, 2003: 5) described 'shameful failings in our ability to protect the most vulnerable children', a reference to the death of eight-year-old Victoria Climbié, whose abuse was not detected by a range of agencies and who died in 2000 from injuries inflicted by her carers. Over a decade later, all of the 'big five' children's charities (Barnardo's, The Children's Society, NSPCC, Action for Children and Save the Children[5]) emphasise the centrality of vulnerable groups or the 'most vulnerable' in their work, and a simple search for 'vulnerable' on their websites (August 2014) returned over 5,000 results. Here, the idea of vulnerable groups would seem to have special relevance as a tool in campaigning policy work aimed at drawing attention to problems experienced by certain 'deserving' children and young people.

Although narratives of vulnerability seem to offer some mitigation against the urge to condemn, behavioural aspects seem to remain significant in the 'realisation' of vulnerability status, even where people might 'officially' be deemed the 'most vulnerable'. Those who might be assumed to fit neatly into a 'most vulnerable' group may in practice have difficulties securing entitlement to support. As one example, vulnerability is especially notable as a prominent motif in official constructions of sexually exploited children and young people (see DH and Home Office, 2000; Beddoe, 2006; DCSF, 2009; DfE, 2011), yet this official classification does not seem to correlate to consistently sympathetic practice responses to young people who fall into this group (see Chapter One; Phoenix, 2012b).

Although useful for designating 'need', tendencies to design and organise policies and interventions based on vulnerable groups identify certain populations as 'different' from 'mainstream' citizens. Writing about the rise of 'vulnerable groups' in the decision making of the European Court of Human Rights, Peroni and Timmer (2013) note that this approach has allowed the court to attend to the constructed disadvantages faced by certain minority populations (especially Roma people), but also links to processes of stigmatisation that operate where vulnerability is delineated at group membership level. Fineman (2013: 16) argues that such aggregated group constructions of vulnerability are 'misleading' and 'pernicious', as they are both 'over- and under-exclusive'. How interventions with vulnerable groups might operate to undermine collective action has also been a concern. McLaughlin (2012) argues that social activism in contemporary society is now based on a tendency to organise according to vulnerability, running contrary to broader collectivist approaches to social movements such as unionisation. He associates a delineation of vulnerable groups with the individualisation of social problems, arguing that this configuration of issues renders unacceptable the analysis of wider social and cultural factors that shape experiences (see also Chapter Two).

When considering issues of stigma, questions arise as to how far those who are deemed as 'vulnerable' might associate themselves with such a label or grouping. Across sociological, policy and official literature, occasional and disparate writings have explored the idea that officially designated 'vulnerable' groups may not identify with the label 'vulnerability'. Writing in the field of interventional development, Chambers (1989: 33) warns that care is needed in the use of the concept of vulnerability as it starts as 'our concept, not necessarily "theirs"'. In relation to people with learning difficulties, Parley (2011: 270) argues that it is other people who decide on 'the vulnerable label or the degree of vulnerability' rather than the individual concerned (see also Wiles, 2011). Official documents (and indeed research) on sexual exploitation often state that even though sexually exploited young people are some of the most vulnerable in society, they may not see themselves in this way (DCSF, 2009; DfE, 2011). Dunn et al (2008) criticise dominant notions of vulnerability as related to external and objective assessments of 'risk', rather than based on understandings of the subjective experience of being vulnerable. The authors argue that discourses of vulnerability evident in policy act to disempower the 'vulnerable adult' by reducing them to a series of risk factors, failing to adequately take account of the experiences through which a person with learning difficulties might ascribe meaning to their life.

McLaughlin (2012) explores the idea of 'vulnerable identities' in detail. He argues that while vulnerable identities have been 'imposed' on individuals through a 'politics of fear' (2012: 112), people have largely been receptive to notions of themselves as vulnerable and as having 'suffered trauma', and have been seduced by the rise of a 'therapeutic identity' (2012: 98). Concerned with overall trends, such analysis perhaps leaves unanswered questions about how particular subgroups of the population may differ in how far they identify with vulnerable identities. Wiles (2011) begins to explore such questions in relation to disability and recipients of care, but differences in how men and women might position themselves in relation to vulnerability, or working-class populations and middle-class populations, for example, would also seem to be worthy of further exploration.

More generally, how far those who are classified as vulnerable are receptive or resistant to notions of their own vulnerability would certainly appear to be an area that warrants further investigation. Considering patterns across policy domains reveals that the designation, support and management of 'vulnerability' has become embedded in governance systems through a wide range of welfare and disciplinary initiatives, being deployed by various actors involved with policy, practice, campaigning and commentary on an array of social problems. Given the subjectivities involved in decision making about who belongs to 'vulnerable groups', vulnerability emerges as especially important at points in welfare and disciplinary systems where professionals exercise judgement. Understandings of the concept also shape how relationships between citizens and the state are cast, and it is to these broader themes that the chapter now turns.

Vulnerability, discretion and subtle social control

One of the ways in which we see 'vulnerability' manifested in policy since 1997 is as tacit moral justification for stronger social control practices. Often, exceptions made on the basis of perceived vulnerability would seem to enhance the power of welfare or criminal justice professionals to make decisions on behalf of those they support. The 'power of professionals' here refers to patterns within particular policy environments, rather than the actions of individuals independent of each other or of certain contexts. In social work analysis, Fawcett (2009) notes that increased emphasis on vulnerability in welfare domains has a tendency to lead inexorably to ideas that reinforce notions of acceptable behaviour. Similarly, Daniel (2010) has argued that the construction of children as vulnerable connects with a sense of them as the passive recipients of our concerns, which results in practitioners within the child protection system frequently overriding the wishes of children. Hasler (2004) and Hollomotz (2009, 2011) share concerns that the conceptualising of disabled people as vulnerable has acted to reinforce the power of disability 'professionals'; protecting people from the risks posed by allowing disabled people the power to control their own destiny at the expense of enabling independence. Empirical work by Hollomotz (2011) even highlights that policies centred on protecting adults with learning difficulties on the basis of their vulnerability can – in practice – *increase* vulnerability, due to a stifling of people's own coping mechanisms to deal with adversity.

Within the area of prostitution policy, some 'liberal' feminist writers have argued that we have witnessed an 'unethical mobilization of the vulnerability' of women who work in the sex industry (Carline, 2011: 331). Using Butler's (2004, 2009) work on 'vulnerability' and 'liveable lives', Carline (2009: 53) argues that vulnerability has been used 'perniciously' in sex work policy. She sees the concept as tied to a positioning of sex workers as victims, the adoption of a 'moralistic agenda' and the criminalisation of prostitution (2009: 38). Scoular and O'Neill (2007) similarly argue that the construction of sex workers as always and inevitably vulnerable is a governance technique that reproduces binary citizenship models, justifying stronger controls where women transgress behavioural norms. Phoenix (2012a) applies these ideas to policy aimed at young people involved in selling sex, or those who are 'sexually exploited'. She has argued that policy in this area has been increasingly based on policing 'wayward' young women's sexual behaviours (Phoenix, 2012a) 'in the name of protection' (Phoenix, 2002).

Policy making on the basis of vulnerability would appear to enable a broadening of the regulatory welfare net, but in the guise of enhanced social justice and 'protection'. A critical reading of the rise of 'vulnerability' in policy might interpret this shift in the context of a trend towards behaviourism, or the intensification of processes by which individuals are appraised and regulated as well as assisted and supported (see Harrison and Sanders, 2014). While a focus on vulnerability is apparently therapeutic, it can be seen to shade into more 'moralising' mechanisms of state governance. For Dunn et al (2008: 241), 'substitute decision-making' on the basis of adults' situational vulnerability could lead to actions that are 'potentially infinite in scope and application'. These authors argue that where laws are based on 'protecting the vulnerable', courts could potentially intervene in the lives of individuals in unprecedented ways where people were deemed to lack the ability to choose the course of action that was least 'risky'. For example, individuals could potentially be prohibited from embarking on cohabitations with abusive partners (Dunn et al, 2008: 241).

As vulnerability classifications are largely ill-defined, they are a point in welfare and disciplinary systems that could potentially be especially prone to being shaped by personal preferences, values, commitments and the individual preoccupations of those who administer them. Writing about discretionary practices within 'street-level' policy administration, Lipsky (1980: 44) notes that where insufficient resources pose 'dilemmas' in processing receivers of services on a 'mass basis', those involved in public service professions necessarily develop techniques for processing categories of cases, resulting in inevitable stereotyping and favouritism. In a context of increasingly selective welfare systems and where attitudes about welfare entitlements for those who fail to meet 'socially acceptable' requirements of behaviour are hardening, service users who conform to commonly held notions of 'deservingness' and ideas about how 'vulnerable' people should behave may find their entitlement to be more secure. Conceptions of vulnerability link with pervasive normative assumptions about 'deservingness' through which the behaviours of individuals and groups are interpreted by state officials and support workers.

The imagining of some groups as 'vulnerable' in policy would especially seem to cause tensions when 'vulnerable' people behave in ways that are deemed 'problematic' (see Phoenix, 2012b). Vulnerability classifications appeal to oversimplified policy binaries related to 'victim' and 'agent', which can result in policies being ill-matched to empirical realities. In relation to child trafficking and migration, O'Connell Davidson (2011: 463) shows that notions of vulnerability are deeply embedded within child migration policies, with 'victim/agent' binaries actively constructing the vulnerability of children who migrate. This, she argues, means that children who do not fall neatly into the category of 'vulnerable victims' are treated more punitively (she also suggests that this is most often the case). It would appear that those who behave in line with common conceptions of vulnerability may be more likely to be accepted as 'worthy' of welfare than those who do not. The practical effects of this may be reductions in support or harsher punishments for those who do not 'perform' their 'vulnerability' sufficiently, a matter that is explored further in subsequent chapters.

How far policies that aim to 'protect vulnerable people' might form part of practices that police and regulate behaviour is open to question. Reviewing domains where the vulnerability zeitgeist has been significant indicates that the rise of 'vulnerability' in policy – paradoxically – may serve to further exclude certain groups and individuals who may be among the most in need of welfare and state support. Vulnerability rationales compete and overlap with other prominent binary understandings about behavioural norms, such as familiar 'undeserving/deserving' dichotomies. Indeed, elements of stigma or labelling would seem to be involved in demarcations of who is vulnerable, perhaps especially when ideas about vulnerability are situated within frameworks of broader power inequalities.

Vulnerability and citizenship

How the rise of vulnerability connects with and maps onto notions of citizenship is particularly contested and complex (see Chapter Two; Brown, 2011b). As was highlighted in Chapter Two, certain theoretically orientated perspectives have advocated vulnerability as a shared human condition, able to act as a conceptual vehicle for the achievement of equality and social justice (see Goodin, 1985; Turner, 2006; Fineman, 2008; Fineman and Grear, 2013). Rather than taking a position of support for the general advancement of vulnerability in social policy, such universal vulnerability approaches instead advocate vulnerability as a concept that can act as a springboard for a recasting of the relationship between citizens and the state based on a universal model of shared and socially constituted precariousness and interdependency. Indeed, it has been argued that recognising and 'living with' vulnerability might have 'transformational effects' in terms of challenging negative stereotypes of dependency (Wiles, 2011: 594), offering a counterweight to ideologies that give primacy to the active, 'purposeful' and economically productive citizen (see Harrison, 2008). Yet from tracing the contours of vulnerability in policy and practice, there are indications of significant 'real-world' challenges that more radical approaches to vulnerability may face. These would seem especially pronounced in policy environments that are increasingly inclined towards selectivism and competition.

Policy commentators have argued that notions of 'the vulnerable' in policy act to single out certain groups as 'other', with vulnerability rationales advanced as patronising and oppressive (Wishart, 2003; Hasler, 2004; Hollomotz, 2011). Wishart (2003: 20) argues that the use of the concept creates images of people with learning difficulties as deficient and as having a 'tragic quality', operating almost as 'victim blaming' and painting those with learning difficulties as inevitably at risk of sexual abuse because of their impairment(s). Roulstone et al (2011) argue that disabled people are often denied the right to be taken seriously as victims in the criminal justice system, with their entitlements to legal protections often diminished due to their status as 'vulnerable'. In other words, where the criminal justice system is preoccupied with a focus on supporting and protecting the 'vulnerable' victim, this negatively affects the apprehension and prosecution of 'perpetrators'. McLaughlin (2012: 112) is highly critical of the institutionalisation of what he calls 'vulnerable identities', arguing that these are a key component of a policy context that 'is no longer primarily concerned with attaining something good but with preventing the worst', opening the door for state intervention into arenas where it does not belong.

Yet while calling groups or individuals 'vulnerable' may be stigmatising or paternalistic in certain contexts, the policy of prioritising 'the vulnerable' would also seem to have important positive effects for some individuals and groups. Harrison (2010; and with Hemingway, 2014) notes a widened application of ideas of dependency and vulnerability, which he argues are often brought together with risk and threat and are connected with legitimating claims for ongoing supplies of secure resources that may otherwise look unreasonable. In the evaluation of New Labour's Vulnerable Children Grant, for example, stakeholders in children's services received the grant's focus on 'vulnerability' very positively, as it was seen as a notion that could help to overcome prejudice around certain identified groups (Kendall et al, 2004b). Labelling groups as 'vulnerable' can circumvent (or at least attempt to circumvent) people being seen as to blame for their problems, acting as an appeal against the impulse to condemn them for their actions or lifestyles (Goodin, 1985; Brown, 2011b), and sometimes triggering vital protections (see Peroni and Timmer, 2013; Campbell, 2014). It is as if 'the vulnerable' occupy the (increasingly rare) position of lacking individual agency to control their life circumstances, so could be considered to transcend standard conditionalities applied to resource allocation. Vulnerability rationales therefore seem to function in some contexts as a moral and practical lever to resources for certain individuals or groups, by which their welfare entitlement is justified or reductions to entitlement contested.

Where vulnerability is not taken as universal, but as something that differentiates people based on differences or deficiencies, it is a concept that overlaps with particularism and the rise of specific interest groups. Focusing on the particular vulnerabilities of one group or another links with tendencies to oversimplify complex social phenomena, leaning towards configuring solutions in ways that ignore wider structural matters and which may undermine more solidaristic approaches. In an era of financial austerity, this has important potential implications for the distribution of resources. For Lévy-Vroelant (2010), tendencies to organise housing policies on the basis of vulnerability place groups into competition for scarce state resources, diverting attention from overall reductions in welfare. The prioritisation of 'the vulnerable' might be seen as sensible financial decision making in an age of limited welfare resources, but how this strategy contributes to competing interests and competition should not go unnoticed. It can serve to legitimate overall reductions in welfare provision on the basis of 'targeting', which might go some way to explaining its prominence in policy rhetoric (see Brown, 2014b).

In the UK, the dominance of economic liberal political orientations would seem to locate attention given to 'the vulnerable' firmly within more 'paternalistic' welfare models. Notions of 'vulnerable groups' serve to underline a particular construction of individuals that is central to economic liberal imaginings of the human subject as 'capable adult', unbound by structural constraints, who needs 'activating' (see Campbell, 1991; Clarke, 2005; Harrison, 2010). In this sense, conceptualising groups as vulnerable focuses attention on the individual and detracts attention from the structural forces that disadvantage people (Wishart, 2003; Hollomotz, 2011). Seen in this way, vulnerability rationales form part of wider trends in social policy, which emphasise self-regulation and 'responsibilisation' (Rose, 1999; Clarke, 2005; Flint, 2006a; Raco, 2009), configuring welfare as a 'gift' for selected individuals rather than a 'right' (see Harrison with Davies, 2001: 65, 74). Universalistic systems of support and security are perhaps more inclined to acknowledge the potential for all to be vulnerable, albeit along a continuum or spectrum of emergent levels of needs, but used within the paradigms of economic liberalism, government prioritisation of 'the vulnerable' most often refocuses public policies around personal accountability rather than rights and collective systems.

Chapter summary

Vulnerability is a powerful and pervasive concept in social policy, reconfiguring and reworking configurations about entitlement and 'deservingness'. On the surface, perhaps, notions of protecting 'the vulnerable' are apparently benign, resonating with the pursuit of 'just' and 'fair' systems of governance and welfare allocation. Further analysis suggests that special exceptions and exemptions made on the basis of situational and innate vulnerability may come at a price. Vulnerability rationales in policy and practice often dovetail with justifications for stronger governmental control and the enhancement of professional power, sometimes at the expense of all citizens but most often in a way that restricts the control that supposedly vulnerable people have over their own lives. Furthermore, labelling groups as vulnerable can be stigmatising. Attention to the issue of 'vulnerable identities' indicates that vulnerability may often be something of a 'top-down' idea, imposed on populations in less powerful positions, a matter that is explored further in later chapters.

Due to variation and flexibility in understandings of vulnerability, organising welfare or disciplinary interventions according to the notion can connect with certain moral preferences and preoccupations at both practitioner and policy-making levels. This seems particularly pertinent in areas where the welfare system is reliant on discretionary processing mechanisms. Questions have been raised here about how far those who do not adequately *perform* vulnerability – such as those who do not accept welfare with deference and gratitude – might be less likely to benefit from policies influenced by vulnerability rationales. From reviewing the ways in which the concept of vulnerability operates in social policy and practice, it can be argued that focusing on 'the vulnerable' provides the façade of being a well-intentioned strategy in a 'just' society, behind which a number of more partisan re-moralising messages may operate in ways that are largely hidden from view. In order to explore some of these broader trends in more detail, investigations now turn to in-depth case study research into how the notion of vulnerability was operationalised in services for 'vulnerable' young people.

Notes

[1] Analysis was conducted July 2014 via the legal database Westlaw UK, which enables searches of archived statutory legislation since 1948, statutory instruments since 1980 and a selection of in-force legislation from earlier dates, with data included until

2013. I am grateful to Matthew Bell and Thompson Reuters for their assistance with this research.

[2] I am grateful for valuable discussions with Jed Meers on vulnerability in housing arenas.

[3] See for example *Now Medical*, a company that can provide medical 'advice' on vulnerability issues to local authorities within a day for £35 to £50: www.nowmedical.co.uk/vulnerability.html

[4] At the time of writing, young people on income support are teenage parents, teenagers living away from parents and young people whose parents have died.

[5] www.barnardos.org.uk; www.childrenssociety.org.uk; www.nspcc.org.uk; www.actionforchildren.org.uk; www.savethechildren.org.uk

FOUR

Vulnerability management

Vulnerability is something that's always there at the forefront; it's always in your mind. (Manager, welfare service for 'vulnerable' children)

... the term 'vulnerability' is common parlance. (Senior manager, Youth Offending Service [YOS])

... it seems like it's the current buzz word. (Project worker, welfare service for 'vulnerable' children)

Introduction

Classifications of vulnerability now shape a range of interventions with people who are seen to require special care or behavioural regulation. Concerns about and responses to social problems are increasingly framed in terms of vulnerability, resulting in social, political and technical processes that seek to classify and manage it. Welfare and disciplinary services target resources at vulnerable groups, assess and prioritise people based on vulnerability and make exceptions to mainstream provision on the basis of vulnerable people's special entitlement or 'need'. Now commonplace in contemporary governance systems, this management of vulnerability tends mainly to operate in 'taken-for-granted' ways. Yet when considered more closely, such delineations and prioritisations raise a number of questions about who is deemed as vulnerable, who is likely to benefit most from the organisation of resources in this way, and what the wider outcomes and effects of frameworks of vulnerability management might be. These are not easy questions to tackle, not least because of the nebulous nature of the concept of vulnerability and the broad range of interpretations attached to it.

This chapter focuses on services for 'vulnerable' young people to explore how those who design and deliver services for this group interpret and apply the notion of vulnerability in their work. Through examining tacit assumptions and subtle mechanisms attached to vulnerability-related practices, the intended and unintended effects of vulnerability rationales are brought into view. The 15 professionals or 'key informants' interviewed for the research were all involved in providing interventions for 'vulnerable' young people in a large northern city in England and were drawn from a range of services and job roles across the statutory, voluntary and private sectors. Interviewees included those who worked in services that are traditionally seen as more 'caring' in nature (such as social care) as well in those that were more 'disciplinary' in orientation (such as the YOS). Informants held a variety of different roles and responsibilities, with frontline workers, managers, commissioners and policy makers all included (for a more detailed discussion of the research methods, see Chapter One; Brown, 2013).

In the next section, an overview is provided of how these interviewees understood vulnerability, with consideration given to which groups of young people tended to be seen as vulnerable. Practical ways in which vulnerability rationales operated in welfare and disciplinary services for young people are then discussed. Following this, practitioner views of the relationship between vulnerability, 'deservingness' and transgression are explored, with some final reflections on the significance of gender in vulnerability constructions. Generally speaking, organising interventions according to vulnerability seemed to offer a conceptual basis for flexible service delivery and was considered a progressive development, but at the same time, the malleability of vulnerability could pose certain problems and led to a rather 'messy' operationalisation. Most importantly perhaps, subtle but potent expectations of particular behaviours were attached to attaining and retaining vulnerability status. Attention to professional territories and orientations highlights that as well as functioning as a trigger for support and assistance for certain individuals or groups, the operationalisation of vulnerability can also work in the direction of excluding those with less compliant behaviours.

Classifications and understandings of vulnerability in practice

There was almost uniform agreement among key informants that the notion of vulnerability was heavily ingrained in the lexis and practices of their professional contexts, most often being used as some sort of classificatory device. Experienced professionals and practitioners earlier on in their career alike commented that the pervasiveness of vulnerability was a relatively new development in the provision of welfare and disciplinary services. Understandings of vulnerability were primarily deficit-orientated but varied considerably in scope, encompassing a range of different concerns (see Table 4.1). Often interviewees would give several accounts of what they understood the concept to mean throughout the course of one interview.

Table 4.1: Practitioner understandings of vulnerability

How vulnerability was understood by informants	Number of interviewees
Related to risk	15
Lack of support systems	5
Behaviours and activities	5
Easily influenced/exploited	5
Poor 'outcomes' (in terms of *Every Child Matters*)	5
Lack of participation/underachievement	4
Less able to cope with difficulties	4
Lack of physical safety	3
Having stresses and difficulties	2
Related to disadvantage	1

It was apparent that vulnerability occupied a similar and overlapping territory to 'risk' at the forefront of the processes by which young people were managed and appraised. Findings in the study supported other work, which has highlighted that 'vulnerability' and 'risk' seem to be concepts used alongside one another in social welfare settings, often without differentiation (see Appleton, 1999; Parley, 2011). Indeed, some informants used the notions almost interchangeably: *"Well, a most vulnerable child could well be a child who's at risk"* (manager, social care). When asked about differences, interviewees often acknowledged some difficulty in articulating the relationship between the two notions, while stressing variance nonetheless:

> *I think vulnerability ... they are very different in the sense that risks is ... erm ... risks I guess are done at various different levels and it can relate to different things and, I think ... I don't know they just are different though aren't they; it's just hard to explain.*
> (Manager, service for 'vulnerable' children)

That risk is a highly contested and subjective term has been extensively chronicled (see Lupton, 1999, for an overview), yet there was a view that vulnerability was more discretionary and less officially defined than risk, with the latter seen as more specific: *"... we have definite risk factors that are organisational and statutory, I'm seeing vulnerability is more of a ... of a state, if that makes sense"* (senior clinical psychologist, child and adolescent mental health service [CAMHS]).

This resonated with arguments put forward by Daniel (2010) and Sarewitz et al (2003), who advance that where risk is used to describe high chances of negative outcomes, vulnerability is used more to describe a *potentiality* for significant adversity occurring, what might be referred to as the 'contingent' nature of vulnerability (see Chapter Two): *"... risk rings different bells, risk is something that can happen, it's a fact, it's an incident, it rings more alarm bells. Vulnerable is a softer word"* (retired commissioner, city council children's unit). According to this understanding, it would seem to follow that a young person could be classified as vulnerable without being viewed as at risk. In this sense, vulnerability seemed to have a more extensive policy and practice reach than the notion of risk.

Close links between vulnerability and resilience were also evident, with the concepts often understood as inversely relational, as highlighted elsewhere (Daniel, 2010; Ecclestone and Lewis, 2014). Vulnerability was often constructed as 'innate' as well as 'situational' or based on particular circumstances or transgressions (see Chapter Two):

> *... disruptive housing or schooling or parental mental health problems or inappropriate peers that are hanging round, things like that. And alongside that they've got, I suppose, low resilience or low coping skills so they've not got the inner strength or self-esteem or confidence to necessarily make the right choices or seek help. So I see it as a bit of a combination of the two really, like poor external factors alongside internally not being as strong or emotionally developed.* (Project worker, young carers' service)

While certain practitioners could consider lack of support systems to be significant in a young person's vulnerability, they could also consider behaviour to be a key factor as well. The government strategy document *Every Child Matters* (DfES, 2003) was often cited as a point of reference for understandings, with vulnerability being seen as related to the risk that a child may not attain the five positive outcomes set out in the document.[1] While some practitioners saw vulnerability as referring to the presence of difficulties in an individual's life, it was also noteworthy that explicit references to structural disadvantages were not often drawn on in discussion. This would suggest that vulnerability is most often drawn on in its psychoemotional configuration, as

Ecclestone argues is the case in educational settings (see Ecclestone and Goodley, 2014; Ecclestone and Lewis, 2014).

Who is vulnerable? Circumstances, behaviours, groups

Table 4.2: Vulnerable groups of young people as cited by key informants

Vulnerable groups or circumstances given as examples	Number of informants
'Sexually exploited' young women[1,2]	9
Parental abuse/neglect/poor parenting	7
Drug and alcohol use[1]	6
Homeless/poorly housed	6
Offending behaviour/getting 'in trouble'[1]	6
Parental drug/alcohol use	5
Parental domestic violence	5
Looked-after children	4
Not achieving at school	4
Mental health issues	4
Learning difficulties	3
Gypsy and Traveller young people	3
Significant health problems	3
Parents who offend	3
Young carers	3
English as a second language	3
Disabled young people	2
Asylum seekers and refugees	2
Those who run away[1]	2
Living in poverty	2
Self-harm[1]	2
Black and minority ethnic backgrounds	2
Parents with mental health issues	2
Not in education, employment or training[1]	2

[1] Denotes what might be seen as 'behavioural' vulnerabilities.

[2] 'Sexual exploitation' might be considered a set of circumstances that young people do not have a choice in, or as a set of behaviours. This issue is considered specifically later in the chapter.

When asked about which young people they considered were vulnerable, informants frequently drew on particular groups as illustrative examples (see Table 4.2), underlining that vulnerability is often denoted by group membership (see Chapter Three).

Examples of vulnerable groups seemed to fall broadly into two categories: young people who were experiencing (or who had experienced) particularly difficult social environments or circumstances; and young people considered to display 'problem' behaviour (marked with a superscript 1 in Table 4.2). Many informants highlighted that 'vulnerable' young people were often those who were dealing with a number of the issues indicated in Table 4.2, or as one commissioner said: *"kids sit in different numbers of vulnerable groups"*. Although categories were associated with vulnerability, the classification was still seen by most as something that operated on an 'individual' basis. The same informant also commented: *"... vulnerability is an assessment that is made about an individual child and so you just don't just become vulnerable because you're in a category"* (Commissioner B, city council children's unit).

There appeared to be some tension between 'universal' and 'particular' notions of the concept of vulnerability. Some informants considered that all children were 'vulnerable' and in other instances it was only seen as a notion applied to particular groups:

> *... it's about recognising that young people and children by their very nature are vulnerable. In terms of development, when a child is born they are massively.... They are about as vulnerable as they can be, and as they grow up and develop it's almost like you're equipping them with the skills to be less vulnerable and more self-sufficient.* (Manager, family intervention project)

That all children were potentially vulnerable seemed to be an aspect of the management of vulnerability that was in some way troublesome when the concept was operationalised:

> *... we can describe almost any young person as vulnerable [laughs] because they are! Young people have to go out and risk take, and find out for themselves what their identity is and what their strengths are, so I think there's a slight problem in that it is not easily defined, and it might be that what I see as vulnerable even what another agency sees as vulnerable, so I think there is some difficulty in that it's a bit of the vague word.* (Senior clinical psychologist, CAMHS)

Discussions of 'inherent' or 'universal' vulnerability (see Chapter Two) were often rooted within developmental approaches to childhood, which were highly influential in classifications.

Across the sample of informants, young people's responses to their circumstances were central to understandings of vulnerability: *"… it's not just about your home and your environment and your relationships but what your own individual personality brings into the equation"* (retired commissioner, city council children's unit). Behaviours were heavily linked with vulnerability classifications. For example, where young people were involved in offending behaviours, they tended to be classified as 'vulnerable' in some way. One informant explained this during discussion about a video vignette of a young offender's life story: *"He wanted to be seen to be hard so he was constantly thinking about what other people think of him and getting into a cycle of drugs, dealing and not telling people; also that made him more vulnerable"* (project worker, welfare service for 'vulnerable' children).

Warner (2008: 32) describes a 'vulnerability/dangerousness axis', where vulnerability can be used to indicate risk posed by an individual as well as to them, a relationship that was supported by key informant narratives. As the retired commissioner commented, calling a young person vulnerable was *"better than saying the child is stupid or is neglected or deviant"*. Close connections between 'deviance' and 'vulnerability' were evident and are returned to later in the chapter. Overall, approaches to defining vulnerability were remarkably varied. Yet differences of opinion about how it might be understood did not seem to affect its popularity. Vulnerability was a notion that professionals regularly drew on and used in a number of ways, which are now explored in more detail.

Subjectivities and practitioner discretion

That vulnerability was a term imbued with subjectivity was advanced uniformly across the interviews (see also Chambers, 1989; Appleton, 1999; Levine et al, 2004; Mackenzie et al, 2014). One informant from a project for 'sexually exploited' young people commented: *"When I describe someone as vulnerable that might mean something different to somebody else"*. When asked about where they saw a vulnerable young person in terms of a spectrum from 'universal needs' to highly 'specialist needs', views varied enormously. One commissioner felt that confusion about vulnerability reflected a lack of clarity from higher up in the commissioning framework: *"A number of government initiatives have used vulnerability in a different way and that's reflected in a local authority structure and the result is a lot of debate and confusion around where boundary lines are drawn around vulnerability"* (Commissioner A, city council children's unit).

Although the nebulousness of vulnerability was met with a certain amount of frustration or disapproval on behalf of some interviewees, others noted that its appeal might in part be linked to its conceptual ambiguity:

> … *[other services for young people] could say 'we're working to support vulnerable young people' and that can mean a hundred different vulnerabilities, a hundred different things, so they'll use that term to encompass everything rather than being specific about what they are going to target.* (Project worker, sexual exploitation service)

Indeed, a more positive reading of the subjectivity of vulnerability would advance that its ambiguity makes it well suited to capturing a rich diversity of experiences of social difficulties (Fineman, 2013; Wallbank and Herring, 2013).

As is the case with many other systems for classifying and managing people who receive welfare or disciplinary interventions, approaches to vulnerability were prone to being heavily shaped by discretionary practices, personal preferences and the individual commitments of those who administer such classifications (see Lipsky, 1980). Differences of opinion about vulnerability were a lens through which the value judgements of welfare professionals were refracted:

> … *there's always differences in people's levels of acceptability I would guess. But the more you work somewhere like here as I'm sure you'll know, the less shocked you get and sometimes you do, probably you'd think, you have different expectations of what people's lives are gonna be. So probably someone, if someone, one of my friends in my personal life saw it they would probably totally think someone else was totally vulnerable where I'd be like it's not, they're alright, that's just their life actually.* (Project worker, antisocial behaviour project)

Such variances indicated that vulnerability might be a relational and culturally specific concept, or one that is (in part, at least) socially constructed, rather than something that is 'innate' or 'natural', an idea returned to in later chapters.

Three informants stood out as having more apparently defined or technical understandings of vulnerability. They were employed at services whose work included discipline-orientated components (the YOS, the family intervention project and the local authority housing unit). Although discretion remained important in how the notion was applied, professionals in these agencies were using vulnerability as an 'official' criterion in delivering their services. The YOS manager described 'vulnerability' directly in line with the definition of the concept in the official Youth Justice Board documents, which refer to it as the risk a young person poses to themselves, rather than to society (see Youth Justice Board, 2006; Phoenix, 2013): *"... 'risk' means risk to the public of serious harm, risk to the public in terms of likelihood of offending, and 'vulnerability' means risk to themselves, either risk to themselves from their own behaviour or because of the behaviour of other people round them"* (senior manager, YOS). The informant from the local authority's housing unit indicated that vulnerability was clearly defined in statutory terms within her setting (see Carr and Hunter, 2008): *"I'm conditioned to think of what it [vulnerability] is in terms of how our legislation sets it out to be honest, and the way that our legislation sets it out is anyone that is less able to fend for themselves if they became street homeless"* (manager, local authority housing service).

As noted previously (see Chapter Two), the legislation the housing practitioner referred to here is a notoriously contentious and heavily litigated dividing line in the provision of social housing resources (Robson and Watchman, 1981; Meers, 2012, 2014). Even where clearer operational definitions were in place, how technical definitions of vulnerability were applied in practice remained largely dependent on practitioner utilisation and understanding of criteria.

Use of vulnerability as a discursive tool: kind or condescending?

Beyond its use as a classificatory system, perhaps the most commonly referred to use of vulnerability in practice was discursive in nature. It was seen to offer a means for referring to young people who had experienced considerable difficulties in a way that indicated that they were not to blame for these problems. This mechanism was valued highly in many cases:

> *... it's about being sensitive, but I think in a way vulnerability is like a kind term [...] it's trying not to put blame on anybody, it's the situation maybe that they're in.* (Project worker, welfare service for 'vulnerable children')

> *... it's an empathetic word, and a word that people kind of like.*
> *It's non-judgemental.* (Senior clinical psychologist, CAMHS)

One informant noted that drawing on the notion of vulnerability offered practitioners a means of actively avoiding the positioning of young people being seen negatively, shaping interventions in a more 'positive' way:

> *... it's used subconsciously, partly to gain another agency's sympathy; you know, if you're making a referral to another agency, as a hook that people will feel more sympathy perhaps towards say a teenager who's an offender who's described as vulnerable because of their background, who may also be an offender. But if you're referring them to an agency who doesn't specialise in offending and started off describing them as an offender, that might sort of limit the response you'd get. Whereas, if you described them as a vulnerable young person who happens to offend, that might get a more sympathetic response.* (Retired commissioner, city council children's unit)

This would seem to support the contention discussed in Chapter Two (see also Brown, 2011b) that labelling people as 'vulnerable' can offer a discursive mechanism that helps to circumvent disadvantaged people being seen as to blame for their problems, acting as an appeal against impulses to condemn them for 'problematic' actions or lifestyles (Goodin, 1985).

Despite drawing heavily on notions of vulnerability in practice, most informants also recognised problems with the idea as a conceptual basis for their work, and two informants eschewed vulnerability-based constructions of young people altogether. Around half of the interviewees mentioned that constructing young people as 'vulnerable' seemed to position them as 'weak' or 'fragile'. The informant from the family intervention project noted that calling someone vulnerable was to *"question somebody's ability to be self-sufficient"*. Vulnerability classifications were seen by some as problematic in that they undermined the extent of young people's agency:

> *... it means sort of a weakness to me and I don't think these young people are weak. They've got lots going and people ... I don't know, they class them as if they're some sort of pathetic, 'can't do this' and 'can't do that', but really if you give them the chance and give them that opportunity. It's a funny one, I wouldn't ever*

refer to anybody as vulnerable, I don't think it's a term I've ever used. (Manager, education service)

As well as the term implying weakness, informants saw 'vulnerability' as potentially individualising problems to some extent (see also Hollomotz, 2011), with comments related to 'labelling' occurring frequently across the interviews: *"... it kind of puts it on them [young people] almost in some ways, like you're vulnerable, rather than looking at it's a vulnerable situation"* (project worker, young carers' service).

Noticeably, despite the pervasive vulnerability-based rhetoric that most of the informants were apparently utilising in their everyday practice, with the exception of two informants (the retired commissioner and the senior clinical psychologist), informants indicated that they actively avoided the term 'vulnerability' when speaking with service users.

There were two principal reasons given for this: first, the word 'vulnerability' was viewed as one that might not be understandable to young people and families: and second, more commonly, informants felt that young people would be resistant to the idea of themselves as 'vulnerable': *"... my reluctance to use it sometimes with young people is because I anticipate it might – it can be perceived like it's a weakness in them. To describe someone as vulnerable cannot really sound very empowering to them, I don't think"* (project worker, young carers' service).

That the use of the term in direct interactions with young people might potentially cause them offence was repeatedly noted:

> *I just think that young people would think, 'you don't know me', you know, 'I can look after myself' sort of thing. It is a bit, I would say derogatory, but it's not that, it's more like, making that young person feel quite young, I guess. Making them feel like they are a child.* (Project worker, 'sexually exploited' young people)

That vulnerability discourses would appear to operate largely outside direct interactions with 'vulnerable groups' raises interesting questions about how far supposedly vulnerable people's feelings about their own identities shape and inform the systems and processes by which they are supported and disciplined. Although vulnerability might be considered as a concept that challenges stigma in certain respects, it can also seem to operate at the expense of marginalising service users' own views of their situations and as potentially reinforcing a labelling of disadvantaged populations as 'problematic' or 'other'.

Organising principle in resource distribution

The classification of vulnerability also operated as an organising principle in the distribution of resources. Perceived vulnerability status acted as a trigger or mechanism whereby young people 'qualified' for interventions, with 11 of the 15 informants commenting that addressing vulnerability was an important part of commissioning processes in services for children and young people. Several commissioners within the local authority infrastructure had job titles referring to particular responsibilities to 'vulnerable groups', and one of the commissioners interviewed explained that the notion was central to his role: *"I use it to characterise services and directions of services, so which bits of services are going to deal with more vulnerable, less vulnerable"* (Commissioner A, city council children's unit). Five of the informants in the case study had been involved in the distribution of New Labour's Vulnerable Children Grant (see Chapter Three), which seemed to have given rise to some of the council's commissioning infrastructure aimed at addressing the particular difficulties of certain 'vulnerable groups'.

Interviewees were in broad agreement that the grant had helped to develop an overarching strategy to support those young people who were in need, although recollections of its implementation indicated that problems defining 'vulnerability' could be problematic when it came to delivering services:

> There were various forms of strategy development locally and nationally with people going: 'Great! This programme is going to deal with vulnerable kids', 'The vulnerable kids, yeah, you know the ones!', 'Yeah! The ones! We all know who the vulnerable kids are!', 'So we're gonna start tomorrow with domestic violence', 'No, they're not the vulnerable ones, the vulnerable ones are the looked after.' You know, I'm not sure if it's any more considered than that, actually. (Commissioner A, city council children's unit)

There were indications from some informants that a narrowing of vulnerability classifications might occur as pressure on welfare resources increased. Talking about a 'vulnerable' young person whom she had struggled to find services for, the senior clinical psychologist commented:

> Often what happens is that in times of economic plenty when government spending is higher, then people are more generous in terms of applying their criteria, and at times where government

spending is restricted, people are a bit more clear about drawing lines around their referral criteria. And so the pool of the young people which don't fit into any category becomes bigger. (Senior clinical psychologist, CAMHS)

This informant was particularly concerned about older young people who were on the cusp of being eligible for adult services, who might be considered less vulnerable due to their more advanced age.

Overuse of the word 'vulnerability' was mentioned repeatedly by a range of informants and tended to be met with disapproval. The social care manager's interview underlined potential problems with overuse, with her suggesting that the word was not enough to indicate that the threshold for a social care intervention had been reached, contrary to some of the practitioner impressions that drawing on this concept acted as a safeguarding 'flag'. The retired commissioner cited above explained that she sat on a panel for a major national grant-giving organisation in the UK and that in applications for funding, vulnerability had *"lost its currency"*: *"[voluntary groups] will routinely say that they work with vulnerable children or young people, and because they all say it, actually it doesn't press any buttons anymore"* (retired commissioner, city council children's unit). That vulnerability seems to work as a kind of 'currency' for competing claims on finite and limited resources is an interesting idea, pointing to the potential for vulnerability discourses to serve dynamics whereby the claims of certain disadvantaged groups are displaced at the expense of others.

Classifications, net-widening and the policing of vulnerability

Vulnerability was commonly utilised within processes of classification and measurement of young people's 'need' for welfare and/or disciplinary interventions, and to determine the urgency and nature of this need. The concept was employed to alert other professionals to serious problems in the case of particular individuals or groups of young people and a perceived requirement of duty that some sort of action be taken to address these. Often, the term 'vulnerability' was considered an effective tool in efforts to activate statutory child protection interventions:

I think there's words that will be used within the social care environment to kind of highlight a young person's needs, as in 'extremely vulnerable' or 'significant risk of harm' … I think they're the ones that will get the support and recognised, because those words are there [...]. You've just gotta say that word [vulnerability] really! [laughs] (Manager, welfare service for 'vulnerable' children)

Despite potential lack of clear meaning, it was standard for consideration of young people's vulnerability to form part of the assessments made by agencies; that is, the procedures by which practitioners judged and made sense of the various situations of young people before interventions were planned and delivered: *"... it might be that from looking at referrals, we identify the children we think are most vulnerable and needed seeing more urgently possibly than others"* (project worker, young carers' service).

Services that had stronger disciplinary components to their practice often had specific tools for its measurement. The assessment of young people's 'vulnerability' was described by the YOS senior manager as *"absolutely critical"* to the organisation's national screening tool, *Asset*, where 'vulnerability' was one of three key factors (along with 'risk' and 'risk of reoffending') on which interventions were decided and planned: *"... having a high vulnerability rating therefore triggers actions and the intervention plan and accountability from that, and the intensity of that intervention"* (senior manager, YOS). This was an intriguing finding as it raised questions about how far vulnerability might be associated with 'net-widening' processes (see Cohen, 1979; McLaughlin and Muncie, 2013: 282-3) or expansionary trends in welfare and disciplinary systems.

In attempts to monitor, assess and address young people's vulnerability, perceived vulnerability tended to trigger more intensive interventions. While more intensive interventions could be considered progressive and 'supportive', there were indications that young people could be deemed 'vulnerable', assigned certain interventions as a result, and then be disciplined if they did not comply with requirements. The most obvious example of this was in the assessment processes for the YOS, where the senior manager indicated that there had been debate on the matter:

> *... if you had two people who went out and committed an offence, who burgled a shed, one of them had no issues whatsoever but our Asset [assessment tool] says, you know, 'fairly minor offence and from a stable background'; and the other one's said 'well fairly minor offence but all these vulnerabilities', one of them [the more 'vulnerable' one] could be sentenced to a more punitive disposal [sanction] than the other one. And actually, that more punitive disposal means a higher restriction on their liberty and more chance*

of breaching it and therefore more chance of going into custody and everything else. So actually, you are being pushed into more punitive disposal on the grounds of your vulnerability, not on the grounds of the seriousness of your offence. (Senior manager, YOS)

The manager here suggests that when a young person is assessed by the YOS as having 'high vulnerability', the responsibility of the agency to act is greater. When asked about instances where young people had 'high vulnerability' but posed a low risk to the public, he explained:

That's the million dollar question really. Things have changed. Some time ago, a young person who came to our service with high levels of vulnerability but low risk of reoffending may have generated a low score and we might have been closer to taking the stance that the risk of reoffending is low, therefore our agency has less to offer. [...] Now that has changed. The expectations have changed on us. You know, we're part of the safeguarding board and that sort of thing, and quite rightly, and you know, let's be honest about where this is driven in terms of the expectations of the inspectorate. When they come in, they're asking us three questions. The three questions are: Do you protect the public from the risk of serious harm? Do you protect the public from the likelihood of offending? And do you safeguard those young people? And we get scored in each one of those categories. (Senior manager, YOS)

A critical reading of such processes might be that mandatory interventions ascribed on the basis of vulnerability may operate to bring more young people into the 'net' of disciplinary processes, intensifying interventions and requirements. In other words, it could be that vulnerability rationales dovetail with a policing of young people's behaviours 'in the name of protection' (see Phoenix, 2002, 2012b, writing about youth prostitution). Such developments might be especially important for those young people already subject to more traditional social control mechanisms.

The vulnerability–transgression nexus: the subtleties beyond the binary

As has been outlined in earlier chapters, tensions would seem to have developed at the policy level between a sense of children and young people being seen either as passive, incompetent and 'vulnerable', or as having full agency in the case of 'wrongdoing' (see Fionda, 2005;

Such and Walker, 2005; Piper, 2008), which vulnerability classifications seem to bring into focus. Piper (2008) suggests that a 'vulnerability/ transgression' binary is a central premise of social policy and practice in relation to children and young people, which was echoed in the narratives of professionals:

> ... writing a social inquiry report you tend to write one that sort of asks the judge or the magistrates to take a lenient line by stressing the things that have happened, the sort of things that have made that young person vulnerable, have determined their behaviour outside of that young person's own sense of who they are. But the judge or magistrates will look at them as the author of their actions and see them as responsible rather than vulnerable and there's a sort of, a kind of two different approaches there really. (Retired commissioner, city council children's unit)

The senior manager in the YOS compared the situation to Victorian understandings of the *"deserving and undeserving"* poor, with young offenders often seen as non-vulnerable and undeserving.

At the same time, there was evidence of a more nuanced and textured understanding of the relationship between vulnerability and transgression, more of a nexus than a binary perhaps. Significant tensions and contradictions were evident in how informants understood the ways in which young people's behavioural transgressions related to their vulnerability: *"... poor behaviour and vulnerability is absolutely the hardest thing to deal with. Without question. Because if you're vulnerable and you're compliant ... you know ... vulnerable and awkward is a totally different ball game"* (Commissioner B, city council children's unit).

As well as noting that certain activities or transgressive conduct could lead to the attainment of vulnerability status (drug taking or offending, for instance), informants also indicated that certain other transgressive activities or behaviours could lead to a withdrawal of this status. 'Compliance' was considered one of the primary factors on which conferring vulnerability status was contingent:

> ... if people are compliant and, you know, accepting of help or appear to be compliant – I think then, generally, workers – well, everybody finds them easier to work with. You know, the youngster who's constantly challenging and in your face and non-compliant with everything, you know, can be quite frustrating to work with and people can sometimes give up on them. (Manager, social care)

Young people's willingness to share personal information that helped to account for problem behaviours seemed to be a key part of 'compliance'. Lack of 'engagement' or motivation for 'change' was a further issue that could mean the withdrawal of services for young people considered vulnerable:

> *You can keep throwing services at families for as long as there are hours in the day but if they don't – I'm not saying something unique you know – if they don't actually want to change or want to do something different or want to have a better something or even see that what you're offering them is better, you're on a hiding to nothing – you're wasting your time.* (Commissioner B, city council children's unit)

Where 'vulnerable' young people repeated or failed to desist from 'problem' behaviours, entitlement to services seemed to be affected.

Lacking contrition for transgressions and being perceived as having 'agency' were also of central importance in how vulnerability was assessed and managed. Commenting on the video vignette of a young offender, which was played as a prompt for discussion in the interviews, the retired commissioner explained: *"... he was making choices from a certain point where he perhaps would be seen as less vulnerable because [...] he was saying, 'well I want to have fun by offending'"* (retired commissioner, city council children's unit). In this quotation, choice is imagined as unbound and rational, and failure to exercise this in an 'appropriate' way leads to the withdrawal of vulnerability status. That vulnerability was contingent on young people behaving in ways that were 'compliant' and which demonstrated willingness to change indicated that when operationalised, vulnerability could serve to reinforce the elevation of the rational, responsibilised and self-regulating subject (see Rose, 1999; Clarke, 2005; Flint, 2006a; Raco, 2009), with potentially disciplinary effects where individuals fail to conform. In the following example, the informant from the housing service describes how her discretion about vulnerability status of particular individuals was shaped by repetition of offending behaviour: *"... if someone's lived at home and they're just being naughty and they keep going into prison, we wouldn't say that's vulnerability, that's just them, they're not abiding by the rules and they just think it's a joke and they think it's a game"* (manager, city council housing service).

Manners and demeanour also seemed to be significant elements of vulnerability classifications. The informant from the antisocial behaviour project felt that *"if someone's cocky and rowdy, stuff like that"* then that could lead to *"people thinking that they're not vulnerable"*. Passaro

(1996) and Cramer's (2005) work on housing provision has highlighted the influence of behaviours such as deference on classifications of vulnerability, which findings in this study seemed to underline.

Taking such discretionary practices and preferences into account, it seemed that behaviour and the *performance of vulnerability* were key factors in how the concept was operationalised at 'street level'. Young people's failure to perform vulnerability in a manner deemed appropriate by service providers and professionals would appear to have significant consequences in the pathways that interventions take. The manager from the local authority housing unit expressed such conditionality about vulnerability in her approach to assessing vulnerability when giving a case example of a young man who had spent several periods in prison and who had sometimes found his own accommodation between custodial sentences. On a further occasion he had been denied support:

> Kate: *So what was your reasoning for finding him not vulnerable?*

> Housing manager: *That basically, he knows exactly, he understands the system, he knows what he's doing. Had he come out of prison, then come to us and said, 'look I don't know what I'm doing, I've got nowhere to go' ... but he was only coming to us, he only came to us once actually and that was after he'd been in prison for a year because no landlord would take him. So he'd already tried to find accommodation himself so he knew exactly what he was doing.*

In this instance 'understanding of the system' seemed to be taken to indicate insufficient performance of vulnerability. As the tone of the quotation indicates, the moral standards of practitioners could assume a prominent role in judgements about vulnerability and appropriate behaviour. The retired commissioner noted similarly: *"Young people's attitudes do shape professional's responses, perhaps more than they should actually."* In this sense, then, vulnerability would seem to be contingent on 'good' behaviour and aligned with conditional or contractual approaches to welfare (see Dwyer, 2004, 2008; Deacon and Patrick, 2011), serving to advance preoccupations with 'correct' and 'appropriate' behaviour and rendering people subject to subtle punitive measures where they fail to conform.

'Cherry-picking' and the pressures of service delivery: excluding the 'most vulnerable'?

That vulnerable people might benefit more from services where they were compliant with individual practitioners' expectations of behaviour would seem an important finding. However, as has been noted in relation to many practices associated with 'street-level bureaucrats' (Lipsky, 1980), wider structures, systems and processes underpinned such judgements and preoccupations. One issue that particularly stood out was the issue of 'cherry-picking', meaning the selection of those young people who were most 'beneficial' to work with.

As services for vulnerable groups were commissioned mainly to tackle specifically defined issues or particular social problems (such as drug use, sexual exploitation or antisocial behaviour), informants implied a tension between the service being able to stick to its agreed performance indicators – aimed at reducing specific difficulties – and the significant challenges that 'vulnerable' young people's behaviour could pose in the course of achieving these targets:

> Social care manager: ... *vulnerability is a phrase that's used a lot, but I guess I tend to think that a lot of the people who provide the services for vulnerable children, if you like, cherry-pick the easy to engage. I'm not sure they always reach the most needy and the most vulnerable.*

> Kate: *Why do you think that?*

> Social care manager: *Well, I guess because if you're being commissioned to provide a service, you want to show that, you know, you've been very successful, so you pick the quick wins [...] I think it can sometimes mean that those who are most vulnerable, most in need, most at risk get less services.*

Some informants alluded to a tension between achieving 'outcomes' and managing 'problem' behaviour. The informant from the education service spoke about her efforts in trying to include a young person who had been volatile in situations with the centre's staff:

> ... *it's just the way she talks, 'fucking bastard' and that sort of stuff, I said it's just not [acceptable] ... and it's starting right back at that and how she dealt with people on a day-to-day basis, but*

you're trying to do that alongside trying to do five lots of GCSE coursework.... (Manager, education service)

It was often implied that working with vulnerable young people who were transgressive required comparatively more resources than where 'vulnerable' young people were well behaved, and there were indications that 'problem' young people would appear to offer the least potential return for services in terms 'improved outcomes'.

Also significant in how services responded to young people who were deemed vulnerable and also transgressive were the various and at times conflicting goals that each service was commissioned to achieve. Differences in the intended 'outcomes' of the various services could cause friction, affecting the pathways that interventions with 'vulnerable' young people took. The informant from the sexual exploitation service spoke of how a young person she was supporting was *"in fear of her life"* due to threats from a group of men she was involved with sexually. Several men had been raping the young woman repeatedly on the grounds that she owed them £300 for drugs. The informant told me how the young person *"hated"* the police because of dealings with them in the past, so was reluctant to cooperate with enforcement agencies who wanted to pursue prosecutions against the men. The informant felt that this had affected how the young person's vulnerability was perceived, as well as service responses:

Project worker: *Sometimes they don't see [the young person] as a victim because she's not saying it, she's not making a statement, you know I've had people ask me if I believe her and I say, 'Of course I believe her.' Not only is it my job to believe the young person, and I do put responsibility on the young people to tell me the truth, I'm not a police officer, I don't need to question them left, right and centre, but I actually do believe her. You know there's some young people who have told stories in the past ... you still need to believe them then, but....*

Kate: *OK so you think there's something about her not taking the action....*

Project worker: *Uncooperative.*

Kate: *Uncooperative. You think that had an effect on how she was perceived?*

Project worker: *Yeah. And what they are willing to do for her. And again it's almost putting blame on her about 'cos she's not doing what we want her to do, she's, you know, involved in it, or she's lying, or you know, she must not be that scared because she doesn't want to do anything about it, although she does want to do stuff about it, you know, she's allowing me to do stuff for her, you know.…*

As this account indicated, moral judgements of particular individuals or values of particular professional approaches seemed to mingle together with an organisation's needs to achieve certain goals or outcomes, with the result being potential withdrawal or alteration of service provision for vulnerable young people who were seen as less 'compliant'. Christie's (1986) notion of the 'ideal victim' would also seem relevant here, with 'agencylessness' to some degree seeming to be important in the realisation of vulnerability status.

When the need to ration limited welfare resources was factored in, vulnerable young people with 'difficult' behaviours could be those whom it made most sense to withdraw services from. One commissioner implied that it was not always possible to continue to support the more 'troublesome' vulnerable young people due to the need to ration resources and target them at those young people who were more receptive:

… *it's exhausting, it's exhausting, you're constantly presenting the child with a new challenge or a different thing or this, that and the other and you just reach a point when you go 'I can't do this anymore'. It's really exhausting when you don't get the response back and you just – you do reach a point when you've got to think of the greater good. That's what happens in society when there aren't endless resources.* (Commissioner B, city council children's unit)

Limited resources and pressures on services to deliver certain 'outcomes', as well as the moral judgements of professionals and influences of wider societal attitudes, were all factors touched on in how interventions played out for vulnerable young people. This seemed to have particular ramifications for those who were less compliant with behavioural norms. Young people's performances of vulnerability were central to vulnerability management, with their behaviours playing an important role in how their vulnerability was perceived and responded to. This relationship between expected behavioural norms and vulnerability seemed to have particular implications in terms of gender.

Vulnerability and gender: the feminisation of vulnerability?

The gendered dimensions of vulnerability have been noted in some of the geo-vulnerability literature on hazards and disasters (see Bradshaw, 2013) and also in the violence literature (see Hollander, 2001). In research conducted for this book, perhaps unsurprisingly, vulnerability appeared to be a state that was much more associated with young women than with young men. Such gendered approaches to vulnerability have a long history. Writing in 1962, Walker saw 'wayward' girls as 'less criminally inclined' than boys, and more vulnerable and 'in need of care and protection' (p 26). Similar attitudes seemed to be evident in current service provision:

> … if you went into a group of YOS staff, and you can include the YOS manager in this, and say 'shut your eyes and think about a vulnerable client', you know, we probably think about the girl that drinks before we think about the six-foot-three person that's done a few robberies, I think without a doubt. [...] how quickly you'll think about that fifteen-year-old boy that lives in a family of chronic domestic violence.… [I don't know]. (Senior manager, YOS)

Most informants felt that by and large young women tended to be seen as more vulnerable than young men, but the story did not end there. Some respondents felt that this was because young women actually *were* more vulnerable in reality, but most felt that young women's association with vulnerability was just more *pronounced* or obvious.

Equally, there were several examples given of how young men's behaviours or demeanour could exclude them from vulnerability classifications. The manager of the education service commented: *"aggression sometimes from young, 15 or 16 … big lads coming in can sort of make you look at them differently. It shouldn't do but it can"*. This would imply that young people's positioning in relation to vulnerability would seem to be shaped by what Connell (1987) has called 'hegemonic masculinities', or dominant male roles related to physical prowess and aggression, which predominate and which may find expression in working-class masculinities (Karner, 1998). The informant from the young carers' service talked about a young man who she had been supporting who had been *"getting into lots of fights"*:

> ... [other professionals] don't normally perceive him as someone that's vulnerable, they perceive him as someone that's strong and – strong-willed and strong-minded and does what he wants. But actually the reasons he's doing that is because underneath it all he's quite vulnerable and scared, I think, and so he puts on a front and takes on people because he's on the attack. (Project worker, young carers' service)

There were resonances here with research that has highlighted the gendered nature of 'antisocial behaviour' (see Brown, 2011a), with some arguing that this can be understood as important identity work and necessary masculinity performance for marginalised young men (see Deuchar, 2010). As the informant from the young carers' service saw it, young men *"tend to go about acting out things in a probably more destructive way"*.

Several informants framed vulnerability gender differences in terms of assumptions about 'agency', commenting that young men tended to be seen as *"being able to look after themselves"*, echoing Donnelly and Kenyon's (1996: 448) findings of the 'myth of male invulnerability' in attitudes to sexual violence. How far such attitudes reflected empirical realities is an interesting question (see Hollander, 2001, for a critique). The YOS senior manager questioned whether this was the case:

> ... when I read the local management reports for people who've committed very serious offences have been, you know, victims of serious ... and you sit there and you read it and you think, I could not have scripted this. If you told me to give someone a worse start in life, I couldn't have done it, you know. And invariably, they're boys actually, and that probably is more hidden when it's boys compared to girls I think, sadly.

Indeed, it could be questioned whether, when operationalised, the concept of vulnerability may paradoxically have the effect of increasing the vulnerability of certain 'troublesome' young men, as they are likely to be excluded from vulnerability classifications. As the project worker at the welfare service for vulnerable children summarised: *"Sometimes boys can be at higher vulnerability or higher risk because they seem as though they can look after themselves"*.

Sexual exploitation as the apex of vulnerability

Sexually exploited young women were the most frequently cited example of vulnerable groups of young people (see Table 4.2). This echoes concerns at government level, where young people in this group are constructed as 'particularly vulnerable' (DCSF, 2009: 49; DH and Home Office, 2000: 21) or the 'most vulnerable' (DfE, 2011: 29; Casey, 2015). Such gendered understandings have a long history, with social control practices within society having tended to be focused on the potentially threatening behaviour of boys and the 'promiscuity' of girls (Hudson, 1989, 2002; O'Neill, 2001; Goldson, 2004), a trend dating back to the 19th century (Shore, 2002). What practitioners understood by 'sexual exploitation' was difficult to pin down, as has been noted in other research (Phoenix, 2012b; Melrose, 2013), but referred to a range of relationships and situations that were deemed 'exploitative' where a young women would 'put herself' at risk.

We can make sense of professional concern about the 'vulnerability' of sexually exploited young women in several ways. It may be that the problem is growing and that more young women are becoming involved in such situations, as reported in the media on a regular basis. However, such preoccupations may reflect more interesting responses to class, gender and vulnerability. Phoenix (2012a) argues that the growing concern with the vulnerability of young women who are sexually exploited can be seen as tied to concerns about the transgression of traditional ideals of femininity and, in particular, the violation of such ideals by working-class girls. She argues that professional concern with this matter is actually connected with the social control of 'wayward' young women's lives by stealth, through a policing of their vulnerability. Comments from the YOS manager indicated that in seeking to protect vulnerable young women, stronger social control mechanisms could be activated:

> We're out to chase [young people] up if they don't turn up but if we put, if we'd said to that person on [the YOS programme] 'my god, you're so vulnerable and you're, you know, at risk of sexual exploitation and everything else, we need to see you 25 hours a week', and we put them on our most intensive programme, which is something called ISS – Intensive Supervision and Surveillance – we are setting them up to fail.

If sexuality was the focus for young women's vulnerability, aggression or deviance was the focus for young men's. A number of informants drew on parallels about the different ways in which vulnerabilities were configured according to gender:

> ... girls and boys do it differently, don't they. With boys, it tends to be crime and getting into bother. With girls, it tends to be getting involved with men who may take advantage of them and being groomed for prostitution, whether that's formal prostitution or more informal prostitution [...] the wider audience, if you like, would see the girl as being more vulnerable and they would perhaps just see the boy as being bad. (Manager, social care)

These heavily gendered approaches to vulnerability were echoed in young people's understandings of the notion and are returned to in later chapters.

Chapter summary

How the concept of vulnerability operates in practice is a complex process. The notion's primary functions were connected to prioritising and distributing resources, serving technical or semi-technical classifications, and also linked with discursive strategies seen as triggering empathy for 'problematic' young people. Yet in terms of what the classification meant for every-day decision making, the subjective nature of the concept seemed to have resulted in fairly substantial variations in application, with discretion central to vulnerability management. In practice, vulnerability classifications were often tied to views about who 'deserved' services the most, with individual judgements about vulnerability shaped by moral and personal preferences as well as wider pressures of service delivery. Ideas about vulnerability were also bound up with traditional ideas about gender norms, indicating that the popularity of the concept in welfare and disciplinary services may have different implications for young men and young women. The interrelationship between behaviour, gender and perceived vulnerability emerges as a complex dynamic underpinning service provision for 'vulnerable' young people.

Vulnerability classifications would appear to function as a way of further drawing 'problem' young people into the reach of welfare and disciplinary interventions. This dynamic could be beneficial in triggering additional support and the concept offered a powerful mechanism thorough which practitioners, managers and commissioners were able to proactively resist condemnation of young people who transgressed. Yet the concept's deployment also seemed to serve more controlling dynamics, where young people who behaved in line with widely held standards of 'appropriate' and 'compliant' behaviours were more likely to benefit from vulnerability classifications. Youth justice research has demonstrated that those young people who are the most likely to behave in the most persistently problematic ways are those who are the most disadvantaged (Wilkinson and Lober, cited in Pitts, 2000; Muncie et al, 2002; Goldson and Muncie, 2006; Jacobson et al, 2010), leading to questions about how far vulnerability discourses – paradoxically – could serve the further marginalisation of the 'most vulnerable' young people. Young men from disadvantaged backgrounds in particular would seem to be especially prone to exclusion from vulnerability classifications. Exploration of how practitioners understand and apply vulnerability has offered substantive insights into how the concept is operationalised, but the voices and views of those on the receiving end of these vulnerability policies and practices are yet to be explored. It is to these matters that the following chapters now turn.

Note

[1] The five outcomes set out in *Every Child Matters* are: 'enjoying and achieving', 'staying safe', 'being healthy', 'making a positive contribution' and 'economic wellbeing'.

FIVE

Vulnerable young people's lives

Introduction

Dominant constructions of vulnerable people tend to imply the idea that they are 'weak' and different from 'ordinary' people, or that they are in need of protection through 'supportive' social interventions. Yet 'vulnerable' people's own perspectives of relationships, trajectories, opportunities, structures and events that shape their 'vulnerabilities' offer a rather different view. This chapter is the first of three to examine vulnerability through considering the experiences and perspectives of vulnerable young people. How those positioned as vulnerable understand their circumstances and make sense of vulnerability is rarely given attention (Chambers, 1989; Parley, 2011; Wiles, 2011), perhaps in part due to tendencies for the voices of 'marginalised' people to be side-lined or overlooked in policy and research (Lister, 2004; Shildrick and MacDonald, 2013). In focusing on the voices and stories of vulnerable young people, the aim over the course of this and the next two chapters is to move beyond the 'official line' on vulnerability, complementing policy and theoretical accounts of the concept (Chapters One to Three) with in-depth exploration of 'lived experiences' of vulnerability.

All three chapters discuss qualitative data from fieldwork conducted in a large city in northern England. The choice of geographical location was based on the city's sizable local authority and relatively substantial infrastructure for supporting vulnerable young people, with a wide range of professionals having responsibilities for commissioning, organising and providing interventions that are often especially targeted at vulnerable groups. The study itself included 25 interviews with young people from a range of different 'vulnerable groups' and also more informal ethnographic work in local youth provision (for a more detailed discussion of the research methods see Chapter One; Brown, 2013). Interviewees were 12 to 18 years old; 14 were female and 11 were male. Young people with a range of different ethnicities were included in the sample, with 17 participants being of White UK ethnic origin. 'Transgressive' young people were deliberately incorporated into the fieldwork; just over half of the young people who were interviewed had offending histories, had criminal behaviours, had been involved in antisocial behaviour and/or had been excluded from school. This strategy yielded especially useful findings in relation to exploring links between vulnerability, care and social control.

This chapter in particular considers the life stories and experiences of vulnerable young people. In the next section, young people's perspectives of difficulties that were significant in their lives are explored, offering a general introduction to the circumstances and social conditions that shaped their 'vulnerability'. The chapter then explores relationships between vulnerability and transgressive or 'problematic' behaviour. Finally, vulnerable young people's hopes for and perceptions of the future are considered. The 'imagined futures' reveal young people's priorities in day-to-day life, perspectives on their vulnerabilities and viewpoints on their 'structural' location in society (see Irwin, 1995), providing insights into interviewees' sense of the opportunities open to them and potential constraints that shaped hopes, aspirations and outlooks. To complement consideration of themes presented here, pen portraits of each young person's life story are also included as an Appendix. These portraits provide a more chronological sense of each young person's lived experience of vulnerability (what might be called their 'journey') and they offer an alternative view on diversity and commonality within the sample.

Just as has been noted in previous chapters, a recurring theme is that vulnerable people might not necessarily always conform to norms of 'acceptable' or 'passive' behaviour that the concept of vulnerability seems to confer on them. A complex interrelationship between 'problem' behaviour and difficult circumstances emerges from the young people's narratives, challenging prominent binary accounts of young people as 'vulnerable victims' or 'dangerous deviants' (see Fionda, 2005; Such and Walker, 2005; Muncie, 2006). Furthermore, alongside the substantive difficulties and challenges in the lives of the vulnerable young people, their voices and perspectives indicate considerable tenacity, determination and optimism. Simplistic and dichotomised constructions of citizens as either 'deserving' or 'undeserving' are called into question. Furthermore, the stories of the young people highlight that although the lives of 'vulnerable' people might be profoundly shaped by institutional or 'structural' factors and forces as well as family or childhood experiences, capacities to resist or shape the development of opportunities or constraints remain important.

Vulnerable youth: difficult lives, multiple disadvantages

The life stories of the young people in the study often revealed layers of complex adversities, which related to both their family contexts and moves towards independence. A range of experiences featured, including abuse and neglect, growing up in the care system, running away, selling sex, homelessness, mental health problems, self-harm and being bullied. The young people frequently reported experiencing multiple issues together, which some researchers emphasise can be particularly problematic (Rossman, 2001; Feinstein and Sabates, 2006; Social Exclusion Task Force, 2007; Barnes et al, 2011). Table 5.1 shows the range of different 'vulnerabilities' experienced by interviewees, after which themes from their stories are then considered in more detail. The names that appear are pseudonyms chosen by the young people.

Abuse and neglect

Problem parental behaviours featured prominently in the young people's life stories. Ten of the 25 young people reported instances or prolonged periods of abuse (physical and/or sexual), as well as emotional neglect. Jay Jay (M, 17) reported that his father used to 'batter him': *"... he used to – not fully punch me – but, like, hit me hard. And I were only a little kid. Like, proper batter me – not proper batter me – but hit me, punch me and that.... And he put my finger in the fire one day and burnt all my finger."* Another young man (mentioned at the start of the book) reported being beaten most days after he was taken to Pakistan for six years to live with his extended family:

> *I used to get beaten up in Pakistan about lots of stupid things really. A brick or a belt or a brush or a tree. That beating started when I was in Pakistan when I was 10 years old. [...] the first two months they were quiet, after that they beat me up until I came here [to England].* (Chris, M, 17)

On his return to the UK, Chris continued to experience violence at home, but was too afraid report it: *"they warned me that if I said anything to anyone ... they threatened me, they'd kill me or they'll do something"*. The serious long-term impacts of negative family experiences such as these have been well documented in childhood studies and behavioural psychology literature (Stainton Rogers et al, 1992; Hooper, 2005; Howe, 2005). Parental neglect was indicated in a number of cases, now considered to be as detrimental to child wellbeing as direct physical

Table 5.1: Vulnerabilities reported by young people in the case study

	Physical abuse/neglect	Sexual abuse	In care	Parental drug/alcohol use	Mental health/self-harm	Bereavement	Homelessness	Refugee/asylum seeker	Learning difficulty	Domestic violence (parents)
Alicia (F, 16)	●		●	●	●	●	●			
Anna (F, 12)							●	●		●
Brook (F, 16)						●	●			●
Charlie (F, 16)	●		●	●						
Chris (M, 17)	●						●			
Elle (F, 14)							●	●		
Hayley (F, 16)					●		●			
Jade A (F, 17)					●				●	
Jade B (F, 16)	●		●	●						●
Jay Jay (M, 17)	●	●								●
'Jeremy Clarkson' (M, 15)							●			
Jess (F, 15)	●	●	●		●					
John (M, 16)					●		●			
Keith (M, 16)	●					●				●
Kotaa (F, 12)						●				●
Laura (F, 16)										
Mackenzie (M, 16)										
Mercedez (F, 15)				●						
Naz (F, 14)		●								●
'Peter Schmeichel' (M, 16)	●		●							
Sam (M, 14)							●	●		
Scott (M, 18)	●	●	●	●	●		●			
Stephanie (F, 16)					●	●				●
Wadren (M, 17)					●					●
'2Pac' (M, 14)										

Running away	Selling sex or favours	Anger issues	Absence from school	School exclusion	Antisocial behaviour	Own drug/ alcohol use	Offending behaviour	Health condition	Caring	Bullying
		•							•	•
		•		•	•					
		•								
•		•		•	•	•	•			
			•							
•	•		•	•						
			•						•	
			•					•		
										•
•										•
			•	•	•	•	•			
			•			•	•			
•	•		•			•	•			
•		•	•	•		•				•
		•	•							
									•	•
		•		•			•		•	
										•
							•			
			•			•	•			
•	•					•	•			

abuse (Egeland et al, 1983; Erikson et al, 1989; Hildyard and Wolfe, 2002; Horwath, 2007). Charlie (F, 16) reported that her mother would call the police and report her children for criminal activities *"when she wanted us out of the house for the day"*. Jade B (F, 16) described how her mother was *"too lazy"* to cook food for her; *"she didn't care about anything apart from men"*. As a result, Jade was often late for school, suffered with illnesses and used to fall asleep in classes *"because I didn't have any food in me"*.

In instances of abuse and neglect, it did not necessarily follow that the young people considered their family environments unsupportive. Affection for parents was often expressed alongside acknowledgements of abuse. Scott (M, 18) had been taken into care after an incident where his mother attacked him with a knife. He had a strong regard for his parents, although events he described often included parental strategies that might be considered unacceptable:

> *We'd always stick together, me and my Mum and my Dad and that. It's like my Dad used to rob pubs, like fruit machines, and he used to come back with grands [thousands of pounds] and stuff like that. I don't know.... We were living ok and, to be honest, my Mum always made sure we had a meal every night and that. But she was still aggressive and she was on heroin and she was on drink, so obviously she had a habit and all my stuff got sold.*

Jay Jay (M, 17) seemed to experience a tension between the negative feelings towards his parents resulting from abuse and the strength of the emotional connection he felt for them in spite of this:

> *... my Mum, I never talk to my Mum. I'm not even near my Dad, don't know my Dad; 'cos what they've done to me ... do you know what I mean. I've still got to see them, and yeah it's my flesh and blood, my Mum and Dad, but at the end of the day, it hurts me for seeing them do that to me. But it doesn't stop me still thinking a lot about them ... I do 'cos it's my Mum and Dad, but can't do owt about it.*

Other young people who had experienced abuse were more condemning about poor treatment from their parents. Jade B (F, 16) at one point described her mother as a *"psychopath"*:

> *We used to go to like contact meetings with social workers, and my Mum, when she did turn up she'd be drunk ... or she just*

> *used to not turn up at all so we used to just sit there waiting for*
> *hours and hours 'cos we hadn't seen her for ages, so we used to*
> *be proper excited to see her … she used to just come in drunk or*
> *she used to come in proper late, or she'd just not turn up at all.*

Jade was one of a number of interviewees who had very little or no contact with their biological parents.

Stories of sexual abuse featured in some of the young people's stories. Jay Jay had been abused by someone his mother had a close relationship with:

> *… it would be about when I were just turning fifteen. My Mum*
> *were with a really good mate of hers, a bloke, and I got touched by*
> *him, so and he got took to thingy and that when I were younger….*
> *To t'police and then nowt come of it.* (Jay Jay, M, 17)

Scott (M, 18) explained that 'something had happened to him' when he was aged 14 in the third care home he lived in, which I understood to mean that he had been sexually abused by a staff member. He described how his experiences in the residential home still caused problems in his life:

> *What happened is never going to go. It's like my girlfriend the*
> *other day, she moved proper quick and I just burst out in shock*
> *and nearly crying and that's because it's how I used to move when*
> *the door opened. I don't know. There's still things there that have*
> *just fucked my head about it and that.*

In each case where young people discussed that they had been sexually abused, disappointment or frustration resulting from inadequate responses to their disclosures was evident, which research has suggested can be especially harmful (Corby, 2001). Naz (F, 14) explained that she was raped by her father when she was five years old, and that her mother's response to this still caused difficulties for her: *"… it's like, my Mum always calls me a slag and stuff and she's always like calling me names and saying that me Dad raped me and this and that"*. Jess (F, 15) had been taken into care after her father sexually abused her. She described a situation with her mother in her doctor's surgery before she went into care: *"… my Mum was just sat there going 'she's got a mental problem, can you put her in a secure unit?', which proper hurt my feelings. 'Cos it's my Mum saying that about me."*

Aside from the direct experiences of sexual abuse, interview narratives often implied high levels of awareness of the sexual abuse of other young people, usually friends, boyfriends or girlfriends. At age 15, Mercedez had an understanding of her boyfriend's experiences of rape:

> ... *Darren said that the woman that did it to him, her husband threatened him with a big knife and saying 'playing fucking sleeping logs, that's the way it is or you're getting stabbed' or whatever, right in his own house, not in their house, in his house.* (Mercedez, F, 15)

One reading of this might be that the possibility of sexual abuse seemed relatively familiar to vulnerable young people.

Family troubles

Beyond abuse and neglect, family contexts described by the young people were largely characterised by multiple difficulties. Family homelessness, parental substance use, domestic violence and parental mental health issues were relatively common experiences across the sample. Many interviewees indicated that they had grown up in an environment where there had been a problematic lack of access to material resources (also see Chapter Seven). Hayley (F, 16) had been responsible for feeding her sister and taking her to school for a number of years, but was not given money to do this. She lived with her father at that time: *"He wouldn't leave me no money for food, so I'd be lending money off of people. It were horrible."* Homelessness was referenced as a point of difficulty in 10 of the accounts and five young people had experienced homelessness along with their parents. While some young people who had lived in hostels experienced this environment as relatively safe, others described it as especially difficult to cope with. Sam (M, 14), whose family were British Pakistani and who was living in a hostel at the time of the interview said: *"in here you've got like [bad] people or summat"*.

Exposure to parental domestic violence was a particular theme in terms of difficult family contexts or 'adversity packages' (Rossman, 2001; see also Hester et al, 2007; Holt et al, 2008). Hayley (F, 16), who had been in an abusive relationship herself, described how her mother intermittently fled from domestic violence incidents: *"My Dad used to be really violent and to grow up watching that it's ... like, my first tooth came out in a hostel for Mums and babies and my brother wasn't even − not eight weeks old."* As well as first-hand experiences of domestic violence, young people were also aware of it having taken place in their families. Wadren (M, 17) said: *"My real Dad was like a complete arsehole. He beat my Mum up, he raped her and did all these horrible things to her."*

In their narratives of complicated family situations, the role that young people played supporting others came across especially prominently. Feelings of responsibility towards loved ones frequently featured, echoing findings from other research, which has underlined that a sense of duty and care towards others is central to experiences of childhood and youth (Such and Walker, 2005). Hayley (F, 16) was homeless and staying temporarily at her grandmother's house. As well as describing how her aunt was in prison for killing a partner, she described quite a range of issues in her family life and efforts to help her family in dealing with these:

> *My Mum's got depression; my Dad's just a stress head and he's telling me that I'm not his daughter anymore; it's like ... he doesn't call me his daughter no more [...] When my Auntie got sent down it was just a bombshell for everyone and I didn't want to speak about how I felt 'cos I felt it would trigger them.*

In four cases, a sense of shared responsibility in family life extended to fuller and more formal caring responsibilities for siblings and parents. The mother of '2Pac' had been diagnosed with multiple sclerosis when he was aged 12, which led to him needing to *"do everything"* in the house, including cooking, cleaning, ironing and washing: *"My life was crap. I hated it. It was like I had to craft my personal life around my Mum because I'd never know if she would be fine or if she would just ... sometimes she can't get out of bed...."* ('2Pac', M, 14).

Even where caring responsibilities were less formalised, the young people described feelings of responsibility towards adults in their families. Mercedez (F, 15) was very concerned that her father might die from his alcohol use:

> *I keep threatening him with it, saying Dad, I want you to be there for my marriage and walk me down aisle, thinking it'd come into his head and think 'right, I can see some sense now'. But there's still nothing ... [so I] said to him 'well, I guess you don't want to walk me down the aisle then'. And then he said 'well I guess I fucking don't then, don't bother asking me'. But that's something that was said that probably weren't ever meant, because you know what these people are like.*

As the tone of Mercedez indicates here, the young people often gave the impression that they were able to manage fairly complicated and difficult family contexts with a substantial degree of independence from adults and parents.

There were a very small number of interviews in which young people gave the impression that their family contexts had been relatively free from such substantive issues, indicating that not all 'vulnerable' young people had come from what might be described as 'disadvantaged' backgrounds. John (M, 16), for example, had attended a public school until he stopped going at the age of 14, when he had started using drugs heavily. Although he argued with his parents extensively and the relationship had eventually broken down, difficulties in his life related to bereavement and drug use rather than complex family circumstances or disadvantage. Laura (F, 16) reported that her greatest difficulties related to meeting new people during the transition to high school and incidents of bullying, which her parents had supported her with. On the whole, however, an absence of difficulties in the young people's family contexts was notable for its rarity.

Difficulties on the journey to adulthood

Many of the young people spoke about difficulties or challenges related to them more as independent 'individuals'. A range of physical and mental health issues were reported, with depression referenced in several interviews. John (M, 16) had recently been sectioned under the Mental Health Act due to concerns about his mental health and drug use, and Scott (M, 18) discussed receiving substantive interventions from the NHS for his mental health issues, which he described as *"schizophrenia"* and *"ADHD"* (attention deficit hyperactivity disorder). Four young people reported self-harming, including one young person (Wadren, M, 17) who had attempted to commit suicide by trying to hang himself.

Instances of bullying also featured frequently, which often seemed related to peer perceptions of difference (see Farrell and Bruce, 1997; Gorman-Smith and Tolan, 1998, 2003; Elgar et al, 2009) and which sometimes included serious physical assaults. Jade A (F, 17), who had learning difficulties, detailed one particularly brutal example after which she was diagnosed with post-traumatic stress disorder:

> ... *I just went down to see the trains and I said to my Mum, 'oh look at this train', and then this girl come up to me and she just basically just said, 'oh you've called me so and so, a slag' and then she just dragged me across the floor, literally by my hair, I had my*

hair down. So she just dragged me across the floor and punched me at the side and my Mum kept saying to her, 'what're you doing, that's my daughter' and then she got punched, I got punched and I was, in my kidneys, I got two black eyes....

Jay Jay (M, 17) reported that he had been hospitalised in one instance of community violence, and was fearful of his safety in certain parts of his estate: *"I got jumped there by two lads, got a bike, put it on my head, started stamping on the bike and that."* Accounts of bullying might be perhaps best understood in the context of evidence suggesting that 'urban youth' are subject to especially high rates of community violence (see Bell and Jenkins, 1993; Gorman-Smith and Tolan, 1998). Consequences of experiencing bullying could be particularly far-reaching when compounded by other problems. Alicia was bullied in one of the care homes she lived in: *"In the end I ended up running away and being homeless and they wouldn't find me anywhere else to live because I was getting bullied at this children's home"* (Alicia, F, 16). She had slept in a tent for one month during this period of homelessness, at the age of 15, with a boyfriend who injected her with heroin.

Like Alicia, six other young people had experienced being homeless as single 'young adults' rather than as children within their family units, living in hostels as they waited for their own tenancies or spending periods sleeping at the houses of friends and relatives. Such stories highlighted that where young people sought independent living, this was from necessity rather than something aspirational, driven mainly by family breakdown or abuse from parents (see also Fitzpatrick, 2000; Randall and Brown, 2001; Monfort, 2009). Brook (F, 16) felt that she could not live with her family due to not getting on with her stepfather and had moved into an adult women's hostel. There had been several incidents involving the police as a result of conflict between her and her stepfather. Chris (M, 17) had experienced physical abuse from his father, who had also threatened to kill him, and had then lived in a hostel with mainly adult male residents. Independent living was in most cases characterised by 'making do' with difficult living arrangements of various forms, but these were in most cases preferable to living with parents or other relatives.

Another theme to emerge from the young people's stories was bereavement, which is increasingly being considered an issue of significance in young people's lives (Corr and Balk, 1996; Thomson et al, 2002; McCarthy, 2006; Goldsmith, 2012). Alicia (F, 16), Brook (F, 16), John (M, 16), Kotaa (F, 12) and Stephanie (F, 16) all mentioned deaths of family members or friends as major difficulties in their lives.

Sometimes the young people had experienced several bereavements in close succession. Kotaa (F, 12), the only Romany Gypsy young person interviewed in the study, had lost her uncle and her father within two years, which she identified as key turning points in her life. For both Kotaa and John, coping with death linked with behavioural matters, as Kotaa explained: *"I started running away from home when my Dad died 'cos I felt that it were people in my house's fault."* This resonated with recent research that has started to make links between bereavement and apparently 'antisocial' behaviour (Goldsmith, 2012).

Finally, 'moving around' was one of the most frequently referenced experiences, discussed in relation to moves within the care system (six interviewees), moving to the UK from abroad (five interviewees) and moving to a different town, city or region within the UK (nine interviewees). All of the young people had moved house a number of times, some indicated that they had moved many times. In some cases, this could be partly in response to aspects of the welfare system, as in Keith's (M, 16) account:

> *I've been at my Nana's for the past five years, but I've had like a couple of month of that because she couldn't get me into – well she got me into school, but she couldn't get help. You know like things I needed, like benefits and stuff like that. 'Cos I'd come from one area and moved straight into another area without letting them know, they couldn't do it all straight away. So she had to send me back to my Dad for a couple of month.*

More commonly, however, a fracturing of the family unit was indicated to be a key factor in house or area moves. Interviewees tended to have lived with different members of their family after or during the breakdown of parental relationships or during periods where their parents were struggling to cope.

In addition, five young people in the sample had moved to the UK from abroad. They had often moved several times since arriving in the UK, to different towns and cities, and had also moved around extensively within the case study city. Difficulty in leaving family members and friends behind in the country of origin was cited as the most problematic aspect of moving to the UK, along with not being able to speak English. Anna (F, 12) had moved from Lithuania at around the age of nine, and had not seen her father for three years:

> Anna: *When I come to England, it was difficult 'cos I can't even talk, I can't understand what somebody talks, and I just stay at*

home. And after, my Mum was talking better than me, but now she can't talk better than me. [smiles]

Kate: *You're really good now, aren't you? And were you scared when you came?*

Anna: *Yeah I were really scared. When we go to the airport and we were waiting for the aeroplane I was really scared and I was crying 'cos I didn't want to leave my Dad.*

Starting school in this country also seemed to be particularly stressful for the young people who had moved from abroad. When I asked Elle (F, 14), who had moved from Eritrea, what her first day at school in the UK was like, she explained that *"it was scary 'cos it was our first day and yeah, I couldn't speak much English at that time"*. Moving house was often experienced at the same time as moving to a different school and there were connections between moving house and periods of absence from school (see also Haveman et al, 1991; Grumen et al, 2008).

The extensive number of moves that the young people had experienced and the tapestry of different 'vulnerabilities' or difficulties that were detailed resonate with research that has indicated that 'socially excluded' or 'vulnerable' young people in particular face an increasingly uncertain world (Furlong and Cartmel, 1997; Johnston et al, 2000; MacDonald et al, 2005). It was not unusual for complex stories of movement and transition to be covered with brevity:

I got adopted when I were four. I stopped with my Mum when she were taking heroin and my Dad were in prison at the time and they couldn't look after me. And then my adopted place was broke down when I were 12, then my Mum died when I were 11 ... . Then it broke down when I was 12 and I went to live with my Grandma, my birth Grandma. And from living with her I went into care. (Alicia, F, 16)

Despite their acknowledgement of the problems that some situations had posed, a tone of acceptance tended to permeate many of the young people's descriptions of the substantial difficulties and transitions they had experienced. That interviewees' narratives consistently framed life events as relatively unremarkable seemed significant. This indicated a 'doxic' (see Bourdieu, 1977) or 'taken-for-granted' dimension to lived realities of vulnerability, which is further explored in later chapters.

Transgression and vulnerability

Connotations attached to the concept of vulnerability would perhaps lead to the assumption that 'vulnerable' people might behave in ways that are seen as submissive or compliant (see Chapters One and Two). The life stories of the vulnerable young people in the study brought such assumptions into question, with 12 of the 25 reporting 'transgressive' or 'problematic' behaviours, including:

- criminal activities (such as theft, assault, criminal damage and the use of prohibited drugs);
- behaviours considered 'antisocial' (incidents on the streets, congregating in groups); and
- aggression and/or violence, which was often described by the young people in terms of 'anger' or 'attitude'.

Ten young people had been excluded from school either temporarily or permanently, six reported heavy use of drugs and/or alcohol and nine had been disciplined within the youth justice system (see Table 5.2 for details of criminal justice system incidents that the young people disclosed). Two had been sentenced to periods in youth offending institutions, and one had been served with an Anti-Social Behaviour Order (ASBO) and had also spent time in an adult prison. Certain 'vulnerable' young people's stories made it clear that they could routinely be involved in activities that would be deemed highly transgressive or problematic:

> ... I got in trouble 'cos that was the first time I ever robbed money off my Nana for drugs. And I got a 12-month Supervision Order, which that just left getting breaches and like I say, 'cos I took more money. So they gave me so many chances and I blew my last chance. (Keith, M, 16)

> I've just come back from Scotland 'cos they had to take me up there because of my behaviour. I was absconding twice a week, just came back, stoned, been prostituting, stood on corners. (Jess, F, 15)

> I used to be shoplifter, innit, and then I thought, well, I might as well just sniff better drugs and go out and do stupid things for stupid amounts of money. So I just ... if you leave an iPod in your car, there's a very, very high chance that iPod will be gone if you don't lock it up, stuff like that, just stupid things. (John, M, 16)

Table 5.2: Criminal justice system incidents detailed by vulnerable young people

Young person	Criminal matters disclosed	Background information
Alicia (F, 16)	Shoplifting, class A drug use (heroin)	Caught for stealing tanning wipes from a shop and a television from a children's home
Brook (F, 16)	Violence, drunk and disorderly, cannabis use	Linked violence with domestic violence incidents between stepfather and mother
Charlie (F, 16)	Charged with criminal damage	Reported it was accidental damage to a glass in the care home she was living in
Hayley (F, 16)	Assaulted police officer	During dispute between family and her ex-boyfriend
Jay Jay (M, 17)	Criminal damage, possession of weapon, threats to kill	Incident with ex-girlfriend after contact with her on Facebook
Jess (F, 15)	Violent behaviour to teachers	During period where her father was sexually abusing her
John (M, 16)	Theft (drug-related), use of a range of class A drugs	Heavy user of mephedrone ('MCAT'). Used to shoplift and steal from stationary cars
Keith (M, 16)	Theft, criminal damage	Stole from his grandmother on a regular basis to fund cocaine use
Scott (M, 18)	Burglary, assault, use of a range of class A drugs, assault (various), drug running (heroin), shoplifting, theft, skipping train fares	Offending began aged 9 with sale of heroin. Had received treatment for a range of mental health issues and had also been served with an ASBO
Wadren (M, 17)	Arrested but not prosecuted for rape, antisocial activities with friends	Ex-girlfriend pressed charges and later dropped them. With friends, set outdoor fires where police were called.

Non-criminal behaviours that might commonly be described as 'antisocial' were also reported in some interviews. Two young men identified themselves as being part of 'gangs' (Scott, 18, and '2Pac', 14), although the account by '2Pac' suggested that this experience was short-lived, ending after his mother told him he had to be home at 6pm of an evening. Several other young men described being involved in low-level nuisance behaviours, such as starting fires and having arguments in public spaces. Scott (M, 18) was the only young person to have been formally disciplined for his antisocial behaviour, having been served with an ASBO and a £280 fine following incidents in a nightclub. This penalty was issued in parallel with criminal charges for other offences.

Anger, aggression and/or challenging behaviour extended into the stories of the young people across the sample, commonly described by the young people in terms of their 'attitude':

> I just … my attitude against the teachers and staff, and just running away, didn't do any work, and ended up punching the staff, throwing chairs out the window. (Jess, F, 15)

> Bad behaviour and getting stoned in school. I think I walked into school drunk one time with my mate, which is probably not the best thing to do. (Brook, F, 16)

Anger issues were often seen by the young people as especially problematic in relation to their participation in more structured environments (see Bottrell, 2007), and in some cases had led to temporary or permanent exclusion from school:

> It's like a classroom innit and it's loads of students and that so it's like they'll be at everyone else and then you'll get frustrated 'cos you won't know what to do – and then the teacher takes their time coming over to you and that so I just get stressed out and then I end up walking out lessons and things like that. (Stephanie, F, 16)

> … my Mum taught us, like, if somebody hit you, you hit them back and, like, if you don't wanna do it, don't do it. And so, if you get into care, it's completely different. It's like if you don't do it, you have to do it. (Charlie, F, 16)

Interviewees did not seem to have excelled in mainstream schools (see also Cooper, 1993; Cole et al, 2001) and many reported a preference for smaller class sizes and specialist teaching units, which the majority had experiences of attending. Stories of anger and challenging behaviour were commonly told about circumstances where young people felt shame or a loss of status:

> I used to mess about a lot but if someone like has a go at me I won't stand there and take it. I won't let people shout at me, you know, so I used to get in trouble a lot 'cos I'd mess about and then

when people tried to tell me off I would like shout back and stuff.
(Mackenzie, M, 16)

Scott was able to offer substantive insights into his experiences and emotions in this respect, explaining how he hated being laughed at:

Scott: *You get embarrassed when someone's laughing at you. It's like a normal reaction. Everyone does. But I just take it more.... My image is everything to me. Like, I don't know. If I don't feel clean that day, I won't go out and stuff like that [...] I have to feel good. I have to – my mouth has to – I don't know, it's weird things, I have to look in the mirror and see if I look all right to go out that day, otherwise I won't go out, and it's just – I don't know. And people look at me on the bus and I think they're just looking at me and my bird says to me, 'That's ok. They could be gay. They could like it. It doesn't mean they're looking at you because they want to fight you and stuff'. But obviously –*

Kate: *Or just a bit – some people just stare at you, not even for any reason do they ... on the bus, it's like –*

Scott: *That's what I <u>mean</u>, but I take it wrongly. I think, 'oh, this top looks bad, or these jeans look horrible' or something and I'll just think that all day. And I'll actually go home and work myself up that much that I go home and get changed.*

Links between anger and aggression, 'vulnerability', mental health issues and 'problem' behaviours are clearly illustrated in this quotation, which have also been highlighted in research with young offenders and 'antisocial' young people (see BIBIC, 2005; Goldson, 2009; Fryson and Yates, 2011).

Of the young people who described transgressive activities in their life stories, the majority implied that they were on a trajectory towards more compliant and conformist behaviours, as is consistent with research indicating that young people 'grow out' of problem behaviour as they get older and experience increased responsibilities (Rutherford, 1992; see also Jessor et al, 1993; Henderson, 1994; Squires and Stephen, 2005). Contrary to populist constructions of young people as taking pride in their problematic behaviours (see Brown, 2011a), almost all of the young people interviewed were inclined towards thoughtful and reflexive accounts of their transgressions. Young people may well be inclined to give different accounts of their transgressions depending on who they are relaying information to and the 'impression' they may be trying to create (see Goffman, 1959, 1963), but in the case study research most of the young people demonstrated sensitivity and a degree of regret as they discussed behaviours that would be considered problematic. Indeed, 'problem' behaviours were most often discussed in terms of their link with difficulties, challenges and problems – or what might be called 'vulnerabilities'.

Relationships between vulnerability and transgression

Attention to lived experiences of vulnerability highlighted that binary understandings of young people as 'vulnerable victims' or 'dangerous wrong-doers' (see Fionda, 2005; Such and Walker, 2005; Muncie, 2006) seemed ill-matched with the complexities of the young people's lives. Complex relationships between patterns or instances of transgression and the presence of 'vulnerabilities' or multiple disadvantages were often apparent in the narratives:

> In 2009, I was abused by my Dad and that was when I got my social worker. They tried to get me a foster home, but because I didn't want to stay there, my behaviour got bad. That's when I was selling sex. (Jess, F, 15)

> When I was home I'd get stressed out a lot 'cos I just I'd be either cleaning or babysitting. And it used – I used to get annoyed and that with myself and then I'd take it out in school. My temper out in school and that.... (Stephanie, F, 16)

If taken as an independent subject of study, young people's stories of 'bad' behaviour could be alarming, casting the story tellers as delinquent. Yet seen in the context of a young person's life story, accounts of transgressions might be understood differently. Sixteen-year-old Alicia had been prosecuted for shoplifting, been involved in selling sex and had been a heroin user in the past. She discussed how she had got involved in some of these transgressions: *"My Mum took heroin so I wanted to know what was so good about it."* Keith (M, 16) had spent time in a 'secure unit' (a form of youth offending institution) for offences related to his heavy cocaine use and theft. He explained how his life started to move towards behaviours considered 'antisocial': *"Because [Dad] were an alcoholic, he were beating me up every day, well not every day but it were like every time he didn't have a drink. So obviously I were roaming the streets 'cos he were drinking all the time."* Rather than 'vulnerability' and 'deviance' being mutually exclusive states, vulnerability in the context of young people's lives might in many cases be best understood as symbiotically and intrinsically linked with transgression.

Scott's case seemed to illustrate this interrelationship particularly vividly. Scott (M, 18) reported the greatest range of difficulties or 'vulnerabilities' in his childhood out of all the young people in the study (see Table 5.1), but he was also the young person with the most prolific offending history. He had become involved in selling heroin at nine years old, had recently assaulted a general practitioner while intoxicated on the drug mephedrone (or 'MCAT'), had repeatedly burgled houses, committed street robberies, and also reported that while using steroids heavily he had assaulted a man *"and proper nearly killed him and everything"*. He made it clear in the interview that he continues to *"work"* or *"go out making money"* (illegally) on the streets. At the age of 18, he had already been incarcerated twice. Alongside such transgressions he reported physical abuse from his parents, serious mental health issues from an early age, sexual abuse while in care, homelessness, parental criminality and growing up in poverty. Parts of his narrative were troubling in terms of the risks he apparently posed to others. Taken in isolation, Scott's continued assaults on others and robberies constituted serious deviance, but set within the more detailed contextual picture of his 'vulnerability' and the adversity he had dealt with, this behaviour was perhaps less easy to dismiss as simple wrong-doing:

Scott: *Say you're trying to knock someone's teeth out, it's just a buzz. And then when they hit you back, I don't know, you just get that nice feeling. It's a good feeling. It feels good. It sounds weird that.*

Kate: *Can you say about why it feels good?*

Scott: *It lets out something. It lets out something that's inside you. It lets out a feeling that's been inside you for a long time. And when you fight, it's like more of that feeling is coming out. So it means that you feel fresher. Even though you could be bruised and cut open the next day, you don't feel as angry because you're letting all that anger out and it just feels good ... sometimes.... It's better than just keeping it bottled up. But, also, you can't keep fighting all the time. That's what I keep getting told. So I'm trying to stop.*

Kate: *So when I said, 'Oh, you were lucky to get away with it' [referring to superficial rather than serious injury], you've sort of got a buzz from it so you sort of don't mind that you've got the –*

Scott: *I've got big scars on my arms and that where I've been attacked with knives and stuff because, I don't know, I've been in [housing estate in the city] and I've been on my own and I've still looked for a fight. I don't know, I like being on the floor getting booted in the head sometimes. I don't know why it is. I think it's how my Mum – with my Mum, innit [...] because my Mum and Dad just hit me quite a lot when I was a kid and that, I don't know, I think that's why I still like to get hit sometimes.*

Tendencies for young people to be seen as less 'vulnerable' where they displayed transgressive behaviours (see Chapter Four) would appear to be particularly significant in cases such as Scott's. Due to his age, the seriousness of his offences and the sustained and repeated nature of his transgressions, Scott would be unlikely to be considered as vulnerable in many respects, even though his life story would indicate that his childhood involved dealing with problems that were among the most multifaceted and extreme in the sample.

That problem behaviours and vulnerability are bedfellows may not necessarily be a position well accommodated in the connotations that the concept of vulnerability carries with it. This would seem problematic in terms of service responses to vulnerability. There were indications that for certain 'vulnerable' young people, transgressions functioned as resistances that were important in order to create a positive identity or necessary manoeuvres in the context of their circumstances (see also Bottrell, 2007). Hayley (F, 16) had self-harmed regularly in the past. A counsellor had assisted her to develop strategies to help her stop hurting herself, but since then, her behaviour in school had become more difficult for others: *"Ever since then I've just been angry 'cos I don't take it out on myself anymore, I take it out on everybody else. So I suppose I'd rather be excluded from school than all cut up"* (Hayley, F, 16).

That young people might perceive certain 'rewards' as well as 'risks' as attached to behavioural transgressions has been documented by other researchers (Hagan, 1991; Hayward, 2002; Bottrell, 2007; Deuchar, 2010), which discourses of vulnerability may flatten out or oversimplify. Chapter Four highlighted that for professionals, lack of compliance on the part of young people often led to them being seen as less 'vulnerable'. Yet the young people's life stories indicated that such resistances may indeed be a common aspect of lived experiences vulnerability, and can be understood within a broader context of coping strategies that young people may see as necessary in order to deal with the challenges and difficulties they face. The 'vulnerable' young people's accounts of their life stories offered powerful challenges to more pathologising narratives of individual inadequacies that permeate dominant constructions of antisocial or criminal youth. Attention to the aspirations of 'vulnerable' young people also provides insights in this area.

Imagined futures

Young people's 'imagined futures' have been a burgeoning area of study in recent decades, considered to offer important insights into young people's social worlds and their outlooks on the societies in which they live (Nilsen, 1999; Brannen and Nilsen, 2002; Thomson and Holland, 2002; Devadason, 2008; Winterton et al, 2011). These have been used as a research tool by youth researchers seeking to understand young people's priorities in day-to-day life, values and sense of their own 'structural' location in society (Irwin, 1995). Many studies have highlighted an increasing array of complex and 'non-linear' progressions into adulthood (Furlong and Cartmel, 1997; Johnston et al, 2000; MacDonald et al, 2005; McDonald et al, 2011), and yet case study findings supported other research that has highlighted how young people's imagined futures remain relatively conventional in nature (Barry, 2001; Croll et al, 2010). Enhanced 'vulnerability' did not seem to result in vastly modified hopes or aspirations relative to other young people.

Somewhat contrary to governmental concerns about the limited aspirations of 'disadvantaged' young people, almost all of the young people interviewed saw education and attending college as a way to secure a better future (see also Bottrell, 2007; Croll et al, 2010). Four young people aspired to go to university, others saw more 'vocational' education as important. 'Jeremy Clarkson' (M, 15) intended to be a mechanic because going to university would be too expensive. '2Pac' (M, 14) also expressed concerns about the costs of university education, but felt it was still necessary: *"To do anything, I have to go, even though it's got to nine grand a year."* It is perhaps worth noting that '2Pac' appeared to have considerably more access to material resources than 'Jeremy Clarkson', who was living in a homeless hostel, which may influence decision making in this respect (see Connor et al, 2001; Forsyth and Furlong, 2003; Callender and Jackson, 2005).

Employment was another core concern for the majority, and constructions of future notions of work could perhaps be viewed as related to economic liberal demands to produce oneself as a 'subject of value' (see Allen and Mendick, 2013). Imagined future professions were highly gendered, as has been consistently highlighted in other research (Francis, 1996, 2001; Kintrea et al, 2011; McDonald et al, 2011). Young women mainly aspired to work with children or as hairdressers and young men predominantly saw themselves as learning a recognised skilled trade or doing a sports-related job (see Table 5.3), with the exceptions of Keith (M, 16) who wanted to be a hairdresser and Brook (F, 16) who wanted to teach sport. The two young people who saw themselves as working in highly skilled 'professional' jobs (a doctor/pharmacist and civil engineer) were from the same Eritrean family, resonating with other research, which has indicated that minority ethnic children tend to have higher aspirations than their white British peers, particularly in the case of those who have moved to the UK from abroad (see Strand, 2007; Morrison Gutman and Akerman, 2008; Fuller, 2009).

Celebrity-influenced aspirations were evident in some of the narratives. Jay Jay (M, 17) had a *"back-up"* strategy of being a plumber, but aspired to become a famous singer and had auditioned for the television show *X-Factor*. Kotaa (F, 12) aspired to be a singer (see Figure 5.1). Other young people indicated that although they desired celebrity

Table 5.3: Vulnerable young people's imagined futures

Imagined profession	Young people
Supporting disadvantaged children	Alicia, Jade A, Jess, John, Mackenzie, Naz, Stephanie
Working with children	Hayley, Laura
Skilled trade (mechanic/plumber)	Jay Jay, 'Jeremy Clarkson', Mackenzie, Scott
Highly skilled professional (doctor/ pharmacist or civil engineer)	Elle, Sam
Hairdresser	Charlie, Keith, Mercedez
Celebrity	Anna, Jay Jay, Kotaa
Sports professions (teacher/coach/ physiotherapist)	Brook, 'Peter Schmeichel', '2Pac'
Army	Chris
Catering	Jade B
Paramedic	Wadren
Unsure	John, Jess, Scott

status, they felt that it was unlikely they would achieve it. Wadren's (M, 17) dream was to play for the football team Manchester United, but he said this *was "never gonna happen"*. As noted in other studies, most of the young people's desired careers were more 'realistic' in their nature (Brown, G., 2011; Kintrea et al, 2011). In some instances, aspirations had been moderated based on both positive and negative life experiences. Brook, who was about to start a Saturday job coaching children in sport, explained:

> *I always wanted to be a policewoman at first, 'til I got arrested. No, even after, I still did wanna be one. But then I realised that I was good at sport and I've always known that, and people have always told me that, so when I got all of these things out of the Academy and that, I just thought I might as well just go for it. So that's what I'm doing.* (Brook, F, 16)

A significant number of the young people wanted their future employment to involve supporting 'disadvantaged' people, as they saw their life experiences as equipping them with insights that would be valuable in such settings. Work and employment tended to be valued predominantly as a route to achieving financial security. 'Peter Schmeichel' (M, 16) wanted to be a football coach, but also indicated that he was more interested in financial reward than vocation, and said that he might instead achieve financial security through marrying *"someone rich"*, like a teacher. Scott (M, 18) hoped for a *"steady job"* and for him, his girlfriend and any children to be *"living well"*. In some instances, employment was seen as a route for securing material goods: *"I want nice things in my life so I know I'll have to work for them, so just a job really and so I can buy a nice house and have things that are nice that I want"* (Alicia, F, 16). As in Alicia's narrative, the desire to purchase a house was commonly mentioned.

Evidence overwhelmingly indicated aspirations structured by powerful normative assumptions about marriage and children (see Thomson et al, 2002): *"I see a nice car and a nice house. I see one of those, you know, one of those cheesy American, like the cheesy English American lives that, like, nice big house, nice wife, nice kids. That's cool"* ('2Pac', M, 14). The only exception was Naz, (F, 14), who said that children 'did her head in' and that she did not want to get married. In some cases, future family scenarios were envisaged with a significant level of detail and consideration:

I know this sounds really childish, but I can still see me and my boyfriend staying together because he's got a wise head on and he ain't like all other knob heads and I've got a wise head on, and we're not like one of them couples who do piss about. And he eventually will get the, you know, finish his college and then get a job and I will, like a year after. Eventually we'll keep having holidays and whatever, but eventually, because he'll be doing mechanics, he'll get his own car, get his own, and then eventually we'll move into a house, hopefully. Our house. Then if it's all still going well, settle down and have kids. We'll still have fun. (Mercedez, F, 15)

Figure 5.1: A young person's imagined future self (Kotaa, F, aged 12) – she hoped to become a singer

Both Brook (F, 16) and Jay Jay (M, 17) said that they wanted their children to *"look up"* to them. Jay Jay thought that this would be achieved if he was *"a good father figure, like someone, like, say I own my own business or I'm a big singer and stuff like that"*. When I asked him the sort of qualities that would make him a good father figure he explained: *"Well, be generous, happy, like always thinking of good things, not bad."* Several interviewees indicated that they wanted their children to have better childhoods than they had experienced themselves, particularly in terms of family stability.

One more surprising theme to emerge was the desire to travel, which appeared in eight interviews. To be able to have holidays often seemed to the young people to be closely associated with the achievement of a suitable disposable income. One of Alicia's (F, 16) main goals was to pay for herself to go on holiday. Jay Jay (M, 17) wanted to have a wife and children and *"have a bit of money behind us so we can go away and that"*, to Barcelona or Cuba. There was also a sense that holidays were opportunities for new experiences and leisure. For his first holiday, Keith (M, 16) wanted to go to Magaluf in Majorca, or Ibiza, because he was *"more of a party person"*. Some young people who mentioned travel also said that they had not yet travelled abroad.

A number of young people struggled with the task of imagining their futures. Their aspirations indicated that they were much more focused on immediate and present day concerns: *"You can't predict your future can you? So you don't know what's going to happen until you reach that age or you just take what comes to you through life"* (Keith, M, 16). John (M, 16) was heavily involved in drug use and mainly saw a future where he would *"stop raving"*. Kotaa (F, 12) said that she wanted *"a modelling career and I want my Mum to be alive when I get married"*, which connected with earlier experiences of the death of her father and her uncle, which had been very difficult for her. Scott (M, 18) was concerned with finding a job. He also wanted to desist from criminal behaviour, as felt that this got him into too much trouble; *"I need to get into boxing or something … so I'm not paggering heads [fighting] on a weekend and that."* Generally speaking, however, more cautious or pessimistic futures represented the minority view. As is consistent with other research on the aspirations of 'disadvantaged' young people, a positive tone permeated the narratives of the young people's imagined futures (see also Brown, 2011; Kintrea et al, 2011). Despite the challenges they had faced, most of the 'vulnerable' young people perceived their futures with optimism and also determination. For Hayley (F, 16), achieving her goals independently was her most important ambition:

I could have so easily just done something purposely to get locked up and just go into prison for, what, three months and come back out and get a flat given to me, money given to me, everything and not have to do anything. But I don't want to do that, I don't want to be one of them lazy people. I want to live a life and go to uni and do what normal people do. I want to, like, prove all my family wrong, the people that just dropped out, like, here, I just want to show them all. When they come back to me and say, 'Yeah, you've done it,' I'll be, like, 'Yeah, without you.'

It may be that some young people employed optimism as a technique to help them to mitigate adverse circumstances (see Benard, 1991; Garmezy, 1991), but such optimism was rarely blind and tended to be characterised by cautious positivity for a future that was imagined with constraints as well as opportunities.

Chapter summary

This chapter has provided insights into the life stories and social worlds of young people who are considered vulnerable. In-depth research highlighted that 'vulnerable' young people had often faced numerous and complex difficulties, which would be likely to confer on them high levels of attention and empathy from professionals involved in the design and delivery of policy and practice interventions. At the same time though, narratives called into question implicit assumptions in vulnerability discourses which can confer expectations of passivity, weakness or absence of human agency on 'vulnerable' people. Lived experiences of vulnerability suggested that vulnerable young people dealt with differentiation and marginalisation in differing ways, including resistance as well as conformity. On the basis of young people's narratives, it would appear that a more nuanced understanding of vulnerability would acknowledge that people's responses to difficulties, challenges and 'vulnerabilities' may often involve transgressions of behavioural norms as well as more 'positive' and socially acceptable strategies. In other words, 'vulnerability' in the context of young people's lives might best be understood as symbiotically and intrinsically linked with (rather than exclusive to) 'transgression'.

Vulnerable young people's imagined futures revealed something of their perceptions of the opportunities and constraints which they saw as structuring their social worlds. Despite seemingly popular concerns about the aspirations of 'disadvantaged' young people, on the whole, vulnerable young people saw positive and relatively conventional futures for themselves, which were firmly in line with economic liberal citizenship ideals of the active and 'responsible' individual (see Rose, 1999; Clarke, 2005). Whilst some interviewees found it difficult to discuss their aspirations in a context of struggling to manage the challenges of day-to-day existence, most of the 'vulnerable' young people in the case study demonstrated substantial reserves of optimism and tenacity despite the significant adversities they had encountered. The present chapter has focused predominantly on the biographically orientated aspects of young people's views of their futures. More structural matters are focused on in Chapter Seven, which considers how young people saw their 'vulnerability' as mediated by relationships, social hierarchies, power dynamics and interventions. Before this, however, we turn to young people's understandings of their 'vulnerability' and their views on being classified in this way.

SIX

Vulnerable identities?

Introduction

While the concept of vulnerability has come to play a significant role in policies, practices and discourses related to disadvantage and social difficulty, how supposedly vulnerable people might understand, construct or respond to being classified in this way has rarely been given consideration. Resistance and receptiveness to 'vulnerable identities' (see McLaughlin, 2012) are little understood, with attention to the implications of vulnerability rationales tending to remain more focused at the level of theoretical or policy concerns. While vulnerability is often assumed to be a kind or empathetic way of framing discussions about 'problematic' circumstances (see Chapter Four), attention to the views of those who are classified as vulnerable reveals that this is not necessarily a perspective shared by the receivers of services (see Wiles, 2011). Similar tensions have been noted in relation to comparable notions such as poverty and social exclusion (Dean and Melrose, 1999; Lister, 2004; Batty and Flint, 2013), indicating possible disconnections between certain conceptual frameworks and lived realities of social and economic difficulties. How far 'vulnerable' citizens' imaginings of their own lives and identities match those carved out in official responses to 'vulnerability' is also open to question.

This chapter seeks to further develop understandings of lived experiences of vulnerability by exploring how supposedly vulnerable people understood the notion and how they experienced being classified in this way. It focuses on how the young people classified as vulnerable made sense of what might be considered the considerable disadvantages and difficulties they had experienced. In considering these matters, the chapter necessarily deals with questions about identity, which is a contested, extensively researched and complex concept. The question of vulnerable identities is approached on the understanding that 'identity' is something fluid, multiple and subject to continuous reassessment (Goffman, 1959; Giddens, 1991), and contingent on the political, social, economic, ideological and interpersonal conditions of the situations in which people find themselves (see Bhavnani and Phoenix, 1994; Hall, 1996; Hunter, 2003). Research findings are therefore reported as a snapshot of the young people's views on their identities at a particular time and place, expressed through conversation with a particular researcher, rather than a definitive view of vulnerable young people's identities. While writers have been critical of tendencies to conflate 'identity', 'self' and 'self-identity' (Lemert, 1994), for present purposes these three terms are used interchangeably to denote the 'practices of self-constitution, recognition and reflection' (Hall, 1996: 13) and 'a sense of belonging(s), the ways in which individuals attach themselves to the social world' (Hunter, 2003: 328).

Vulnerability was a notion that all 25 young people who were interviewed in the study were able to connect with and respond to. However, in a number of cases, the young people were unfamiliar with the word 'vulnerability', so in order to achieve mutual understanding during interview conversations, I sometimes used various proxies such as 'difficulties' or 'difficult lives' to introduce or discuss the notion of vulnerability. Although proxy adaptions of the term 'vulnerability' were necessary to operationalise the concept in the research process, the term itself was brought into the conversation through specially designed interview tasks (see Chapter One) and used wherever possible. Most of the young people were familiar with the word and after informal clarification of meaning seemed to feel comfortable using it. A small number even spontaneously employed the term 'vulnerable' to position themselves before being asked about vulnerability directly, indicating that it was a concept that featured in their frame of reference.

Next, the chapter explores the various meanings that vulnerability had for the young people, focusing particularly on the centrality of blame and deservingness in understandings of the concept. It then considers the considerable resistance to vulnerability classifications that was evident in most of the interview narratives, exploring young people's perspectives on the implications of being considered 'vulnerable'. As responses to vulnerability classifications could be ambiguous or mixed, instances where the young people were more inclined to accept or embrace the designation are then also considered. Finally, reflections on the optimistic ways in which the young people approached their identities are included.

In acknowledging young people's resistance to the concept of vulnerability, the aim here is not to seek to advance that the young people were not 'vulnerable'. Instead, the hope is to contribute to debates about the extent to which a range of discursive practices related to 'at-risk' or 'problem' people may serve narratives that can reinforce misunderstandings about the social worlds and circumstances of those from less privileged backgrounds. The analysis highlights that 'official' vulnerability classifications often function as sites where differences of opinion and judgements about acceptable behaviour are played out. The responses of the vulnerable young people to their vulnerability classifications and the difficulties they had faced illuminate a more textured picture of vulnerability than many policy and research accounts seem to leave room for. In considering 'vulnerable identities', broader questions emerge about how 'precarious' or 'risky' situations that certain groups are exposed to might be most usefully conceptualised in policy, practice and research.

Young people's understandings of vulnerability

As previous chapters have highlighted, vulnerability means different things to different people; a subjectivity that was further underlined during the interviews with the young people. Almost uniformly across these interviews, vulnerability was associated with personal weakness and deficit. Instances of young people connecting it with anything positive were limited and the concept's dissonance with the young people's conceptions of their ability to exercise human agency was a recurring theme. Most commonly, its meaning was associated with naivety or a lack of self-determination. Although John (M, 16) felt that he was vulnerable in some ways, mainly related to his substance use, his resistance to being thought of in this way was based on his idea of himself as an active agent: *"I can be very, very strong-minded. It just depends on what subject. I can think for me sen [myself]."* Sometimes this sense of the concept as indicative of a lack of control over one's own circumstances was linked with an ability to reject various 'temptations' such as sex or drug use: *"I think [someone's vulnerability] depends what kind of stage you are at in your head, whether you can walk away from something like or say, 'oh yeah, I'll do that'"* (Alicia, F, 16). In several instances, the young people discussed vulnerability in terms of how far a person's 'head was screwed on'.

Another pronounced understanding related to a lack of capacity to protect oneself from others. In discussion of this interpretation of vulnerability, there was a notable gender dimension to the forms that third-party malign forces were seen to take. In young men's narratives, being vulnerable was frequently related to a lack of physical power and resulting threat of victimisation: *"It's like how you can back yourself up and that 'cos if you're vulnerable people will take the mick out of you, and you just have to tell 'em about yourself"* ('Peter Schmeichel', M, 16). '2Pac' also saw his vulnerability as something indicative of potential for violent or aggressive behaviour: *"They [peers] go on about my Mum and that's when it turns a bit vicious. So that's where I'm most vulnerable."* Physical prowess and the ability to deal with confrontations were sometimes implied as the antithesis of vulnerability, and the concept was often linked with 'hyper-masculine' identity constructions:

> *I'm vulnerable because I keep thinking in my head I'm losing my reputation now. It's like I went out the other night and no one ever used to start on me because − I'm not saying I'm a big dog and that − look at me; I'm tall and skinny. I don't think I'm hard or owt. I've got a name for myself though.* (Scott, M, 18)

That young men tended to see vulnerability in terms of (lack of) physical aggression or prowess seemed to indicate that the idea of 'hegemonic masculinities' might be useful for understanding young men's lived experiences of vulnerability (see Chapter Five; Connell, 1987), where traditional and normative male roles often linked with patterns of aggression underscore the 'most honoured way of being a man' (Connell and Messerschmidt, 2005: 832).

Whereas vulnerability was associated with 'masculinity deficit' for young men, it tended to be seen as tied to the sexuality of young women. When asked what she took 'vulnerable' to mean, Charlie (F, 16) replied, *"Easy to, like, use"*; wording echoed in many other interviews. The ease with which interviewees saw that young women could be 'taken advantage of' was frequently commented on. Female vulnerability was sometimes associated with socialising and situations where drugs might be used. The young people's gendered understandings of vulnerability echoed practitioner accounts (see Chapter Four), resonating with longstanding and highly gendered care and control practices, which have focused on the potentially threatening behaviour of boys and the 'promiscuity' of girls (Hudson, 1989, 2002; O'Neill, 2001; Goldson, 2004). Implying notions of exploitation, some young people understood the sexual vulnerability of young women to be related to them dealing with a lack of financial security: *"Anyone can give her money and stuff or do summat, to have sex with her and stuff"* (Naz, F, 14).

Just as professionals had indicated that gendered imaginings of vulnerability had implications for how the institutional gaze fell on young people, this was also evident in interviews with young people. Alicia (F, 16) felt that 'vulnerability' tended to be a classification applied to young women rather than young men:

Alicia: ... *women are seen more as vulnerable than men, aren't they?*

Kate: *What makes you say that?*

Alicia: *They just are. I don't think I've ever heard of someone saying 'he's a vulnerable lad' ever, but I've heard loads and loads of people say 'oh, she's a vulnerable girl' and all this. But never, like with workers and things, have I heard 'oh, he's a vulnerable lad'. Maybe because lads like do the wrong thing, don't they ... I don't know. They probably think 'lads can look after themselves'.*

Only two young men talked about the sexual vulnerability of males, both of whom had been sexually abused. Indeed, more sexuality-based understandings of vulnerability were particularly apparent in the narratives of the three young women who had experience of selling sex or 'favours' and the four young people who had been sexually abused.

In certain interviews, rather than seeing vulnerability as tied into one particular type of personal inadequacy, some young people seemed to conceptualise the notion in terms of more general precariousness. Keith (M, 16) said that vulnerability *"comes in all different shapes and sizes"*. Kotaa (F, 12) used the metaphor of a boat:

> *It's like for example say you have a boat and then 'cos you're so close to your Mum and stuff it starts to rock 'cos you're taken away from her and then it starts to rock a bit more because you don't know anything and you've been taken to a different country, then it starts rocking even more and then you get pregnant at a certain age.*

The young people's understandings of vulnerability often seemed to offer insights into the challenges they had faced or were currently facing in their own lives. Imaginings of vulnerability were frequently laced with references to relationships being unequal in power, difficulties arising from this, the need to carefully convey an impression of strength in order to stay safe, and also the management of emotional strains connected to difficult life events.

A less personally orientated meaning attached to vulnerability was that it related in some way to life opportunities and social support systems. For example, especially notable in the narratives of young people who had moved to the UK from abroad or who were from black and minority ethnic families was that vulnerability related to lack of success at school. 'Jeremy Clarkson' (M, 15), who lived in a homeless hostel and was of British Bangladeshi heritage, explained vulnerability as follows:

> You find that some like in my class that are smart or something, I don't think they could have huge problems 'cos like they're getting their grades, they're getting good education so they can get into uni. But obviously if someone else that, that are taking drugs and stuff and is not concentrating then they have big problems more with them, that get in the way to go to college or they might not get a place in college.

The idea that society shaped young people's vulnerability appeared in 18 of the 25 young people's interviews, with the implication being that it was contingent on systems that were in place to help young people deal with challenges and setbacks. Again, this represented certain similarities with professional views of vulnerability. Jay Jay (M, 17) stayed for most of the week with an older couple he helped to look after. He did not have very much contact with his parents (see the Appendix) and saw his vulnerability as shaped by the support networks around him:

> Kate: ... if workers did say that you were vulnerable, would you agree with them?
>
> Jay Jay: I would agree and I wouldn't agree. I would because I've ... I ain't got a lot of family behind, I have got a lot of family behind me, yeah, but I never hardly talk to my really close family. And I aren't vulnerable because like the people who do look after me, they're the ones what'll stick by me and don't let owt happen to me.

There were frequent indications that interviewees saw vulnerability as something that varied over time, sometimes as support systems altered. Some young people indicated that they saw vulnerability as contingent on past situations. John (M, 16) felt that vulnerability related to decision making, but *"your past also changes that decision"*. For Keith, life experience was central to his understandings of the concept:

> It depends on your history of your life and stuff like that. So you could have had the best life that you've ever had, but something bad could have happened one day and your vulnerability is changed and stuff like that. So it's all the history of your life. (Keith, M, 16)

This more 'socially constituted' view of vulnerability resonated to some extent with academic ideas about the concept being able to bring into focus the political, economic and social processes that mediate opportunities and disadvantage in society (see Chapter Two; also Wishart, 2003; Butler, 2004; Fineman, 2008). That vulnerability could be imagined as mitigated by relationships and external factors seemed important in terms of how supposedly vulnerable young people might receive interventions, a matter that is explored in Chapter Seven.

Blame and rational actor understandings of behaviour

As has been widely chronicled, powerful narratives that condemn the lifestyles and behaviours of less well-off groups (see Jones, 2011; Tyler, 2013) and which frame lower social and economic positioning as personally and individually constituted (Dorling, 2010; Shildrick and MacDonald, 2013) now characterise much contemporary discussion of poverty and disadvantage. Such discursive practices can be understood as the latest echoes of long-running debates and contested demarcations of 'deserving' and 'undeserving' people in society. While vulnerability discourses often seem to be deployed by those interested in more structural approaches to disadvantage, attention to the perspectives of those classified as vulnerable in the present study highlighted that vulnerability did not occupy a position outside 'blaming' narratives, and that the notion was similarly pervaded by ideas about deservingness. Discussions of vulnerability with people classified as vulnerable seemed firmly aligned towards what Batty and Flint (2013: 2) have called 'regimes of judgement', or moral assessments of the social spaces in which marginalised individuals might orientate themselves. In Scott's (M, 18) case, he referenced his vulnerability as a context for his offending history:

> I started going to that kind of big life of crime when, basically, I left my Mum and I was in care because I was vulnerable and that. I didn't really want to be in there, so I was running all the time. And every time I ran away, I was getting into trouble.

As with practitioners, the young people's various conceptualisations of vulnerability were almost always framed within understandings about young people's 'culpability' and agency.

When asked their views on whether people in particular situations were vulnerable, interviewees tended to assess how far 'choice' had been exercised. After watching a short video vignette of a young offender telling his life story, Alicia (F, 16) said:

> *No I wouldn't say he's vulnerable. He chose to sell weed [cannabis], didn't he? So he made that decision himself, it's not someone else saying it to him why don't you sell weed or trying to like persuade him to do something like that, he's made that decision on his own to do that.*

In discussions about vulnerability and transgression, the young people were apparently largely in agreement with what might be understood as 'rational-actor' configurations of offending behaviour prominent in official and public understandings of young people's transgressions (Smith, 2003; Goldson and Muncie, 2006; Hopkins Burke, 2008). As Brook (F, 16) explained:

> *… he chose that life. So if he chose it, like he said there, he had fun doing it, so no, I've got no sympathy for him. The other lass [teenage mother] I had, but not him. She didn't choose that life. She had to do that. She got forced, if you like. He didn't get forced to do that. He was in school. He had an education. He spoke English. He's English. So, you know, he made life bad for himself.*

Although most interviewees saw vulnerability as contingent on a person not having 'chosen' the problem circumstances they had found themselves in, perceived intersections between vulnerability, choice and deservingness were not always clear cut.

There seemed to be a point at which the seriousness of circumstance meant that despite the part an individual had played in the situation developing, they should be seen as vulnerable and (by implication) deserving. The video vignette of the young offender's life story often elicited such understandings:

> *He had good parents, he didn't come from a background, a really bad background, he decided to go in, to get involved with those type of people, it was his choice, no one made him do that. He could've said no and walked away from them and not get involved in that sort of thing. Whereas I think now, I think he really does need someone to help him and just give him a little bit of encouragement and support.* (Jade A, F, 17)

There are some resonances here with Goodin's (1985: 129) argument that the concept of vulnerability can open up empathetic responses to our understandings of human difficulty, possibly extending into how those who have faced difficulties might understand the situations of others in similar circumstances.

While the idea of choosing particular behaviours was central in most discussions of vulnerability, narratives of 'free choice' competed and overlapped with the idea that disadvantages structured individual actions. Scott (M, 18) seemed to see himself as vulnerable and also exercising considerable agency at the same time:

> Kate: *So you saw yourself as vulnerable when you were in care because some of your behaviour was bad?*
>
> Scott: *Yeah. I chose that though. I chose to do that. I did it for the money. I didn't do it because I wanted to be liked. I didn't give a fuck what anyone thought about me. I did it because I wanted money. I wanted to get my money.*

Despite some fairly pronounced verdicts about blame and transgression, discussions of vulnerability often exposed tensions in how the young people made sense of culpability and victimhood. When they were asked to make judgements about the vulnerability of young people who had transgressed behavioural norms, interviewees frequently commented that they found this 'hard'. When Charlie (F, 16), a young person who had offended in the past, was asked about whether 'young offenders' were vulnerable she answered: *"I don't think they're vulnerable. They're just stupid. Well, they might be a bit vulnerable. I don't know."* This could perhaps be indicative of a certain level of ambivalence by the young people towards their own transgressions.

Even where transgressions were judged harshly, within the same interview there were often comments that indicated an understanding that young people's vulnerability could be 'structural', or due to patterns of disadvantage and lack of opportunity. Although Scott (M, 18) indicated that he had 'decided' to commit crimes, he did not appear to extend the 'rational–actor' model to all young people: *"It's the kids out there that are born on council estates, born into a gang and have to choose whether to live or die, they're the people that you've got to feel sorry for, people that have got no choice."*

Generally speaking, despite some consistent themes in the young people's understandings of vulnerability, interviewees tended to interpret the concept in multiple and various ways. Meanings that the interviewees ascribed to vulnerability often seemed shaped by their own life experiences, reinforcing that the notion is highly subjective and often tied to a variety of different normative assumptions and individual perceptions of the social world.

Vulnerable? Not me, not now

One of the most striking themes in the interviewees' discussions of vulnerability was their rejection of their status as 'vulnerable'. To a certain extent this may be unsurprising, as similar reactions have been noted previously with vulnerable adults (see Beard et al, 2009; Wiles, 2011) and in relation to notions such as poverty (Lister, 2004; Batty and Flint, 2013) and social exclusion (Dean with Melrose, 1999). However, that shame and stigma might extend into vulnerability discourses seems intriguing given that the notion is often employed as a way of referring to social difficulties in a less stigmatising way. For Hayley (F, 16), vulnerability implied judgements about behaviour, which seemed unfair to her:

> Kate: *If a worker – that you had – said that they felt that you were vulnerable –*
>
> Hayley: *I wouldn't like it.*
>
> Kate: *And why's that?*
>
> Hayley: *It means, like … you're not vulnerable, you're just different. To me, vulnerable means, like, that's personal. To me, it's like, I've put myself there, where other people have done it to me. So it's like fair enough I am vulnerable, but it's not my fault.*

Discussions revealed that being labelled as vulnerable could incite feelings of anger and resentment, as evident in Alicia's (F, 16) narrative:

> Alicia: *I think they just give loads of kids that name in care, 'vulnerable'.*
>
> Kate: *Go on…*
>
> Alicia: *I don't know I just think they do give it loads of kids … like, say they're vulnerable, even if they aren't.*

Across some of the literature on vulnerability, concerns have been raised about the potential for the concept to function as a problematic label that encourages assumptions about particular groups as being weak and passive (Wishart, 2003; Lein, 2009; Hollomotz, 2009; Parley, 2011). Certainly among the young people interviewed there was some evidence of resistance to notions of vulnerability on this basis, as in Brook's (F, 16) case:

> Kate: *Some workers might call you vulnerable. What do you think about that? Do you agree with them?*
>
> Brook: *No. I don't, no.*
>
> Kate: *Why not?*
>
> Brook: *'Cos no one wants to think of themselves as vulnerable, do they? I think I'm perfectly fine.*
>
> Kate: *What makes you say nobody wants to think of themselves as vulnerable?*
>
> Brook: *Because the word 'vulnerable', it sounds like you're a self-harmer or summat, doesn't it? … 'Vulnerable'.*

Rather than the 'otherness' or abnormality that vulnerability seemed to imply to interviewees, the young people instead saw their social worlds as mundane and everyday. Discussions of vulnerability therefore highlighted 'doxic' (see Bourdieu, 1977) or 'taken-for-granted' understandings of the considerable difficulties that had been relayed in accounts of life stories, with the label-quality of the term 'vulnerability' seeming somehow to undermine the young people's sense of their lives as ordinary or unexceptional.

Many of the young people saw vulnerability as something that applied to other people, but not to themselves. As Shildrick and MacDonald (2013: 293) found in their study of those seen as living in poverty, 'close points of comparison' seemed to be evident and interviewees often considered vulnerability to be something that applied to those who were considerably worse off than themselves. Charlie (F, 16) felt that her being in care was an *"awkward situation"* whereas being vulnerable *"is like someone living on the street and getting into crack [cocaine] and stuff"*. The young people frequently expressed a view that although they might have had struggles in their own lives, other people's situations were worse: *"... all mine is like basically having to clean up and that I never got like ... never got hit or owt like that, never got abused or anything like that so I'd be least at risk"* (Stephanie, F, 16).

As cited in the opening paragraph of Chapter One, Chris (M, 17) had been taken against his will to Pakistan, where for six years he was regularly beaten by his uncle. He had also fled from his abusive father in the UK, been homeless for a period and had recently secured his own tenancy. He explained (as cited at the opening of the book): *"People have even more difficulties than me. This might not be such a big thing. I've seen other people have more difficulties even worser than these. Yeah it's difficult, but not difficult difficult, I'd say"* (Chris, M, 17). That a young person can be considered vulnerable by official agencies and not see themselves in this way might well indicate that vulnerability is a concept that is to a considerable extent culturally specific and relational.

In the following passage, Alicia (F, 16) describes herself as *"a little bit"* vulnerable when she was involved in heroin use and prostitution at the age of 14, which was in marked contrast to her keyworker's view of her vulnerability as *"off the scale"*. When I asked if she thought she was vulnerable, she said:

> *I don't know. A little bit with heroin, like he [boyfriend] were the only one that ever injected me and I wanted to make him happy by letting him do that. And I wanted to make him happy by getting money to get heroin and things like that. So that's probably where I wor' a bit, but ... I think the only reason I was vulnerable is 'cos I were like upset at that time and I wont [wasn't] in the right place in my head.*

Insights about the strengths and limitations of using relational concepts in social research and policy can be found in the literature on 'social exclusion' (see Room, 1995, Levitas, 1998; Young, 1999; MacGregor, 2003), a popular notion in the New Labour period partly as it was considered less stigmatising than 'poverty'. Vulnerability discourses would seem in some respects to be the latest incarnation of attempts to engage sensitively with the situations of marginalised people, perhaps inclined again to fall short of capturing the complexity and nuance of the circumstances and identities that it is deployed to describe.

The implications of being 'vulnerable': care and control

Some of the young people who were interviewed recounted direct experiences of instances of vulnerability classifications. Many had opinions on what judgements about their vulnerability meant for them and how these might affect their daily lives. Although Chris (M, 17) said that he had felt vulnerable while he lived in a homeless hostel for adult males, being classified as vulnerable was experienced as posing more risk than it offered protection: *"It doesn't feel good if you say 'vulnerable'. 'Cos what if someone listens, they* [workers] *say 'you're vulnerable', they* [other people] *can do anything – they get advantage."*

As highlighted in earlier chapters, it appeared that for receivers of services, vulnerability classifications could be experienced as a gateway to extra support or assistance, as an entry point for social control, or in some cases as a mixture of such processes. Jade A (F, 17), who had learning difficulties, felt that she was not vulnerable because of support from her friends and family, but she recognised that being seen in this way was an opportunity in some respects:

> Kate: *How do you think you'd react if somebody said you did [need special support]?*

> Jade A: *I don't know, I think I would, it would surprise me really. But I would, if it were there for me I would take it.*

> Kate: *Would you?*

> Jade A: *I would take it because then I know that I've got someone there that can help me. If it wasn't there in place, then you know, then I would just get on with my life.*

Keith (M, 16) relayed direct experiences of the way the Youth Offending Service (YOS) used 'vulnerability' in the assessment of young offenders and in determining interventions for this group (see Chapter Three; and also Youth Justice Board, 2006, Appendix 12: 7):

> Keith: *I was vulnerable before I went into [secure unit].*

> Kate: *Were you?*

> Keith: *Yeah. They put me down as 'vulnerable' for some reason. […] It were my YOS worker that told them to do it. I think my YOS worker didn't want me going into [youth offending institution] or anywhere like that. So she said that I were vulnerable in certain ways. In how I were, do you know, just certain ways in my life as being, stuff like that.*

Kate: *Can you remember what sorts of things?*

Keith: *My Dad beating me up, that's what made me vulnerable, my YOS worker said.*

Secure units tend to be viewed by practitioners in the youth justice system as offering a more supportive environment for young people than youth offending institutions (see Goldson, 2002c). That vulnerability classifications could be experienced as beneficial in how they provoked differential treatment is consistent with other work highlighting the potentially positive aspects of labels (see Gallagher, 1976; Quicke and Winter, 1994; Riddick, 2000). Keith (M, 16) certainly saw some benefits of being classified in this way: *"… you did have that little bit more support than other people did have. But it wasn't as much, but that little bit more support were better than no support I thought. So alt' support I got while I were in [the secure unit], I took it all in."* Accounts such as Keith's indicated that practitioner discretion in classifications of vulnerability could operate to mediate or 'soften' disciplinary responses to transgressive young people, echoing insights from professionals (see Chapter Four).

At the same time, however, there was also a perception that being seen as vulnerable could entail stronger controls on behaviour. Naz (F, 14) was to some degree receptive to the idea of herself as vulnerable in situations where she was spending time with older men, often in their houses during periods where she had run away. She said that these men *"might think that it's alright to do stuff"*. However, she felt that it was important to conceal her vulnerability as far as possible from controlling influences, in order that she could keep taking risks she enjoyed:

Kate: *… if people were to describe you as vulnerable, how would it make you feel?*

Naz: *I'd say to 'em 'I'm not vulnerable and I'm all right and I'm safe, and I'm gonna go out' and stuff.*

Kate: *OK. Why?*

Naz: *I don't know, 'cos like, my Mum will carry on with me and stuff, like, say stuff to me and that.*

Similarly, John (M, 16) indicated that certain behavioural restrictions could be associated with being seen as 'vulnerable':

Kate: *Did anyone ever say you were vulnerable?*

John: *Yeah, all the time.*

Kate: *Can you give me an example?*

John: *'We think you're taking too many drugs.' I don't know really, they just gave me a great big lecture on how I'm ruining my life … I've got so many good chances going for me and all I can do is take drugs, and not look at life and just drop out of college and put myself in vulnerable situations.*

That vulnerability appeared to be connected in some ways to normative judgements about behaviour was a recurring theme: *"I think I'm doing well for myself, and if [social worker] just said that I was vulnerable, then it'd make me feel like I'm doing loads of things I shouldn't be"* (Charlie, F, 16). For some of the young people, caring and controlling implications seemed to be seen as interrelated. Alicia (F, 16), who described attending a school for *"vulnerable girls"* when she was selling sex, seemed to sum up the dualism involved:

Kate: *What do you think [saying they are vulnerable] means for young people, do you know?*

Alicia: *They really are protecting them a lot more, or something like that, and they are – they don't get to do as much things.*

Whether it was experienced and perceived as a mechanism for care, control or both of these things simultaneously, there was a sense from the young people that the label of 'vulnerability' had practical effects on their lives.

Ambiguities in resistance: vulnerability as a site of tensions

Resistance to vulnerability classifications often seemed to illuminate a clash between more official views of young people's lives and interviewees' own sense of their circumstances. Vulnerability's connection with judgements about behaviour meant that there could be a defiant tone when the young people distanced themselves from professional views, as in Charlie's (F, 16) interview:

Kate: *What about if workers said that you were vulnerable?*

Charlie: *I'd tell them to shut up.*

Kate: *Why?*

Charlie: *'Cos I'm not vulnerable. They just chat a load of shit.*

Alongside what could be quite fierce rejections of the label of vulnerability, the young people sometimes indicated that a personal tension lay behind this. Although Jess (F, 15) said that she would respond to being called vulnerable by saying *"I'm not vulnerable"* and *"walking off"*, she also indicated that something more reflexive would accompany this reaction: *"I'd be questioning myself. And then I'd start crying 'cos I couldn't decide between the two sides. One side of me'd be like 'am I?' and the other side'd be like … I'd be questioning myself, but then I'd be reassuring myself."* Discussions such as this seemed to indicate that self-assessments of behaviour and vulnerability were fluid and subject to revision and reassessment, and also potentially influenced through relations with others.

Indeed, there was an impression given by some interviewees that they saw their vulnerability as dependent on the context in which they were asked to reflect on it. It was not unusual for the young people to position themselves as vulnerable *to some extent* at one point in the interview and then later to distance themselves from the classification. For example, Hayley (F, 16) said that the nature of the relationship she had with the person calling her 'vulnerable' was important:

> *If it was a worker and, obviously, I knew her, like say – my CAMHS [child and adolescent mental health service] worker I wouldn't like it. At this age where I am now and I've learnt that I have got a voice, I'd probably kick off. Whereas with my [counselling] worker at [college], we had that better relationship, I'd probably go, 'Please don't call me that', and she'd find a different word.*

There are many variables that would seem to influence how a particular label is received by an individual (see Hargreaves, 1976) and Quicke and Winter's (1994) argument that the way a label is received is to a large extent context dependent is perhaps relevant here.

Power struggles seem pertinent in such dynamics. John (M, 16), who had been sectioned for his own safety due to heavy drug use, said that people had told him he was vulnerable *"all the time"*, which for him was problematic: *"I've got to figure it out for me sen [myself], otherwise I'm not going to do it. I'm not going to do it for anyone but myself ... I wouldn't see myself as vulnerable but if I took the time to look at it, I suppose I was."* John seemed to accept his vulnerability with hindsight, but that it was not something he would have been receptive to at a time of tensions with others about his behaviour. Such struggles would seem significant in terms of how vulnerability classifications might play out. Bottrell (2007: 598) argues that while 'deficit positioning' of young people is popularly pursued by official agencies and can provide opportunities for young people to access support, this may promote opposition among young people who, she argues, pursue resistance as 'necessary identity work, given the context of their marginalisation' (2007: 597). Vulnerability-based constructions of young people's identity would seem likely to be rejected by those who are more inclined to use resistance as a way of managing in difficult circumstances, which has ramifications in terms of which young people are most likely to 'perform' vulnerability according to practitioner and policy preferences (see Chapter Four).

As in John's narrative, interviewees were much more receptive to the idea that they had been vulnerable at certain times in the past – or would be at points in the future – than that they might be vulnerable in the present. Chris (M, 17) felt that he was vulnerable when he was being physically abused by his family in Pakistan and in the UK: *"I had no idea. I couldn't do anything, couldn't see anything. I just do what they say. I don't know a thing. Then I had no idea what life was like, no idea what to do."* However, his view of his situation at the time of the interview, as a young man of 17 who had recently moved into his own accommodation, was that *"I am absolutely not vulnerable at all"*. Hayley (F, 16) was about to leave full-time education, and felt that she might be vulnerable in the future: *"So I'd have no one from here [support project] and have no Mum and no Dad and be on my own. I think I would be vulnerable then, especially with the past I've had as well."* A sense of future precariousness is something that Emmel and Hughes (2010) argue characterises experiences of being vulnerable, and there were certainly echoes of this in some of the young people's narratives, which is explored further in the following chapter.

Receptiveness to vulnerability classifications

Alongside resistance to the idea that they were 'vulnerable', most of the young people also indicated that they saw themselves as vulnerable to a certain (qualified) extent. Only one young person responded positively to the idea without ambivalence or resistance – Mercedez (F, 15):

> Kate: ... *if they said about you now, that you were vulnerable, would you...*

> Mercedez: *What, would I agree? Yeah, because I don't know what's coming up next. I don't know if my Mum and Dad are going to start drinking when this new thing's [parenting programme is] starting, which I can imagine happening, or I don't know – I don't know what's coming. I don't know if they're going to go down the right path and just recover, unlikely, or they're just going to go from drinking to drinking more and more. I don't know it 'cos that's down to them, not us.*

That Mercedez was overwhelmingly receptive to her vulnerability classification was intriguing. She was one of a small number of young people who had actively sought out support from agencies to deal with the problems she faced at home (rather than being persuaded or compelled to seek help). She also saw her vulnerability as predominantly shaped by her parents' drug use; something outside of her control and which she judged harshly. This may have been a factor in how she framed and made sense of her difficulties.

Vulnerability labels were not ubiquitously seen as harmful or damaging. In some cases, official vulnerability classifications provided validation of young people's difficult experiences, perhaps particularly in circumstances where they might feel judged for transgressions. The way in which Keith (M, 16) discussed how his YOS worker applied a vulnerability classification to him appeared to indicate that this had altered his view of himself:

> Kate: ... *when your worker said to you that you were vulnerable because of what happened with your Dad, what did you feel about that?*

> Keith: *I was shocked because I didn't know. I didn't see myself as vulnerable.*

This again underlines the potentially beneficial implications of labelling that have been noted by some disability writers, indicating how differential treatment can be positive (Gallagher, 1976; Quicke and Winter, 1994; Riddick, 2000), and to some extent the young people's narratives indicated that vulnerability might have such effects in relation to mitigating harsher judgements about their behaviour.

Two other young people (Wadren, M, 17 and '2Pac', M, 14) could be described as *fairly* receptive to notions of themselves as vulnerable, although they still qualified this in some limited way. Wadren said *"in a way I'd agree with them"* as he suffered from depression, and '2Pac' saw his vulnerability as related to being bullied. Both of these interviewees were notable for how keenly they stressed access to relatively high levels of disposable income and both said that they did not live in social housing, opening up the possibility that more 'middle-class' identities and orientations could perhaps be more inclined to draw on or accept the deployment of vulnerability classifications. McLaughlin (2012) has argued that the ascendance of vulnerability as a concept in social policy has led to a rise in 'vulnerable identities' being taken on within contemporary society. However, there would seem to be differentiated patterns in terms of how far this might be the case. Evidence from the present study about young people's responses to their supposed vulnerability would lead to questions about how far 'vulnerable identities' have been accepted uniformly, and how different social groups might respond to vulnerability classifications.

One of the most intriguing aspects of how the young people conceptualised their identities was their receptiveness to the idea that they had had 'difficult lives', in contrast to their resistance to 'vulnerability' classifications. Although Jay Jay (M, 17) did not feel that he was vulnerable because he had people who supported him, when the question was phrased slightly differently, there was a different response:

Kate: *Do you think that you're someone who's had a difficult life?*

Jay Jay: *Yeah, very difficult life. Now I'm trying to sort myself here, coming here and getting some qualifications.*

Brook (F, 16), who was highly resistant to notions of vulnerability (see above), was candid about how she saw her upbringing:

... *in a way, like, I have been dragged up and I haven't had time to slowly see things and have a normal life. I've got a normal life but, yeah, I think I got dragged up really and that's why it's so clear now 'cos bad things like violence and domestic violence and that happened at a young age.*

Again, understandings of difficulties were often constructed in relation to other people's lives and experiences. Kotaa (F, 12) felt she had had *"a little bit"* of a difficult life, as *"some people have Mums and Dads and some people's Mums and Dads don't argue and some people like don't have to move house and stuff like that when they're still young and when they start new schools more people go from that school with them".*

The way in which the young people responded positively to the idea of themselves as having experienced difficulties, and yet largely negatively to vulnerability classifications, may well suggest that the deficit-orientated connotations of vulnerability may be especially problematic when the notion is operationalised. John (M, 16) argued that the concept of vulnerability was unhelpful in this respect:

> *... don't tell them [young people] that they're vulnerable. Find out why you think they're vulnerable first instead of just telling them they're vulnerable, 'cos they're gonna put up a block and go like, 'well no I'm not'.... So don't just have a shot in the dark, with the word 'you're vulnerable'. You should try and figure it out first.*

Although vulnerability discourses largely represent attempts by policy makers and practitioners to take an empathetic approach to supposedly 'vulnerable' people's lives, the deficit-orientated nature of the notion seems to pose inescapable limitations in terms of how such constructions might resonate with the receivers of services.

Optimism, resistance and 'vulnerable identities'

The young people in the study certainly felt that their lives had not been free from difficulties or problems, but they often had a positive view of how they had dealt with setbacks. Indeed, ideas about resourcefulness and strength were often key features of 'lived experiences' of vulnerability, just as has been noted in relation to poverty (see Batty and Flint, 2013; Shildrick and MacDonald, 2013). Experiences that many professionals would consider as harmful and damaging were consistently framed as having equipped interviewees with valuable life skills: *"I'd seen it all. So now, by the time I've got to this stage, I know what's right and I know what's wrong"* (Brook, F, 16).

Relative maturity quite often featured as a beneficial effect of what might otherwise be considered adverse life experiences:

> *... growing up and getting my house, I think that changed me a lot. Getting my own house, I grew up quite a lot when I got me own house. Like other people my age, like I look at like lads in my college, my age, and they're proper immature. And I think*

like being in care I think it makes you more mature as well and how to deal with things better. (Alicia, F, 16)

Ability to cope with difficulties was highly valued by the young people, and drawing on the concept of vulnerability seemed to some extent to undermine or invalidate their perceptions of their ability to do this. Mackenzie's (M, 16) response to his supposed vulnerability was one example:

Kate: *If somebody said, 'oh I think that your diabetes and the time out of school makes you a bit vulnerable', what would you say to them?*

Mackenzie: *Probably maybe like the amount of time I had off of school 'cos obviously like doing my exams and that is harder for me like revising and stuff harder 'cos some of the stuff I don't know but that's – that were my own fault so I don't want people to like feel sorry for me or owt 'cos I can still cope with it.*

Again, the importance of optimism as a technique of mitigating difficulties was underlined (see also Chapter Five; Benard, 1991; Garmezy, 1991).

Even though some of the young people who were interviewed had experienced what might be judged to be extreme hardship and injustices, discussions of life's setbacks and challenges tended to have a distinctly optimistic tone. Hayley (F, 16) was homeless and was about to leave school. Her life circumstances seemed particularly concerning and precarious and her support workers shared this view. Although she was frank about the problems in her life and saw herself as potentially vulnerable in the future, an upbeat tone underpinned her account:

I see things as, like, positives and negatives now. That sort of calms … I don't look at the negatives, just think of the positive and it helps you pull through. Obviously, I'm getting a house soon; I'm on the waiting list, so I'm just looking forward to that. I've got college waiting for me in September, I've got – even though it's not ideal the way I see my Mum and my Dad separately and got to go over to my Mum's or to my Dad's and arrange everything first, but the relationships there are a lot better now.

The young people's narratives of vulnerability highlighted that apparently vulnerable receivers of services do not necessarily see their lives as problematic in the same way that policy makers and practitioners do. While listening to and accommodating voices of marginalised subjects who reject 'vulnerable identities' would seem to somehow risk accepting their possibly internalised regimes of responsibilisation and individualised accounts of marginality (see Frost and Hoggett, 2008), the fact remains that vulnerability narratives seem to flatten out and over-simplify the identities and lived realties of social and economic problems. In particular, the rise of vulnerability rationales potentially underestimates sources of positive self-esteem and assets that supposedly 'vulnerable' populations might have access to.

Chapter summary

How the young people in the study conceptualised 'vulnerability' offered insights into the social worlds they inhabited, characterised by unequal power relations and access to precarious support systems, which needed careful attention and management. The young people classified as vulnerable understood the notion as largely related to individual deficit or personal inadequacies, with interviewees interpreting the notion in a number of ways, such as a lack of self-determination or a weakness to third-party influences. There were also indications of gendered interpretations of vulnerability, with the concept being seen as related to the sexuality of young women and deficiencies in what might be called 'hyper-masculinity' in the case of young men. This again raises interesting questions about how far the notion might relate and map on to matters of difference (see also Chapters Three and Four). Views of vulnerability were firmly anchored in prominent and long-running narratives about deserving and undeserving citizens. Ideas about culpability, blame and 'rational-actor' models of transgression permeated the young people's understandings of the notion, but discussion of vulnerability usually revealed some ambiguity and complexity in how far being vulnerable related to the power to 'choose' certain behaviours or circumstances. Most of the young people indicated that they saw vulnerability as socially constituted to some extent, and understood it as something that was shaped by support systems and relationships.

Classifications of vulnerability seemed incongruent with the young people's own perceptions of their ability to cope with life's difficulties and setbacks, making them dissonant with identities centred on resourcefulness and fortitude. Attention to how far the young people positioned themselves within a frame of vulnerability revealed the concept to be socially and culturally constructed, and associated with the particular social space that a person inhabits. The notion had relative and also moral dimensions, which would seem important in how vulnerability classifications might play out in everyday care and control practices and interventions. Being categorised as 'vulnerable' was viewed by the young people as a gateway to extra assistance and also as an entry point for the regulation of their behaviour, highlighting the complex ways in which vulnerability serves tightly enmeshed care and social control practices. Resistances to vulnerability narratives were to some extent bound up with struggles about the regulation of behaviour and disagreements about what constituted acceptable circumstances and events. It would seem that vulnerability-based constructions of young people's identity may more likely be rejected by those who are inclined to use resistance as a way of managing in difficult circumstances, again pointing to the fact that discourses of vulnerability may benefit those with more compliant behaviours when the concept is operationalised.

Although they could be receptive to being classified as vulnerable within certain social and relational contexts, generally speaking, the young people's narratives were characterised by a resistance to the idea that they were vulnerable. This indicated that the vulnerability zeitgeist is much more of a 'top-down' rather than 'grass roots' phenomenon. Resistance to vulnerability and vulnerable identities is perhaps unsurprising given how far dependency has been positioned as the antithesis of 'normal' and 'acceptable' citizenship (see Campbell, 1991; Harrison, 2008) and as personal inadequacy rather than an inevitable consequence of human embodiment (see Butler, 2004). While often being deployed as a discursive strategy aimed at avoiding labelling and stigmatisation, it is evident that shame and stigma, which have been associated with notions such as 'poverty', seem to be similarly pervasive in relation to vulnerability discourses. Vulnerability would seem to share a seat at the table along with various discursive practices that sharpen divisions in how more affluent citizens think and talk about those who are less privileged. In other words, seen from the perspectives of those who are seen as vulnerable, vulnerability may well contribute to 'othering' rather than 'including' (see Lister, 2004). Before further consideration is given to the potentially excluding ramifications of vulnerability, one further chapter explores how it may be mediated by support systems, relationships and interventions.

SEVEN

The social mediation of vulnerability

Introduction

This chapter explores vulnerable young people's perspectives of broader structural factors that had an effect on their lived experiences of vulnerability. The chapter speaks partly to developmental issues, which were central to the young people's understandings of how vulnerability was mediated. Social psychologists and childhood scholars have given extensive attention the ways in which children and young people's relationships with carers and dynamics within their families affect their later lives (Bowlby, 1969; Rutter, 1990; Bynner, 2001), and young people's views on how these factors link with vulnerability are explored. It also gazes beyond family environments, giving consideration to welfare and disciplinary strategies that affected the young people's 'vulnerability'. Social hierarches are brought into view, as these pervaded the young people's stories and accounts, albeit implicitly rather than being expressly articulated. A central concern is to explore young people's perspectives as a way of generating insights into how policy and practice interventions might more effectively alleviate difficulty, foster wellbeing and develop engagement with groups who might sometimes be considered 'difficult to reach' or 'vulnerable'.

Previous chapters have highlighted how close relationships between vulnerability and transgression influence the ways that interventions take shape, and particular attention is given here to the young people's experiences of processes where they were being 'supported' and/or were being 'controlled' or disciplined. In consideration of care and control processes it should be noted that 'caring' and 'controlling' mechanisms are not taken to be mutually exclusive features of social policy interventions but rather are seen as inextricably woven together in the delivery and ethos of services (Squires, 1990; Phoenix, 2008; Flint, 2009; Wacquant, 2009), perhaps especially where 'vulnerable' people under the age of 18 are concerned. In giving attention to the close relationships between care and social control in welfare and disciplinary systems, insights are generated about how supposedly vulnerable people received and perceived some of the tensions that result from long-running tendencies to frame young citizens in terms of their status as 'deserving' or 'undeserving' (Goldson, 2002a, 2004).

In the next section, developmental factors that the young people felt influenced their vulnerability are explored, such as family, friends and transitions within home environments. Then, an overview is provided of the welfare and disciplinary services that the young people discussed in their interviews, highlighting the range and types of interventions that they had received. The young people's views on what aspects of interventions they considered as having been helpful (or unhelpful) in reducing their vulnerability are considered. Within this more general view, the young people's experiences of the 'care/control' process (see Goldson, 2004) are highlighted. Finally, the chapter explores the young people's understandings of broader social structures and hierarchies that they perceived as having influenced their vulnerability, with particular attention given to matters such as financial resources, gender and age-related power dynamics.

That children and young people are less inclined to articulate or acknowledge the role of structural forces in their experiences has been noted by researchers (MacDonald et al, 2005; Heath et al, 2009) and as with other 'marginalised groups', children and young people's interview narratives can often be underpinned by a 'discourse of individualisation' (see McNaughton, 2006). Given that this was likely to be a factor in interviews with 'vulnerable' young people, interview tasks such as video vignettes and life-mapping activities were designed with a particular eye on drawing out more structural matters for discussion, as well as leaving space for consideration of biographies and family relationships. While the interventions and social processes that are considered in the chapter are likely to represent something of a partial view of state and family involvement in vulnerable young people's lives, the focus on interviewees' own views offers a rather different and rarer account of how social systems and processes shape the lives of supposedly vulnerable people. The chapter therefore engages the with young people's experiences as 'vulnerable' receivers of services and as potentially marginalised young citizens, exploring further the ways in which vulnerability might be socially, economically and politically constituted.

Childhood development and vulnerability

When asked about what factors shaped their lives most, the young people most often focused on biographical events and family experiences. The most common matter cited as having had the greatest influence on their vulnerability was their relationship with their parents, and of particular relevance were disruptions such as parental domestic violence, separation and shifts in living arrangements that often followed new parental relationships or separations. Such 'adversities' or 'maltreatments' have been given extensive attention in the psychosocial child development literature (Bowlby, 1969; Rutter, 1990; Luthar, 2006; Cleaver et al, 2007, 2011). Keith (M, 16) felt that witnessing violence and acrimony in his parents' relationship had enduring effects on his own life: *"… it's awful when you see your Mum and Dad arguing over I don't know what. It's awful though when you see it. So I think that's where it started all from round about there [on life map]. It's all gone downhill not uphill like it's meant to."* Also, there were instances where the young people set out the importance of relationships with family members as 'protective' influences in their lives. Brook (F, 16), who lived in a homeless hostel, felt that her mother was the most important 'helpful' factor in her life:

> *It's just how mums do. I don't know how they do it. They just do it, don't they? […] Making me laugh, treating me, you know, telling me not to ruin my life. But basically telling me not to be like me brother and be a shithouse really and not get owt out of life in grades….*

Where parents were considered by the young people to have helped them in life, in all but one case (Laura, F, 16) it was mothers who were referred to rather than fathers.[1]

In some cases, the young people indicated links between family behaviours and attitudes and access to social welfare resources on offer. Jade A (F, 17), who had learning difficulties, felt that her mother's determination and hard work had been very important for being able to access the support that she needed:

> *She used to ring up, the phone bill used to be really surprising, she used to ring people up saying, 'oh no you have to report to this one, that one, other places' and it just got to be where eventually we got to have a meeting with these people, they come to your house and then they helped.*

In the two cases where the young people had severe health problems or disabilities, mothers seemed to have provided an important gateway to wider systems of support, raising questions about how those with less proactive parents might fare in terms of access to support.

The importance of grandparents was especially pronounced in some of the young people's discussions about practical and emotional support. This is consistent with other research that has recognised the significance of grandparents in children's lives (Dench et al, 2000; Rutter and Evans, 2011) and the crucial role in 'firefighting' (or coping with difficulties or crises) that grandparents often play in low-income families (Emmel et al, 2011; Hughes and Emmel, 2011). Since moving to the UK from Lithuania, Anna (F, 12) missed her grandmother very much:

> ... she's the best, she can do anything ... I was with her about three months and I don't need a dad or mum, she can be that. And she's like, I can tell any secret, and like, about my Mum, what I don't like about her, and I tell her [grandmother] and she don't tell anybody. [...] if you've got headache and in my country it's like [she gets] a load of flowers, put it in tea, and she makes me drink that!

The idea of grandparents being 'like parents' was mentioned repeatedly, echoing Hughes and Emmel's (2011) findings that the type of support that grandparents offered could be characterised as 'rescue' and 'repair': *"... my Nana's been like my second mother. So obviously, obviously I love my Mum like you're meant to, but I love my Nana more in a way, because my Nana's been there for me"* (Mercedez, F, 15). Three of the young people had spent extensive periods living with their grandparents full time, and several others had lived with grandparents for shorter periods or during family crises.

Although parents and grandparents were the primary focus of much of the discussion about the mediation of vulnerability, there were various other more developmental factors that seemed relevant. For three young people, boyfriends/girlfriends had been an important source of mutual emotional support and understanding, and friends were also discussed by some interviewees in terms of them being important sources of emotional and practical support. Charlie (F, 16), who was in care, discussed how a friend who was also in the care system was one of the most important sources of support in her life: *"She used to come to my house and, like, get me and tell me to sort my head out [...] 'Cos she is in care, she gets everything as well, doesn't she? She understands."* Whereas for young women their friendships were more important in terms of emotional support, for young men, peers and friends were often discussed as being important for their physical protection (or lack of).

The young people's life stories were characterised by what could be viewed as considerable transitions of various kinds (see Chapter Five) – in family life, in living arrangements and in their 'journey' through welfare services. In discussions of 'what had helped' and 'what had not helped' them in life, transitions were a common theme: *"I ain't had a stable life, I never have, never will. Been moving from place to place all the time, never had a stable life in one home"* (Jay Jay, M, 17). For 'Peter Schmeichel' (M, 16), who had also been in care, moving to another city was the thing he felt had been most difficult in his life: *"I went to live with family in Birmingham, but most of the people that I know are in* [case study city] *so that's why I didn't like going."*

The difficulty of coping with multiple transitions was similarly noticeable in the narratives of other young people in care (see also Jackson and Thomas, 1999; Leathers, 2002; Munro and Hardy, 2006; Ofsted, 2012). Charlie (F, 16), for example, said that she was moved 15 times in three years between various foster carers and care homes. For the five young people who had experienced moving to the UK from abroad, not being able to speak English was a particular issue: *"It was really hard 'cos when you go t' shop and you need to buy something, my Mum would say to buy me sugar but I bought her salt!"* (Anna, F, 12). English language services in school were considered by this subgroup as one of the most beneficial interventions they had received, highlighting the importance of language in undermining or cultivating feelings of safety, security or 'vulnerability' (see also Rutter, 2003; Sirriyeh, 2008).

Studies that have explored relationships between structure and agency in young people's biographies have argued that as young people make sense of their identities over time, they may increasingly recognise that 'doing well' at particular endeavours (such as school subjects, craft-related undertakings, the arts or sports) can lead to various investments and returns that may become significant in their trajectories (Honneth, 1995; Henderson et al, 2007). This sense of young people developing particular skills or competencies was not very pronounced in interview discussions with the young people, but in instances where young people did refer to a sense of competency or virtuosity for a particular skill, the impression was given that this was a key source of pride or 'resilience'. Brook (F, 16) talked about how her *"talent"* for sport had resulted in major positive changes taking place in her life. She planned to study and teach sport in her adult life, and was about to start a Saturday job as a coach to children. Scott (M, 18) saw his talent as how 'streetwise' he was. While he saw this as problematic in many ways, aptitude in this area also seemed important to him:

I'm streetwise. I'm not paranoid about the streets. I'm a night-time person and I cheer up more in the night because I like the dark. I love being out in the dark and stuff [...] Since I was a kid I've worked – thingi'd ont streets, been ont streets and stuff like that.
(Scott, M, 18)

That instances of young people describing their aptitudes or particular skills were relatively infrequent across the interviews could perhaps indicate that 'vulnerable' young people may have less-developed senses of their aptitudes, raising questions about the potential for interventions and services to offer support in this area (see Gilligan, 2000, for consideration of this).

Experiences of care and social control processes

Seeking to explore young people's experiences of vulnerability in a wider social context, the remainder of this chapter focuses on the structures, processes and interventions that the young people understood as shaping their biographies and 'vulnerabilities'. Table 7.1 highlights some key trends within the sample and Table 7.2 shows the full range of the interventions that the young people detailed. Service involvement in the young people's lives varied over time and was much more frequent and substantive in some cases than in others; the numbers of services cited in each interview ranged from two up to 16, with the average being around five or six.

In some cases, the range and number of interventions was extensive and young people described a catalogue of interventions that they had received throughout their whole lifecourse. Of the 25 young people interviewed, 15 had received interventions that could be seen as more social control-orientated in that they were compulsory or there were sanctions for failure to cooperate. These were mainly provided by social services, the police and the Youth Offending Service (YOS), but also in some instances education services (for example via 'attendance officers' with the power to issue Parenting Orders). General themes arising from young people's accounts of the interventions they had received are considered in more detail below, as well as the particular issues related to balances of care and control.

The mediation of vulnerability through interventions

The young people saw a broad range of services as influential in their lives, but there was little continuity or correlation in their perceptions

Table 7.1: Key intervention patterns

Intervention domain	Patterns from vulnerable young people's interview narratives
Child protection issues	• 10 interviewees had been on the Child Protection Register, indicating relatively intensive state intervention and monitoring via social care at various points in their childhoods • 6 young people were in looked-after care with the local authority
Mental health provision	• 12 young people discussed having had mental health interventions • Of these, 7 cited formal psychiatric interventions from Child and Adolescent Mental Health Services, and 11 cited other 'informal' counselling, usually via voluntary sector agencies • 'Informal' counselling had often been experienced along with 'formal' interventions, indicating that certain 'vulnerable' young people had received substantially more mental health input than others • There was a notable overlap in terms of those who had experience of mental health interventions and the youth justice system (see BIBIC, 2005; Goldson, 2009; Fryson and Yates, 2011)
Youth justice	• 8 young people had received formal youth justice interventions via the Youth Offending Service • The number of services discussed by interviewees with experience of the youth justice system was substantially higher (average of 9 services) than for those not involved with the system (average of 4). This may be because these young people had greater 'needs' or because they were better connected with local provision • Of the 8 young people who had been involved with the Youth Offending Service, 6 had been on the Child Protection Register

of the helpfulness (or otherwise) of particular agencies or interventions. Instead, the characteristics or particular aspects of services or individuals who provided interventions seemed to be more influential in how the young people saw vulnerability as mediated, along with some key themes that were common to discussions of this.

The usefulness or limitations of 'talking-orientated' interventions was one such issue that featured commonly. In certain instances, counselling or discussion-based services were viewed as having helped to reduce vulnerability, but this was usually seen as due to the rapport that the young people had enjoyed with a particular person (or people) as a result. Mercedez (F, 16) felt that the only factor helping to reduce her vulnerability was support from her keyworker at a young carers' service: *"She's just a leg-end* [legend] *int' she. She just – I don't know, I can just sort of get it out and feel – I don't have to feel – I feel comfortable in*

Table 7.2: Welfare and disciplinary interventions described by vulnerable young people

	Fostering & adoption	Residential care homes	Social care	Social care child protection 'Register	Young people's housing provider	Hostels (adult /young person/family)	Local authority housing services	Specialist residential care	CAMHS	Voluntary sector support service
Alicia (F, 16)	•	•	•	•	•		•	•	•	
Anna (F, 12)						•	•			•
Brook (F, 16)			•	•	•	•	•			
Charlie (F, 16)	•	•	•	•			•			
Chris (M, 17)			•		•	•	•			•
Elle (F, 14)						•	•			•
Hayley (F, 16)						•	•		•	
Jade A (F, 17)									•	••*
Jade B (F, 16)	•		•	•						
Jay Jay (M, 17)			•							
'Jeremy Clarkson' (M,15)						•	•			•
Jess (M, 15)		•	•	•				•	•	•
John (M, 16)							•	•	•	
Keith (M, 16)										
Kotaa (F, 12)			•	•						•
Laura (F, 16)										
Mackenzie (M, 16)										
Mercedez (F, 15)			•	•						•
Naz (F, 14)			•	•						••*
'Peter Schmeichel' (M, 16)	•		•	•						
Sam (M,14)						•				•
Scott (M, 18)		•	•	•		•	•	•	•	
Stephanie (F, 16)			•							
Wadren (M, 17)			•						•	
'2Pac' (M, 14)										•

Note *: Two different services were described.

Specialist education provider	Connexions	Police (victim)	Youth services	Mentor /teacher	Young people's drugs service	Youth Offending Service	Youth offending institution/ secure unit/prison	Police (perpetrator)	Other
•					•	•			Leaving care team
		•				•		•	Sports academy
•				•	•				Children's rights team
		•	•	•					
									Language support
•								•	Counselling service
		•	•						
•			•						
•	•	•	•	•		•		•	
	•			•					
			•			•		•	
•					•	•		•	Public school
•			•			•	•	•	
•			•						
•				•					
				•					School attendance officer
		•							
•									
									Language support
•	•		•		•	•	••*	•	Anti-Social Behaviour Unit, probation
			•	•					
		•	•					•	
				•					Church group, participation group

front of her." Scott (M, 18) felt that the best thing about his local youth project was the way they talked to him:

> *They talk to you normal. They have a joke with you. They don't talk to you like you're in here because you're a dude, because you're a div. They talk to you like you're normal. They treat you normal. Not like you're a different race, like you're an alien or something, or a rebel or something.*

Most often, however, therapeutic value seemed to be attributed to action-orientated or more 'practically inclined' interventions. Jade B (F, 16), for example, valued the help of her foster carers above all the other interventions that she had received: *"… they let me live at their house and they do a lot for me, they cook for me and I can talk to them whenever I want and they buy me stuff."* Charlie (F, 16) had been particularly affected by a mentor from her school who took a more 'hands-on' approach to interventions:

> Charlie: *… he came to my house once 'cos I wouldn't get out of bed to go to college.*
>
> Kate: *And that was important to you?*
>
> Charlie: *It was. Then I felt that I'd have to go to college now or he'd just come to my house every day. So since then I've been going to college really.*
>
> Kate: *And who was that?*
>
> Charlie: *[Name]. He just got one of the staff to knock on my door: 'Your teacher's here' and I thought 'What the fuck?! The teacher's here to wake me up.' He told me the day before though, 'If you don't get up, I'm coming to your house,' but I didn't think he actually would. But he did.*

The limitations of talking-orientated interventions were frequently noted. Alicia (F, 16) who was in looked-after care, and had used heroin and sold sex, felt that *"talking wouldn't make things go away or anything like that"*. As well as 'speaking' interventions being seen as ineffectual, there could sometimes be criticisms that they were intrusive: *"I was speaking about things I didn't really want to be speaking to … like, the people, just like they were intruding in my life and made me talk and I didn't want to talk"* (Hayley, F, 16). Furthermore, interviewees noted that as talking-based interventions were short term, problems often seemed to recur once interventions finished: *"… as soon as I left there, I got worse, my anger got worse and everything because, when I was going there, I was happy. And then when you leave there, obviously you've still got all these emotions and anger and I just…."* (Scott, M, 18). Naz (F, 14) had a history of running away, which improved during an intervention from a voluntary sector young project, but deteriorated again shortly after: *"… when I stopped going and my Mum started, like, being all bad again to me and stuff, and then I just used to climb out my window and jump on the roof and off the roof, and get ladders, my mates used to bring ladders"* (Naz, F, 14). Comments such as this opened up questions about how far the often complex and enduring nature of young people's difficulties might be somewhat mismatched with service models based on short-term speaking interventions.

Timely and appropriate action was consistently cited by the young people as a facet of service delivery that was of central importance. Where gaining access to a certain service was delayed, this could be seen as limiting usefulness. Scott (M, 18) described burgling houses while he waited weeks for his benefits claims to be backdated; Alicia (F, 16) described how she only received access to support for sexual exploitation after she had already stopped selling sex. Once engaged with a particular service, response times of workers or lack of flexibility were often cited as the reason why interventions were seen as valuable (or not). John (M, 16), who had used drugs heavily, felt that there were periods related to his 'come-downs' that were missed opportunities for support: *"When someone's actually like that, book another* [appointment] *for like two days to see if they're still like that […] 'cos it might have changed entirely by next week."* Where services were not delivered in a timely way, this could have particularly pervasive implications, as short-term options for coping with delays often seemed extremely limited. Alicia (F, 16) lived in a high-crime area and felt that she had been left particularly vulnerable due to delays in a response from her housing provider to a broken front door: *"They left me without a door handle, so I put an ironing board behind my door to shut it of a night, for three days."*

In the majority of the descriptions of problems with timeliness, the young people did not simply refer to the practical effects of delays in services; there often also seemed to be important therapeutic implications. As one example, Mercedez (F, 16) had contacted her social worker via text message at a time of crisis, and her social worker had taken four days to respond: *"… it felt like she were pissing me about because she's saying I can trust her and I can say, you know, I can ring – text her whenever I can – and it's like, well obviously, not at all."*

Several interviewees implied that they felt undervalued, hurt or even foolish if they sought a particular response from a service or individual practitioner and did not get this. Jay Jay (M, 17), who had been sexually abused by a male friend of his mother's, had reported this to the police but the man had not been charged. He had also been physically assaulted by two other young men several years after, and saw these incidents as part of a catalogue of inaction and delays from enforcement agencies:

> *Alt' stuff that I've told them, they're just putting it in a sleeve or something, that's what it feels like to me, so they're not doing owt about it. 'Cos about the attack, that wor bad, how my face was smashed in like that, couldn't even see. I've got permanent ear damage in my left ear … they took pictures, everything. The pictures were bad as well, 'cos I seen them myself. And then they just, like they just went 'I'll get in touch with you' and they never got in touch back and that's when I told them about getting in touch, and that's when they still didn't do nowt about it, and that's why I'll never have faith in police, never ever.*

Lower levels of resources to deal with difficulties seemed to mean that timely and responsive welfare interventions could take on enhanced significance in vulnerable young people's lives, especially perhaps where family support systems were weaker.

The importance that interviewees attached to being listened to and having their opinions valued was another issue of major significance in young people's views about how vulnerability was mediated. Being *"treated like"* or called *"a kid"* was highly disapproved of by most of the interviewees. Chris (M, 17) reported that although he was shy, being called *"a kid"* by his social worker had led him to raise this with her: *"I just told her off really, I said 'don't call me a kid, I don't like you calling me that'."* Sometimes, young people linked their 'problematic' behaviours to circumstances where they felt they were not listened to. For Scott (M, 18), expelled from school at the age of 13, feeling foolish when he was not listened to connected to problems with anger:

> *I couldn't stand the teacher because he'd never listened to me. I'd put my hand up and everything and they'd never talk to me. And that's when I used to flip a chair over and walk out and shit because I'm not going to waste my time putting my hand up, like I did,*

> *and them just turning me down like I'm some kind of doyle [fool].*
> *So I turned round and just walked out and stuff.*

The young people's 'voice' and opinions being taken seriously by agencies or practitioners was seen as forming the basis of a trusting relationship and catalyst for addressing vulnerability. For Wadren (M, 17), what he most valued about the local youth project he was engaged with was related to 'respect': *"They don't treat you like a kid. They speak to you as an adult, which I like. I get sick and tired of being spoken to like I'm a little two-year-old kid. I'm a 17-year-old boy. I'm nearly 18 for God's sake. I'm nearly an adult."*

Societal ambivalence about young people's citizenship status and capacity for decision making and responsibility might well be a relevant context in which to view these comments (see also Goldson, 2002a, 2004; Muncie, 2006), and the space for interventions to take account of vulnerable young people's voices seems especially significant in the delicate balances of care and control involved in interventions with vulnerable young people.

The care, control and consultation balancing act

Control without consultation was a major theme in 12 of the young people's interviews. In all but one case, this appeared during interviews with those who could be considered as 'transgressive'. Alicia (F, 16) had been involved with various compulsory interventions and resistance to control without consultation was particularly prominent in her narrative:

> *Social services never really used to like, you never used to like go, like get to go see where you were gonna be living first, things that, they just used to take you and leave you there whether you liked it or not. At one time I'd even said that I never ever wanted to live in children's home, the social worker took me to this children's home and I'd said I didn't wanna live there, and she left me there. And in the end I ended up running away and being homeless and they wouldn't find me anywhere else to live.*

A tension between the 'protection' and 'control' that young people experienced as a result of interventions seemed difficult for some interviewees to reconcile. Jess (F, 15), who had been selling sex since the age of 14, explained: *"[Social worker] helped by putting me in care, but she didn't really help me 'cos I'm not allowed to go out by myself 'cos I put myself in too much risk."*

Disapproval of not being 'asked' or 'told' prior to compulsory interventions was also a theme. John (M, 16) had been sectioned under the Mental Health Act due to concerns about his drug use, which had been a particularly frightening experience for him. He recognised a need for the intervention, but he felt that he should have been informed beforehand:

> *I just could have been informed to what was like going on, instead of, 'we think you need help, we think you need help'.... Explain to me why we think you need help and not when you're blatantly wrecked when the police arrive, especially when you're on acid.*

Tensions between professionals' need (and legal obligation) to 'protect' vulnerable children from harm and young people's desire (and right) to 'choose' or to be consulted with are something that would appear to become more acute the greater the degree of 'risk' a young person is deemed to be at (see also Brown, 2006) and seemed especially pertinent to how interventions might mediate young people's vulnerability.

When encouraged to reflect on the duty of practitioners to keep young people safe, interviewees sometimes indicated that while they disapproved of compulsory interventions at the time these had taken place, they saw benefits to this course of action with hindsight. Charlie (F, 16) had not wanted to be taken into care at the time this had happened, but reflected that it had helped her in life: *"Probably if I didn't go into care, I'd be a little tramp and probably dossing it up at home."* However, there were other cases where the young people felt that the balance was misjudged in an enduring way: *"... some things they do are alright but you don't think they are at the time. And other things they aren't all right though that they do"* (Alicia, F, 16).

The results of resistance to control mechanisms for 'vulnerable' young people could be extremely concerning, as the young people often described disengagement from services and greater safety risks as a result. Some indicated that they recognised the potentially controlling forces that could be activated as a result of accessing more 'caring' interventions, and this could make them reluctant to access the support that was on offer. Despite his own concerns about his drug use, John (M, 16) concealed the extent of it from his drugs worker, *"... then I wouldn't get me head drilled over the negative consequences"*. Jess (F, 15) had been sexually abused by her father, after which her behaviour deteriorated, but she did not tell anyone as she was concerned about the involvement from services that would likely follow: *"I knew if I said something that they could go to the police. And it just, I just didn't want that. There were enough going on without a big riot with my parents."* That vulnerable young people could be reluctant to access protective mechanisms due to a desire to avoid control or surveillance seemed particularly significant for the young people who were more transgressive.

In terms of factors that influenced young people's responses and resistance to more controlling interventions, feelings of loyalty or protection towards parents and other family members were another significant matter. Of the 10 young people who had experiences of the Child Protection Register, around half disagreed with judgements made about their parents' potential to cause harm to them. Even where the young people appeared to feel that their parents posed some risk to them, there could be strong reactions to compulsory social care interventions. Scott (M, 18) recognised that he had been in danger when his mother threatened him with a knife when he was 14, but despite this, demonstrated considerable resistance to the monitoring of his wellbeing, saying that social services *"were pricks"*:

> ... *butting in too much. As soon as I got a bruise, man, that's it, they'd jump on me. I don't know. I think it's right that a kid has a bruise. I think you should worry if a kid doesn't have a bruise, if you know what I mean, because they fall over and stuff like that and it means they're doing something. Like they're messing about, they're playing. But as soon as I get bruise now, they jump on me: 'His Mum's beating him again.'*

Perceived voyeurism or meddlesomeness appeared several times as a basis for resistance to compulsory interventions, indicating a possible clash of expectations between young people and professionals. While professionals seemed to expect vulnerable young people to give accounts of reasons for their vulnerability (see Chapter Four), this seemed unlikely to be well received in some cases. Brook (F, 16) said that her YOS worker was a *"bastard"* because: *"Basically, he wanted to know the ins and outs of a cat's arse. He wanted to know everything. Things that he didn't need to know, he just wanted to know."*

There was also sometimes strong resistance to interventions where the young people felt that their behaviours were negatively judged. School was seen as a particularly problematic environment in this respect:

> *... they [teachers] didn't give me the chance even when, like,*
> *I don't know because I get stressed a lot and the teachers knew*
> *that, then they used to say to me, 'If you feel yourself getting bad,*
> *excuse yourself from the lesson', and that were fine, that was what*
> *was settled and there were so many teachers, like, that obviously*
> *taught the subjects, that didn't like me, and I'd say, 'Please can*
> *I be excused?' and they'd be, like, 'No', and it'd be, like, 'Well,*
> *I've got this to show you', and they'd, like, 'No, you're not*
> *leaving my lesson' and it's like, I'd get even more angrier and I'd*
> *just end up flipping out and do summat bad that I'd get excluded.*
> (Hayley, F, 16)

As Hayley's narrative indicates, that responses to behaviour were seen as appropriate and 'just' was key to young people's positive engagement with provision, but perhaps particularly in terms of more controlling or compulsory interventions.

Despite the prevalence of resistance to social control-orientated interventions, a small number of the young people seemed to respond positively to certain directive or compulsory interventions, perhaps especially from the youth justice service, which could often be seen as an important source of support. Keith (M, 16) felt that he had benefited from time he had spent in a secure unit, where he had stopped using drugs and had re-engaged with education and with his family:

> *People nudging me, not nudging me but trying to push me down*
> *the right road. [...] Push me the right way. Give you that big*
> *shove you need. 'Cos some kids just need that shove to get them*
> *into the right way. I'm one of them kids, I know I need that big*
> *push [...] Basically I need someone to get me, pick me up, put me*
> *there and just stick me to the floor so I can build my way round.*

Taken together, these findings suggest that how controlling interventions were received by the 'vulnerable' young people depended on a range of factors, including personal outlooks, the relationship they had with those providing the interventions and also the amount of consultation that was involved prior to compulsion.

There appeared to be considerable complexity and ambivalence in young people's attitudes towards how professionals should organise and balance various facets of their work, underlining the intricate balancing acts that are involved in the provision of support and disciplinary interventions for vulnerable young people. Moving beyond such experiences of particular interventions, interviewees also provided insights into more structural dimensions to vulnerability, which related to matters of difference, and these broader social hierarchies form the focus of the final part of the chapter.

Vulnerability in context: wider structural influences

There were several forms of social hierarchy, inequalities or patterns of difference that were considered as mediating vulnerability, namely: social and economic factors, gender and age-related power differentials. Sexuality was referred to in some cases, usually in discussion of gender. Such a range of coverage seemed to underline a connection between lived experiences of vulnerability and matters of social positioning, patterns of inequality and intersectional differences, as well as the relational and socially constituted dimensions of the concept of vulnerability (see Chapter Six). It is worth noting here that sampling is likely to have influenced which structural matters emerged most prominently in the interviews. The numbers of black and minority ethnic young people and disabled young people were small, and so ethnicity and disability may have been unlikely to emerge as significant themes.

Many of the young people reported childhood experiences that related to poverty or material disadvantage (see Chapter Five) and most interviewees indicated that they saw vulnerability as shaped by economic factors or access to resources. At 12 years old, Anna displayed what might be considered an astute awareness of the financial problems that influenced the opportunities that she had access to:

> ... you need to pay for loads of things and that's if like, if you have kids, you can't go to work 'cos you can't leave them [...] Like some of them [young people] have got good education and they get good work and you feel like if they're the only kid in the family then they can get money from their Mum and get what they want. 'Cos right, when I ask my Mum for something, to buy me it, only for me, anything like a phone, she's like 'no 'cos your big brother gonna need it'.

Stephanie (F, 16) felt that people *"can do everything with money"* so people with more money were less vulnerable:

> With people on the dole as well they can't really afford much. 'Cos you only get paid so much on the – so it's like harder for them. 'Cos if like if they borrow money off people and they pay

that debt off when they get that money and that they've only got a little money to provide for themselves. So it's a lot harder.

A small number of interviewees understood access to resources as important because of their influence on where a person lived, which was perceived as closely linked with future life experiences and opportunities. Susceptibility to community violence was also cited frequently as a factor that was deemed to influence the vulnerability of young people (particularly young men), which was tied to geographical locality:

> *... where I live I had – there's like people like not like gangs as such but like people who go round robbing people and stuff and it just makes everything harder and stuff 'cos you have to worry about where you're going and who you're gonna be with and all stuff like that.* (Mackenzie, M, 16)

Brook (F, 16) saw financial resources as providing access to gaining training that may eventually lead to employment, a view shared by a number of the older interviewees. A more common view, however, was that access to resources was important in that it offered some sort of mitigation against stresses and strains:

> *When you've got money, like, everything seems to be fine, there's, like, no stress to lead to family arguments or things like that.* (Hayley, F, 16)

> *If you've got enough money you can just – not buy everything – but having money makes stuff easier doesn't it like you can buy like buy stuff to help you rather than having to do it all yourself like.* (Mackenzie, M, 16)

Such views resonate with Emmel and Hughes' (2010) understanding of vulnerability as linked to an individual's (lack of) capacity to cope with crises and stresses due to limited material resources.

The significance of gender was another notable theme in discussions of what mediated vulnerability. As in other research on social hierarchies and vulnerability (see Hollander, 2001), almost uniformly, young women were seen as more vulnerable than young men based on assumptions about the inherent vulnerability of female bodies in terms of their smaller size and potential as a target of sexual violence:

... with violent relationships and things like that it's, like, I've been in one myself, and it's always the girl that's vulnerable and it's bad to say, 'cos sometimes it's probably the other way round, but you don't hear of Action Aid for men, it's all for women. (Hayley, F, 16)

You see women are more vulnerable than men are. 'Cos men can stand up for themselves, some women can't stand up for themselves towards another man wragging them around sayin' ... trying to rape them, you know what I mean? If they see a vulnerable woman they're going to go target her aren't they? (Keith, M, 16)

For Brook (F, 16), possible problems in her future centred around her choice of partner: *"not finding the right man and finding a straight arse instead, so it all goes wrong"*. Young women's sexuality was often seen as shaping and influencing their vulnerability. As Jay Jay (M, 17) said, *"it's harder for young women because there's a lot more danger out there for women than there is for men"*. Asked to elaborate he said, *"there's paedophiles and stuff like that"*. Jade A (F, 17) felt that young women's vulnerability related to their self-image, resonating with concerns about what McRobbie (2007) calls the 'normative discontent' experienced by young women in relation to their body image: *"Because girls are like, the image and how they look and the body and how they fit in with guys and stuff like that and how they fit in around other people and stuff like that...."* (Jade A, F, 17).

A lack of economic independence was also seen as augmenting young women's vulnerability in some cases:

... [girls] have to think, like, like, the girl we saw, about their life, what they're going to do, what they're thinking, like, what are the people you know I mean what like about their family, their children.... (Sam, M, 14)

'Cos like girls that are pregnant and stuff they go, when they're on their own and they can't afford money and stuff to pay the bills and stuff they go out and sleep with guys and get loads of money and stuff. (Naz, F, 14)

Hollander (2001) argues that gendered imaginings of vulnerability are problematic as they reinforce the perceived 'naturalness' of female vulnerability and male dangerousness, shading into processes which then shape and reinforce how vulnerability is constituted in relation to social inequalities, and there was certainly evidence of such understandings in the young people's accounts.

Only one young person (Mercedez, F, 15) seemed to feel that vulnerability was experienced equally by both men and women. Both her father and her boyfriend had been raped, and she felt that *"we're all really vulnerable"*. Where gender was seen as contributing to young men's vulnerability, this was largely due to the problems related to the need for young men to act in 'hyper-masculine' ways, which it was perceived could bring physical dangers and threats. Mackenzie (M, 16), however, was unusual in that he was the only young man to suggest that he saw young men as more vulnerable than young women. This, he implied, was due to society's responses to normative gender roles of young people: *"They just have more like stereotypes like the police and stuff always think it's always boys that are causing trouble in school and they always think it's boys that always cause trouble and stuff."*

In certain interviews, young people seemed to indicate that they saw an interrelationship between class, gender and vulnerability, offering interesting insights in terms of the intersectionality of different social hierarchies. Hayley (F, 16) gave the impression that she understood 'hyper-masculinity' almost as a direct response to vulnerability in young men from certain inner–city areas:

Hayley: *Like you can tell when someone's had to bring themselves up.*

Kate: *What sorts of things would you be able to tell about, what might make you think someone's brought themselves up?*

Hayley: *Well, I think when children, like, say boys when they're on a bus and they're standing up and they're just staring at people, they're rude and their back's just up all the time.*

Kate: *Do you think them people, do you think they're vulnerable?*

Hayley: *Yeah.*

Kate: *Why?*

Hayley: *They're just doing that to protect themselves, it's obvious and they think it's a good look. But it's not; you can tell that they've had some shit in their life and there's obviously a need. They want someone there, but they ain't got no one there.*

Naz (F, 14) seemed to feel that young women's opportunities and behaviours were shaped by opportunities resulting from class and gender: *"Some people, when they're older, they might not be going to college and stuff. They might just be going out with people and stuff, people and stuff like that and like, getting drunk and like doing stuff with 'em. Like sexual stuff with 'em and that."*

Overall, young women tended to be positioned by the young people as vulnerable because of their bodily weakness or lack of independence from men, whereas where young men were considered vulnerable it was seen more as a failure to perform normative levels of 'hyper-masculinity', which certain interviewees felt resulted in varied behavioural strategies to mitigate this. After her assertion that all young people were vulnerable, Mercedez (F, 15) offered a particularly direct view of this relationship between behaviour, gender and vulnerability: *"Lasses are bitches, boys are arseholes. Normal."*

Power imbalances resulting from age-related status was one other prominent theme in discussions of how 'vulnerability' was constituted, and the importance attached to issues related to 'voice' discussed earlier in the chapter might well be best understood in such a context. The young people's accounts provided insights into experiences of being part of a social group who, due to age, were sometimes in positions where they felt marginalised. Adults were often seen as taking advantage of or failing to exercise their relative position of power. Chris (M, 17) indicated that beatings he experienced from family members in Pakistan were due partly to structural responses: *"there was no control there, no one was doing nothing"*. Mercedez (F, 16) felt that her mother and father manipulated the welfare system to avoid control, and that due to their status as adults, this disadvantaged her: *"I just think it's funny that when* [social worker] *comes – 'right make sure that's clean and go'. Right. 'Yes, everything's fine' – no it's not."*

Frustrations were evident in relation to instances where adult accounts of certain situations were believed over young people's. In some cases, the young people indicated that they thought that some 'official' agencies could be prejudiced against them. Charlie (F, 16) felt that within the care system, staff involved in her care had *"just made loads of shit up"*. Indeed, she felt that the Children's Rights Service had played a substantial role in mediating her vulnerability through advocacy work: *"They were just like, 'We hear this thing all the time', and they know how the carers are."* The importance of advocacy in the mediation of age-related power differentials was mentioned by others also. Wadren (M, 17) said: *"We need more people who can ask us for our opinion, not just say it for us."* Given the particular relationship between young people being 'vulnerable' and assumptions about the need for them to be controlled for their own safety, it could be argued that such age-related power dynamics might be especially significant in welfare provision for this particular group.

Although the interviewees saw vulnerability as mediated by structural factors in certain respects, more often than not, discussions also suggested a view that vulnerability was considered to be largely up to individuals to address. As Keith (M, 16) explained:

> It's not your YOT [Youth Offending Team] worker's decision; it's your decision to change your life. It's not – there's only one person that can do it and it's not anybody else, it's you that can only help change your life. It's only you that can do anything. It's only you that can do it.

Some young people seemed to be grappling with a contradiction between a sense of themselves as disadvantaged and also as capable agents. Asked if she thought money helped people with difficulties in life, Jade B (F, 16) said: *"It does in a way and it doesn't, because money doesn't solve all your issues."* Where the young people indicated views that individuals were in control of their lives and that money did not shape vulnerability, there was usually some degree of conflict in their narratives in relation to this, as in Jay Jay's (M, 17) interview: *"… you can have exactly the same future with money or without money 'cos you can be the same person with money that you are without money. But people can do owt with money, can't they?"*

Rather than revealing young people to be expecting state assistance to address inequalities and vulnerabilities, dependency on the state was predominantly viewed as undesirable. Hayley (F, 16) was homeless, had been *"disowned"* by her mother and father and was about to leave education: *"I wanna do it on me own, to be honest with you. I wanna be able to say, when I've done it all, you know, 'I did that on me own'."*

For some of the older young people who had experienced more direct dependency on state resources, there was evidence of feelings of resentment. Scott (M, 18) felt that claiming benefits had been a struggle and had become more entrenched in crime as a means of supporting himself and his girlfriend:

> I thought, 'fuck it, if the government's not going to help me, I'm not going to help myself'. And I thought, 'fuck it, I'm going to do what I want to do, me', and I went sour for a bit. I went that sour that I thought, 'fuck t' government, fuck t' Jobseeker's [Allowance].

I'll never be a doley.' I said I'd fucking never take anything from the government and what they've done for me. And that's when I just started making money [committing robberies].

Narratives that drew on structural understandings of vulnerability competed and overlapped with young people's sense of themselves as capable and active agents, indicating both a substantive degree of 'responsibilisation' for social difficulties and also simultaneous appreciation of the ways in which wider systems and processes were implicated in shaping vulnerability.

Chapter summary

The young people's lived experiences of vulnerability were mediated and shaped by formative relationships and events in childhood and youth, and also by interventions, institutions and social hierarchies. Families were central to the young people's understandings of what factors influenced vulnerability, as well as extended family networks, friends and boyfriends/girlfriends in some cases. For certain 'vulnerable' young people, the role of welfare services in shaping vulnerability appeared as particularly significant given limited recourse to other options and avenues of support when dealing with difficulties. The young people had received a wide range of interventions, which included both support-orientated and more control-inclined involvement. Rather than particular types of intervention being seen as beneficial, how far welfare and disciplinary interventions might address young people's vulnerability was perceived by interviewees as being tied to a range of issues, such as:

- relationships they developed with their support workers;
- the timespan and practical impact of a given intervention;
- the timeliness and flexibility of provision; and
- the suitability and proportionality of action taken.

The importance of young people feeling that their voices were listened to was central, a matter that seemed perhaps especially problematic where young people were deemed to be 'transgressive' or in situations where they might be deemed 'at risk'. Balances of care and control were shown to be highly significant in the ways in which interventions were received, and where the young people experienced interventions as unfair or overly controlling this was usually met with resistance or disengagement, which could in turn lead to further escalation of 'vulnerability'.

Interesting questions about how vulnerability is constituted according to social hierarchies and divisions were raised by the young people's narrative accounts. A number of key structural determinants were seen as influential, such as access to financial resources, gender and age-based power dynamics, opening up possibilities that other dimensions of difference may well be important in how lived experiences of vulnerability are socially, politically and economically constituted. Although a certain amount of ambivalence accompanied discussions of how far material resources structured vulnerability, gender was almost unanimously seen as a key determining factor, supporting research findings in earlier chapters that highlighted 'vulnerability' as a highly gendered concept.

This chapter was the last of four to report from case study research investigating the perspectives of vulnerable young people and professionals involved in care and control processes for the group. Taken together, these chapters have revealed something of the textured and nuanced ways in which vulnerability is operationalised and experienced. The various lenses through which vulnerability has been explored have shown a range of divergences, commonalties and recurring themes, which are now reflected on and brought together with more theoretical insights in the concluding chapter.

Note

[1] Three of the young people's fathers had died, which may have had some effect on the prominence of the discussion of mothers in the interviews.

EIGHT

Vulnerability, behavioural regulation and 'revolting subjects'

Introduction

Vulnerability now plays a significant role in contemporary systems of governance, in the social construction of social problems and in shaping lived realities of adversity. The concept informs hegemonic social practices related to individuals or groups who are often heavily disadvantaged or 'in need', reframing welfare debates in subtle ways that have important implications for configurations of 'deservingness' and citizenship. Questioning the rise of vulnerability in policy and practice offers crucial clues to understanding how social divisions are elaborated, maintained and experienced, as well as providing insights into new forms of social organisation and power. Developments that target and prioritise 'the vulnerable' take on further significance in a climate of economic difficulty and welfare retrenchment, arguably contributing to processes that ration limited resources among those at the 'bottom' rather than encouraging questions about the distribution of resources and opportunities across society. As well as being an increasingly popular discursive motif, vulnerability is now a vital ingredient for understanding care and social control mechanisms across local, national, regional and global contexts.

In the UK, vulnerability rationales have been influential in a wide range of welfare and disciplinary provisions, including: interventions with children and young people (see Fawcett, 2009; Daniel, 2010; Ecclestone and Lewis, 2014); the protection of 'vulnerable adults' (see Wishart, 2003; Dunn et al, 2008; Hollomotz, 2011); social housing (see Niner, 1989; Carr and Hunter, 2008); and apparatus for tackling crime and disorder (see Furedi, 2008; Waiton, 2008; Richards, 2011).

The concept's reach stretches well beyond the UK, through institutions such as the European Court of Human Rights (see Peroni and Timmer, 2013) and the United Nations (UNDP, 2014), featuring prominently in attempts to understand and address global problems such as poverty, natural disasters, armed conflict, financial crises, unemployment and environmental changes (Chambers, 1989; Butler, 2004; Adger, 2006; Furedi, 2008). Vulnerability appears to be a conceptual zeitgeist or 'spirit of the time' in contemporary policy and practice (see also Brown, 2014a); reflecting and influencing welfare and disciplinary processes in multifarious ways and extending into a vast array of policy matters, from violence against women to volcanoes.

This chapter draws together findings on vulnerability, focusing on empirical outcomes and philosophical concerns that are tied in with debates about the governance of 'vulnerable' citizens' lives. Tensions over understandings of vulnerability are highlighted and key dimensions of the concept reviewed. The potentially progressive aspects of vulnerability rationales are evaluated and how the concept maps on to notions of citizenship is explored. Following the thread of vulnerability in earlier chapters through theories, policies, practices, identities and lived experiences has illuminated its eclectic and multifarious implications. In order to further explore these, this concluding chapter draws in places on ideas about 'governmentalities', theorisations advanced by Foucault (1980) to describe the nuanced and far-reaching nature and rationalities of political and social practices connected to the exercise of state power and social control. According to Foucault's governmentality ideas, state power is dispersed across society via the social practices of a variety of governing authorities, and through systems of thought. This formulation emphasises individual actions and subjectivities and their role in and effect on such processes, with government power acting in 'both an upwards and a downwards direction' (Foucault, 1980: 91). Such ideas are useful when reflecting on vulnerability, given the textured ways in which social structures are woven in with the agency of those who design, deliver and receive services when the notion is operationalised.

The chapter advances that vulnerability discourses frame relationships between state and citizen in ways that open up opportunities for enhanced support and also for the intensification of social control for 'problematic' populations. In a context where 'contractual governance' and conditionality are becoming more widespread (Crawford, 2003; Dwyer, 2004; Harrison and Sanders, 2014), with social rights increasingly subject to devaluation (Harrison with Hemingway, 2014: 28), apparently inclusive vulnerability rationales in social policy can mutate to activate subtle but pervasive disciplinary effects on those who fail to conform to standards of 'appropriate' or 'acceptable' behaviour. Put simply, the rise of vulnerability in policy and practice can operate to further exclude those who might be considered the most vulnerable.

Overview of findings

This book approached and considered vulnerability from a variety of different viewpoints, including the perspectives of 'vulnerable' people themselves, with the aim of advancing a more critical view of the concept. Chapter One set out the contours and relevance of the vulnerability zeitgeist in contemporary social policy and practice, exploring its relevance in citizenship, welfare and social control debates. It also provided an overview of the ontological approach and methods used in the research on which the book primarily draws. Chapter Two then explored theories of vulnerability and charted some of the principal ways in which the concept has been drawn on in social science literatures, highlighting how its conceptual dimensions vary according to disciplinary contexts and theoretical positions. A number of commonly occurring configurations were outlined, which included:

- vulnerability as 'innate' and tied especially to particular aspects of the lifecourse;
- vulnerability as 'situational' or relating to 'problematic' circumstances, in which the accountability and agency of the 'vulnerable person' are implicated;
- writings that focus on spatial and often internationally or geographically orientated ideas about vulnerable populations;
- 'universal vulnerability' ideas, which advance vulnerability as a concept able to offer a powerful model for a new, emancipatory and socially just reconfiguration of the relationship between citizens and the state, and/or a more sophisticated way of understanding the nature of human embodiment or experience;
- vulnerability as understood against the backdrop of the 'risk society'.

Chapter Three charted the rise and significance of the concept of vulnerability across various key social policy domains. The complex ways in which ideas about vulnerability resonate within a context of economic liberal democracies were explored, highlighting that the notion can be viewed as part of systems by which certain individuals and groups are reviewed and monitored as well as supported and assisted.

Findings from empirical case study research illuminated how vulnerability was operationalised in service interventions for 'vulnerable' young people in a large city in the north of England (Chapters Four to Seven). This case study utilised qualitative methods including interviews with 25 'vulnerable' young people and 15 interviews with practitioners and policy makers involved in services supporting vulnerable young people, and more informal ethnographic immersion in practitioner worlds through meetings, conversations and interactions. It offered rich insights into how vulnerability was used by practitioners and local policy makers and how it was lived by young people.

Chapter Four discussed how professionals understood and drew on vulnerability in their work, illustrating its role in both supportive and more regulatory inclinations. Chapter Five focused on the life stories and imagined futures of young people classified as vulnerable, showing how they had often faced numerous and complex difficulties. The chapter underlined close relationships between vulnerability and 'deviant' or criminal behaviour. Young people's imagined futures were also explored, revealing largely conventional aspirations in most instances. Determination, optimism and a sense of competency were distinctive features of the interview narratives, qualities not commonly associated with supposedly vulnerable people. Young people's understandings of vulnerability were the focus of Chapter Six, with particular attention given to their responses to being classified as 'vulnerable'. The deficit-orientated connotations of the notion emerged as a key focus for resistance. Finally, Chapter Seven sought to explore the ways in which young people saw their vulnerability as shaped and influenced, highlighting the significance of formative relationships, events in childhood and youth, and also processes, institutions, interventions and wider social hierarchies. Delicate balances of care, control and consultation appeared as especially significant to the ways in which vulnerable young people received welfare and disciplinary interventions and classifications of vulnerability.

Together, the four chapters that focused on the case study showed the diverse, ad-hoc, multidimensional and at times inconsistent ways in which the notion of vulnerability is significant in care and control processes and in the lives of those who are classified as 'vulnerable'. Over the course of the book, theoretical, policy, practice and experiential insights raised a number of substantive themes, which are now considered in more detail.

Mismatched understandings of vulnerability: expectations and realities

How the young people in the case study lived and understood vulnerability offered insights into the social worlds they inhabited, characterised by unequal power relations, significant challenges and precarious support systems that needed careful attention and management. Prevalent in the 'vulnerable' young people's narratives were stories of familial abuse, neglect and/or sexual abuse, as well as complex and multiple disturbances that had arisen within family contexts, such as domestic violence, parental substance misuse, mental health issues and caring responsibilities. Alongside family circumstances there were difficulties related to moving towards independence, including precarious living arrangements and homelessness, running away, selling sex, personal mental health problems, self-harming and being 'bullied' or victimised by peers. To a certain extent, welfare and disciplinary professionals' views of vulnerability (Chapter Four) resonated with the 'vulnerable' young people's life stories, in that the identifiers of vulnerable groups to some degree mirrored the circumstances and experiences described by the young people. Indeed, this was perhaps to be expected given that the sampling of young interviewees was to some extent shaped by practitioner and policy framings of vulnerability.

Yet there were important differences in approaches to and interpretations of vulnerability, which provided insights into mismatched expectations and understandings of the social world. While most of the young people saw themselves as having faced substantial difficulties, they largely distanced themselves from classifications of vulnerability (Chapter Six), as has been highlighted by other researchers (see Wiles, 2011, writing on older people) and in relation to comparable notions such as poverty (Batty and Flint, 2013; Shildrick and MacDonald, 2013). Indeed, the practitioners interviewed for the research were aware of this potential resistance (Chapter Four) and most avoided using the term 'vulnerability' in direct work with service users. Unsurprisingly, being classified as vulnerable seemed to be generally seen by most of the young people as an affront to their sense of human agency and capacity to cope with their circumstances. While 'vulnerability' was generally considered by practitioners to be a less stigmatising denigration than 'risk', this was not necessarily a view shared by the receivers of services. A female interviewee in local authority care (Charlie, F, 16) indicated disapproval of the term as follows: *"I think I'm doing well for myself, and if* [social worker] *said that I was vulnerable, then it'd make me feel like I was doing loads of things I shouldn't be"* (previously quoted in Chapter Six). The young people's discussions about vulnerability revealed tensions with adults and professionals over what circumstances constituted 'risks', and behaviours that professionals classified as engendering vulnerability could be seen by young people as strategies that helped with 'getting by'.

Meanings ascribed to vulnerability by the interviewees often seemed shaped by their own life experiences, reinforcing the idea that vulnerability is highly subjective and frequently tied to a variety of normative assumptions and individual perceptions of the social world. The claim might be advanced that vulnerability is to some extent a relative and culturally specific concept. In his work on 'habitus', Bourdieu (1984: 165) argued that the way the social world is understood and experienced depends on an agent's sense of belonging or position within a particular social space and processes of classification. This would seem a useful point of reference in making sense of the tensions between more 'official' understandings of vulnerability at the policy level, practitioner expectations and assumptions, and perceptions and lived experiences of vulnerability as set out by the receivers of services. Although it would seem useful in describing and designating spaces of precariousness, vulnerability is bound up with what Bourdieu (1977) calls 'doxa', or taken-for-granted assumptions about the social world orientated via an individual's sense of place within it. In other words, vulnerability seems heavily contingent on the person who is classifying or delineating it. This is not to say that it has no common currency and utility in practice arrangements. As Sheppard (2006: 52) argues, while researchers from the 'outside' may seek to contest definitions used in practice, from the 'inside' (frontline practice) characterisations can be legitimate and to some degree 'objective'. Authors interested in universal vulnerability stress how the notion can offer a counterweight to narratives that place emphasis on productivity, activity and independence (see Chapter Two). However, given that 'vulnerable' people would seem largely resistant to notions of themselves as vulnerable, it might be questioned whether vulnerability is an appropriate way of conceptualising adversity.

As indicated above, supposedly vulnerable receivers of services do not necessarily see their lives as problematic in the same way that policy makers and practitioners might. Therefore, when operationalised, the concept of vulnerability opens up tensions about how far vulnerability judgements take account of the views expressed by the individual or group in question, and the extent to which these should be overridden. While 'vulnerable' people appear to place importance on acknowledgement of their capabilities as active agents in their own lives (Chapter Six), accommodating such a position possibly risks shifting the locus of concern for social problems further towards what might be considered a 'responsibilisation' of those people concerned. The relationship between vulnerability and agency is therefore a contentious one. Vulnerability appears to do something to 'taint consent' (Collins, 2013: 31), intimating that the individual in question might not appreciate or understand what is best for them, opening up important and often ethically controversial avenues for state support and control. In the case study, mismatched understandings about vulnerability appeared to form part of a broader gap in perception between official understandings and lived realities of vulnerability, among which there featured some complex and sometimes contradictory ideas and expectations about the behaviour of vulnerable people.

Deservingness and the vulnerability–transgression nexus

Often deployed in contestations or demarcations of 'deserving' and 'undeserving' people in society, different understandings and interpretations of vulnerability indicated something wider about the realities and lived experiences of social divisions. At surface level, classifying an individual or group as vulnerable would appear to have the effect of positioning them as 'deserving', due to the connotations that the concept has (see Goodin, 1985). Yet when vulnerability classifications are examined more closely, a much more nuanced picture emerges. Often, where citizens are described as vulnerable, there can also be a subtext implied: that an individual or group also represents some sort of threat to social order and needs to be controlled. Useful illustrative examples include constructions of groups such as sex workers (Phoenix and Oerton, 2005; Scoular and O'Neill, 2007), people with mental health problems (Warner, 2008), 'troubled families' (see Centre for Social Justice, 2010) and even people who might commit acts of terrorism (Richards, 2011; Coppock and McGovern, 2014). Similarly to risk, vulnerability serves a dual purpose in discourses related to precariousness. It not only highlights that the person or population is 'at risk' but also indicates that they are 'a risk' to others or to society (see also Warner, 2008). Just as is the case with other supposedly vulnerable groups, young people are often described as vulnerable when they display behaviours that are deemed problematic. As one retired local authority commissioner explained, calling young people 'vulnerable' is *"better than saying the child is stupid or is neglected or deviant"* (previously quoted in Chapter Four).

Demarcations of deservingness that operate via vulnerability classifications are complicated by an often close-knit relationship between vulnerability and transgression, as demonstrated in the stories and narrative accounts of 'vulnerable' young people in this book (see Chapter Five). Interviewees' descriptions of their lives, experiences and behaviours undermined dichotomous understandings of 'youth', which tend to appear at the policy level, where young people are often represented as either 'transgressive' or 'vulnerable' (see Fionda,

2005; Such and Walker, 2005). Life stories (also see the Appendix) clearly illustrated links between anger and aggression, 'vulnerability', mental health issues and 'problem' behaviours, which have also been well documented elsewhere in research with young offenders and 'antisocial' young people (see BIBIC, 2005; Goldson, 2009; Fryson and Yates, 2011). In the face of what could be considered profound disadvantages and difficulties, transgressive behaviours such as criminal activities, antisocial behaviour or what young people called 'attitude' could be viewed as important 'identity work' to preserve dignity and self-worth or as a strategy for mitigating against social marginalisation (see also Bottrell, 2007; Frost and Hoggett, 2008; Deuchar, 2010; Fryson and Yates, 2011; Goldsmith, 2012).

The performance of vulnerability

A strange contradiction seemed to emerge in relation to the vulnerability–transgression nexus. At the same time as recognising links between vulnerability and 'deviance', policy makers and practitioners also seemed more likely to see a young person as 'vulnerable' if they were deemed to have exercised only minimal agency in arriving in difficult circumstances, were compliant in offering information about the causes of their 'vulnerability' and took a more active approach to changing their situation. Amenability, acquiescence and responsiveness all seemed central to the achievement of vulnerability status, or as one informant phrased this *"attitudes do shape professional's responses, perhaps more than they should actually"* (quoted previously in Chapter Four). The *performance* of behaviours associated with vulnerability was therefore an important part of being classified as 'vulnerable'.

The relationship between 'deservingness' and vulnerability appears to have particular ramifications for those perceived as assertive, aggressive and/or strong-willed, who might well be less likely to 'perform' vulnerability according to practitioner and policy preferences. As noted by one key informant (see Chapter Four), *"if someone's cocky and rowdy and stuff like that"* then this could lead to *"people thinking that they're not vulnerable"*. Frost and Hoggett (2008) argue that enlightenment liberalism's elevation of the rational and autonomous subject renders those who experience social suffering – including the harms inflicted by economic liberal governance systems – unable to act in their own best interests and often 'done to' by policy interventions. This, argue Frost and Hoggett (2008: 49), represents a 'double suffering' where 'dysfunctional' defences and 'adaptive' forms of coping with social and material inequalities and injustices trigger repressive mechanisms, which in turn intensify suffering. Such arguments are relevant here in that vulnerability discourses could contribute to a double suffering where disadvantaged individuals in difficult situations are disciplined where they fail to successfully navigate a tightrope between somewhat contradictory preoccupations about *lack of agency* and also *active* agency.

The vulnerability–transgression nexus is also bound up with normative assumptions about gender and appropriate behaviour. There was evidence to suggest that young women seemed to enjoy a more secure attachment to vulnerability status than young men, although this may not necessarily match the empirical realities of young people's situations and experiences. While it is possible that young women actually *are* more vulnerable, it may be that their association with vulnerability is *more pronounced* or obvious due to the 'performance' of gender (Butler, 1990). Young men's social worlds could be seen as heavily influenced by the threat or realities of community violence, which perhaps tend to receive less attention than the sexual vulnerability of young women (see Chapter Four; also Hollander, 2001). As the informant from the Youth Offending Service indicated (previously quoted in Chapter Four), when practitioners imagined a 'vulnerable' young person, *"we probably think about the girl that drinks before we think about the six-foot-three person that's done a few robberies"*. Performances of what could be considered 'hegemonic masculinities' (Connell, 1987) seemed to constitute important 'identity work' for some young men (see Deuchar, 2010), but such behaviours could be interpreted as 'transgressive' and might therefore mean that young men risked exclusion from vulnerability classifications. This raised questions about how far the vulnerability–transgression nexus might be relevant to other dimensions of 'difference', such as ethnicity, disability and sexuality. Various assumptions, expectations and realties attached to vulnerability revealed the concept to be a site of tensions and contradictions in processes that configured and reconfigured deservingness. More generally, mismatched understandings of vulnerability highlighted the subjectivity and nebulousness of the notion, raising broader questions about its conceptual dimensions.

Dimensions of vulnerability

Vulnerability rationales form part of a set of other popular and prominent concepts commonly used by researchers, practitioners and policy makers to refer to lower-income or less well-off groups, of which some of the most prominent include risk, resilience (see Chandler, 2014; Ecclestone and Lewis, 2014), need ('priority need' in the case of housing) and adversity (see Daniel, 2010), with risk perhaps having received the most sociological attention (Culpitt, 1999; Lupton, 1999; Taylor-Gooby, 2000; Sarewitz et al, 2003; Misztal, 2011). A further key policy idea within the same constellation is that of 'troubled families', which merges the notions of 'troubled' and 'troublesome' (Levitas, 2012; Ribbens McCarthy et al, 2013). All of these notions can prove difficult to define and have amorphous boundaries, but have in common that they are drawn on within social policy and practice to describe individuals or groups who are seen as requiring particular state 'support' and/or control. In certain respects, then, vulnerability rationales might be taken to be the latest incarnation or manifestation of long-running concerns about 'problematic' populations (Murray, 1990; Welshman, 2013), a form of 'sociological shorthand' (Bagguley and Mann, 1992: 113) for referring to those who might concern us, phrased in an apparently non-judgemental way. Yet questions remain about why enduring social problems that have been core social policy concerns for centuries are now increasingly configured in terms of vulnerability, and what if anything is different or novel about drawing on vulnerability as a way of explaining and understanding them.

Towards the individualisation of social problems?

Generally, individuals and groups who are commonly positioned as vulnerable (see Chapters Two and Three) include those who might be considered disadvantaged or less well-off. However, narratives of vulnerability stretch wider than socioeconomic disadvantage, raising questions about how far a focus on vulnerability might advance or obscure more structural accounts of social problems. In some ways, vulnerability could be understood as associated with what Wacquant (2009: 4) calls 'generalized socialised insecurity' produced by the erosion of wage work and related cultural and class solidarities, or perhaps with Standing's (2011) 'precariat', a social class who lack labour-related security as a result of widespread deregulation of the labour market. Yet vulnerability rationales also bring into focus the situations of those who face precariousness due to ill-health, age, particular circumstances such as domestic violence and sex work, or dangers in the communities where they live. Although class was one factor that permeated the young people's and informants' narratives, intimations of vulnerability stretched in many other directions. Indeed, vulnerability discourses seem rather well suited to accounts that position class in the background of social difficulties. This might variously be considered an advantage or a major limitation of tendencies to frame social problems in terms of vulnerability, depending on one's view of how precariousness should be understood.

Vulnerability rationales seem associated with ontological concerns about risk, insecurity and powerlessness, and the 'risk society' thesis (Beck, 1992) is often drawn on to explain the prominence of ideas about vulnerability (see Chapter Two). Beck (2009) himself notes similarities, and other theorists have also closely aligned these concepts (Furedi, 2008; Waiton, 2008; Misztal, 2011). The in-depth empirical case study research underlined a deep connection between vulnerability and risk, with risk frequently drawn on by practitioners and strategists as a reference point in their definitions of vulnerability (see Chapter Four). Similarly to risk, attention to vulnerability is often located in deficit-based approaches to social issues, or what Ecclestone (in Ecclestone and Goodley, 2014: 7) sees as 'profound pessimism' about severe social problems or crises in contemporary society (see also Furedi, 2007, 2008; McLaughlin, 2012) and defeatism about potential for radical social transformation. Much of the theorising on risk has highlighted how certain concepts seem particularly well suited to the measurement, auditing and assessment of people against the model of economic liberal citizenship ideals – centred on the independent, rational, capable individual – which may go some way to accounting for the popularity of vulnerability as a tool in policy and practice (see also Campbell, 1991; Lupton, 1999; Kemshall, 2002). 'Risk' tends to assume centre stage in such analysis, yet 'vulnerability' would seem to have a similar significance in welfare and disciplinary settings, drawing attention to how people are deficient in the requisite skills or qualities required of supposedly 'normal' or 'capable' citizens.

Resilience is another concept closely connected with vulnerability in theory, policy and practice (see Chapters One to Four). According to developmental or normative concerns, resilience/vulnerability-focused accounts of social problems facilitate an approach centred on assessing the likelihood of potential harm or suffering, and identifying and utilising existing capabilities to safeguard against this. Such an approach has been drawn on to advance recognition of the complexity of contemporary social problems (see Chandler, 2014) and the alleviation of suffering on a global, regional, local and individual level. However, critical scholars have noted the potential of resilience/vulnerability thinking to frame social problems in ways that obscure their deeply political composition (Ecclestone and Lewis, 2014), inclining developments towards a prioritisation of 'emotional need' or 'positive adaptation' rather than structural disadvantage. Used in a normative sense, vulnerability rationales arguably strip experiences of precariousness from their historical, political and economic constitution and reorientate the official gaze away from such matters, authenticating the rise of psychological and behavioural explanations and accounts of social problems (see Jones et al, 2013). In other words, vulnerability discourses reframe the harsh lived realities of politically and economically structured social divisions as situations of misfortune or misadventure.

At the same time, however, vulnerability is a concept that serves to underline something of the role of mid-level social systems in how social difficulties are experienced. Vulnerability's contingent nature alludes to the possibilities of people coping (or not coping) in situations of precariousness. When carefully theorised, it has been used by some social researchers to highlight the dynamic nature of disadvantage or deprivation, and the role of structures and institutions in creating such 'social spaces of vulnerability' (Emmel and Hughes, 2010, 2014). In the geo-vulnerability literature (see Chapter Two), we find deliberate attempts to focus on structural accounts of vulnerability, which are orientated firmly towards political or economic solutions, and such analyses have also been advanced by the 'universal vulnerability' writings (see also Chapter Two; a matter also returned to below). Vulnerability is also a concept that can be utilised to highlight precariousness over time (see Emmel and Hughes, 2010, 2014). Discussing global environmental dangers, Beck (2009: 178) argues that 'a sociological conception of vulnerability has a pronounced reference to the future, yet it combines with this a profound rootedness in the past'.

When defined in a way that accommodates structure, vulnerability captures something of the dynamic nature of social problems, appealing to what might be seen as a core social policy idea: that when people are experiencing difficulties, interventions can mediate the severity or impact of these. Generally, however, both the policy review in Chapter Three and the practice realities covered in Chapters Four to Seven indicated that when viewed against a policy environment and political leadership consensus that 'downgrades structural factors' in social difficulties (Harrison with Hemingway, 2014: 30), vulnerability rationales seem to reinforce systems of thought that frame disadvantage as circumstantial and 'individual'. As it appears in contemporary policy, the vulnerability zeitgeist is inextricably bound up with social pathologies.

The reach of vulnerability: extending care and control

Given its malleability and plurality of meanings, vulnerability is potentially further-reaching and more dynamic than concepts such as risk in terms of who is implicated via governance arrangements when such ideas are operationalised. This reflects what I have referred to as the 'contingent nature' of vulnerability (see Chapter Two). The concept seems to be linked with the *potential* for an undesirable situation or predicament, rather than tangible and *immediate concerns* about a negative outcome (as in the case of risk; see Sarewitz et al, 2003). Risk, as Van Loon (2008: 50) argues, 'implies a calculation'; vulnerability somehow seems more open to interpretation (see also Misztal, 2011: 33). As one clinical psychologist said in discussion with me (Chapter Four), vulnerability to her was more of a *"state"*, whereas there were *"definite factors"* associated with risk. As the idea of someone being 'vulnerable' is increasingly used as a standalone term (instead of someone being vulnerable to something specific; see Furedi, 2007, 2008), policies aimed at addressing presumed vulnerabilities are likely to be broader-reaching than where they address risk or need, or even the development of resilience. As one example, interviews with informants (Chapter Four) indicated that as the youth justice system had become increasingly concerned with addressing vulnerability, this seemed to have widened and intensified the scope of surveillance, support and interventions.

Such expansionist tendencies are not necessarily to be condemned, and indeed may be interpreted by some as a move in the direction of progressive social care practices. Indeed, for certain groups or individuals, there are important advantages associated with social welfare organised around vulnerability. Being classified as vulnerable frequently offers a route to accessing additional state resources, and also seems to act against the urge for officials to condemn transgressions that might otherwise be seen more pejoratively. As one example, a 16-year-old young man interviewed for the case study who had served a custodial sentence for drugs and theft offences described how his classification as vulnerable (related predominantly to being regularly beaten by his father) meant that his sentence was served in a secure unit rather than the harsher environment of the youth offending institution. Delineations of vulnerability could therefore be seen as offering important protections for extremely marginalised populations, which has been highlighted in relation to groups such as Roma populations in Europe (Peroni and Timmer, 2013) or street sex workers in the UK (especially via the 'Merseyside model' of interventions; see Campbell, 2014).

One key aspect of vulnerability that distinguishes it from other notions is the particularly pronounced ethical dimension to the concept (see Goodin, 1985; Mackenzie, 2009; Mackenzie et al, 2013). It is imbued with connotations of empathy and caring or therapeutic approaches. As one key informant put it, vulnerability is a *"kind word"*. Yet such 'therapeutic' approaches may not be as benign as they at first appear (see Harrison and Sanders, 2006) and in practice may also result in encroachments on the activities or behaviours of 'vulnerable' groups. Ideas about vulnerability often imply that officials or professionals 'know better' than the receivers of services, and that without interventions service users might not make 'appropriate' decisions (see also Hasler, 2004; Dunn et al, 2008; Hollomotz, 2011). This *paternalistic or controlling dimension* to vulnerability is subtle and seldom recognised, with the veiled nature of the regulatory implications in itself almost a defining element of the concept. Discourses of vulnerability therefore could be said to give licence to governmental interventions and surveillance 'in the name of protection' (see Phoenix, 2002). Analysing policies on teenage parenting, Van Loon (2008: 59) uses Foucault's notion of governmentality to argue that vulnerability 'is a specific label that can be deployed to justify targeted actions towards/against specific groups of people. It enables governmentality to adopt a cloak of "concern and care" or what Foucault [...] has termed "pastoral power"'.

This *cloak of concern* is one of the most significant factors that marks vulnerability out as conceptually distinctive in contemporary governmentalities. As its regulatory effects are largely masked, these can potentially slip by unnoticed. Vulnerability's connotations of benevolence can make it a particularly effective conceptual mechanism for the transference of power from the receivers of services to professionals who design, implement or manage welfare and disciplinary provision.

Dynamic dimensions and beyond the discursive

Contributions drawing on governmentality ideas have provided particularly useful insights. However, analysis within this book has also indicated that it is important to avoid painting a mechanistic picture. Practice conditions at the 'front line' showed a more textured or nuanced process than simply those in power exercising control through the imposition of vulnerability classifications. Chapter Six highlighted that the young people in the study were largely resistant to being described as 'vulnerable', but depending on bonds with their workers and their situational circumstances, it could be a classification that they were receptive to, or even be positively received and validating. How they reacted and responded to the classification was therefore a dynamic negotiation. Equally, in practitioner worlds, while 'vulnerability' emerged as imprecise, its degree of shared meanings, tacit understandings and potential for useful ambiguities made it a concept that helped to organise interventions and resources in flexible ways. This could bring distinct advantages to particular individuals or groups who were less well-off.

Although exploring particular terminology might emphasise the pertinence of certain discursive 'tools', empirical work in this research also highlighted that systems of ideas and practices that shape the lives of people who are described as 'vulnerable', 'excluded', 'at risk' or 'troubled' move beyond the discursive. Tracing the contours of operationalised vulnerability has indicated that while particular rationales, discourses and technical mechanisms are important, these form part of a wider set of processes and social systems that shape and mediate realities. Ultimately, vulnerability is a malleable notion, imbued and affected by the possibly irreducible impact of consciousness of both the user and the receiver of the label. In other words, effects and meanings of vulnerability classifications in policy and in practice are always likely to be moderated at grassroots by the receivers of interventions and by the dynamic interactions between the 'vulnerable' person and those intervening on the basis of 'vulnerability'. Such processes change and shift through time, and alter according to situational factors. Discourses of vulnerability are therefore unlikely to be fixed. Uses of the term reflect relational power dynamics between individuals, with personal interactions in turn structured and influenced by wider institutional factors and forces persisting over time.

The vulnerable citizen: the social division of social control

How the concept of vulnerability features in configurations of the relationship between citizens and the state seems particularly contested and complex (see also Brown, 2011b, 2014b). It has been argued by some scholars that vulnerability is a notion able to offer a new conceptual foundation for citizenship, based on our shared human frailties and interdependencies (see Chapter Two; Beckett, 2006; Turner, 2006; Fineman, 2008; Fineman and Grear, 2013). According to Fineman and Grear (2013: 2), vulnerability citizenship models are able to offer a powerful challenge to what they call the 'mythical (and equally destructive) autonomous liberal subject of neoliberal rhetoric', replacing it with an acceptance and embracement of interdependency that can be cultivated to forge a stronger civil society (see also Goodin, 1985; Campbell, 1991; Turner, 2006).

Such accounts position us all as vulnerable by virtue of our human embodiment or corporeality (Harrison, 2008) but in ways that vary according to biological, social, geographical and political factors (see also Butler, 2004; Wiles, 2011). Shared humanity is the focus here, with vulnerability put forward as a mechanism for disrupting tendencies for citizens to compete for resources, and one that can challenge negative stereotypes of dependency. 'Universal vulnerability' ideas have been used across a wide range of policy arenas including housing (Carr, 2013), European legal systems (Timmer, 2013), family law (Wallbank and Herring, 2013), caring (Kittay, 1999; Dodds, 2007; Wiles, 2011), disability (Beckett, 2006; Goodley, in Ecclestone and Goodley, 2014) and even tsunamis (Clark, 2007). That social responsibilities should be structured according to vulnerability (see Goodin, 1985) also holds appeal for those interested in classic libertarian or small-state citizenship ideas, which prioritise citizens' mutual recognition of each other's worth and the exercise of civic responsibilities (see Ramsay, 2008; Anderson and Honneth, 2009).

Universal vulnerability ideas offer a way of exploring the subjectivities of human experience while also minimising potential risks of over-reifying agency and capacity. They provide avenues for investigating resistance and passivity without necessarily reinforcing negative ideas about dependency and lack of capacity. They also seem to offer an alternative to 'productivist' accounts, which prioritise autonomy and purposive economic action as core components of existence. Vulnerability approaches to personhood and social responsibilities perhaps have possibilities to move beyond normative assumptions about human agency where 'agency is good, and the absence of agency is bad' (Hoggett, 2001: 43). Yet concerns remain about what placing the vulnerable citizen at the heart of democratic society might mean for the augmentation of regulatory mechanisms, erosion of liberties and undermining of possibilities for collective social organisation.

Authors such as Ecclestone (in Ecclestone and Goodley, 2014) have argued that the rise of vulnerability discourses represents a move towards the denigration of the liberal and neoliberal rational subject. Importantly, it should be noted that this position is not to argue that widespread and intensifying feelings of structural, physical or emotional precariousness are not *real*, just that to respond to these through vulnerability rationales is to be deeply pessimistic and to legitimise therapeutic ways of responding to political and economic problems. Seen through a Foucauldian lens, the vulnerability zeitgeist might be seen to pave the way for a more repressive governance of a new 'passive subject' (see Jones et al, 2013) in a society where different social groups compete for resources based on their various fractured vulnerable identities (see McLaughlin, 2012). In policy-orientated explorations of vulnerability, problems with the paternalism fostered by vulnerability rationales have been noted in various assessments of a range of domains, including housing (Lévy-Vroelant, 2010), mental health law (Dunn et al, 2007), disability (Wishart, 2003; Hollomotz, 2011) and youth (Van Loon, 2008; McLeod, 2012). Despite the power and appeal of universal vulnerability approaches, there certainly seems to be a danger that the radical and progressive potential of vulnerability is open to being undermined and subverted when it is operationalised, perhaps especially in highly conditional and selectivist welfare contexts.

Although beneficial to certain specific individuals and groups, overall, vulnerability rationales in social policy seem to undermine structural accounts of disadvantage and 'rights-based' approaches to citizenship, advancing reconfigurations of welfare as a 'gift' rather than a 'right' (see Harrison with Davis, 2001: 61, 74). Although discussions about resources going to 'the most vulnerable' can imply an ethical rationale for targeting resources at those who require them most (see also Brown, 2014b), findings from the empirical research described in this book resonate with other commentaries that have linked vulnerability with: welfare reduction (Kemshall, 2002); competition (see also Lévy-Vroelant, 2010); an undermining of collective approaches (McLaughlin, 2012); and the erosion of social rights (Brown, 2014b).

As regards the potential of vulnerability rationales to open doors for stronger control mechanisms and the denigration of the 'rational' citizen, Harrison and Sanders' (2014: 11) idea of the 'social division of social control' is able to offer useful insights here.

Drawing on the social division of welfare thesis (Titmuss, 1958; Sinfield, 1978) – which highlighted the role of institutions in bringing assistance and support to a much wider range of individuals and households than might be imagined by too narrow a focus on 'welfare' – Harrison and Sanders (2014) bring into focus the differentiation in degrees of social control across contemporary society. They argue that just as upper- and middle-income groups have maximised the use of universal systems of welfare, gaining disproportionately from state-sponsored intergenerational advantages via tax arrangements, legal processes and occupational welfare, so have social control mechanisms been adopted and experienced differentially. Whereas 'nudge' techniques have been deemed appropriate for the better placed (centring on incentivisation rather than coercion), different strategies are pursued when it comes to 'disadvantaged' or 'vulnerable' groups, including harsher treatment, selectivism and disciplinary conditionalities that might inflict indignity or suffering (Harrison and Sanders, 2014).

Wacquant's (2009: 43) metaphor of the 'centaur state' with a 'liberal head mounted on an authoritarian body' similarly depicts such variegated processes of social control. Wacquant (2009: 43) argues that while neoliberal states such as the United States apply a doctrine of laissez-faire 'upstream', when moving to cope with consequent social inequalities they are 'brutally paternalistic and punitive downstream'. Rather than representing a move in the direction of confirming one particular configuration of the relationship between citizens and the state, the rise of vulnerability in contemporary governmentalities might best be seen as a part of such differentiated and divided practices of social control, enabling more intensified behavioural regulation of the less well placed while better-off citizens are subjected to less impinging persuasions.

Subtle shades of care and social control: towards a more excluding society

Vulnerability is aligned with systems that create and sustain binary oppositions about the deserving and undeserving within society, in subtle and often undetected ways. Its connections with deservingness and undertones of weakness and defencelessness combine to form a potent conceptual prism, which can support exclusions where people fail to perform their vulnerability sufficiently. Where individuals are 'vulnerable' and also 'non-compliant' or transgressive, they pose particular challenges to services. Commissioned often on the condition that they demonstrate improved outcomes in relation to specific social problems, services supporting vulnerable groups may be inclined to target resources at those who are most responsive to them. Accounts from key informants in the present research indicated that services might 'cherry-pick' the more compliant vulnerable young people (see Chapter Four). This seemed to stem partly from a funding context that was focused on particular vulnerabilities or problems, as well as workload and cost implications of working with more challenging individuals, but was also the result of moral judgements made by practitioners and policy makers about who deserved help or required discipline the most.

One of the concerns illustrated in this book has been that vulnerability is often contingent on 'good' behaviour and aligned with conditional or contractual approaches to welfare (see Dywer, 2004, 2008; Deacon and Patrick, 2011). At the same time as gesturing towards inclusion and empathy, vulnerability rationales also configure transgressive people as less legitimate in their claims on resources than those who behave in more conformist ways. People who mobilise resistance as a coping strategy or resource for 'getting by' are perhaps less likely to enjoy the benefits of vulnerability status. Given that those who are most heavily sanctioned for problematic and criminal behaviour have often grappled with the greatest structural disadvantages (see Wilkinson and Lober, in Pitts, 2000; Muncie et al, 2002; Goldson and Muncie, 2006; Jacobson et al, 2010), it seems inescapable that vulnerability classifications are unlikely to work in the favour of such citizens.

This brings us to the central contention of the book. Behavioural conditionalities attached to vulnerability mean that – paradoxically – the concept can operate to further exclude those who might be considered among the most vulnerable in society. As such, despite triggering important protections for certain individuals and groups some of the time, the rise of vulnerability in policy more generally represents a key development in progressions 'towards a more excluding society' (Harrison with Hemingway, 2014).

Within a context of economic liberal policy frameworks, hegemonic social practices related to vulnerability are intimately connected with regulatory welfare. Governmental and practitioner discourses drawing on vulnerability can be seen as part of wider disciplinary processes that subject those who are less well-off to sanctions, disapprovals or the withdrawal of support where they fail to conform. Furthermore, within a climate of welfare retrenchment, organising welfare on the basis of vulnerability can help to justify overall reductions in entitlements. In focusing attention on resources and situations at the lower end of the income and opportunity spectrum, the vulnerability zeitgeist serves to divert attention away from a society-wide view of social advantages and disadvantages. Targeting resources at the most vulnerable has the effect of placing various different groups and interests into a competition over scarce resources on the basis of 'deservingness' (see Chapter Three), with those who are the most compliant arguably finding their entitlements more secure.

As vulnerability delineations are most often applied by those in more powerful positions to define those in less powerful ones, elements of stigma or labelling also seem to be involved in such demarcations. In highly selective welfare systems, classifications of vulnerability can act as a signifier of social worth, yet at the same time, vulnerability denotes how certain populations and groups are 'different' from the mainstream. In this sense, then, vulnerability rationales serve to 'otherise' rather than include, but the language of vulnerability reframes this exclusion as something more palatable and benign, dressing it in a cloak of concern. In her consideration of growing contemporary distaste for less well-off classes or 'revolting subjects', Tyler (2013: 8) argues that stigmatisation operates as a form of neoliberal governance that 'legitimises the reproduction and entrenchment of inequalities and injustices'. It might be argued that vulnerability discourses serve rather than disrupt such a trend, in ways that are frequently veiled or hidden from view. As they currently feature in policy and practice, paternalistic vulnerability rationales would certainly seem problematic in their potential to exacerbate rather than bridge social divisions.

Implications for policy, practice and research

While policy and practice recommendations might risk oversimplifying complexities and replacing one set of normative assumptions about vulnerability with another, brief reflections about how findings can be taken forward are advanced here. Three key recommendations seem pertinent.

First, vulnerability-based approaches should be further scrutinised and the assumption that they are always and inevitably progressive should be treated with care. A more cautious approach to the notion might include closer attention to defining what is meant by vulnerability and how it is to be understood when drawn on as a conceptual tool in policy, practice and research. One useful approach to vulnerability might be that it is *biological and inevitable in some respects*, but that it is *structured by social inequalities and institutional forces that persist over time,* and also *shaped by the choices, views and experiences of individual social actors.* More understanding about the perspectives of receivers of services, and a greater diversity of voices in policy and practice, may go some way to helping to address disjunctures in understandings of vulnerability and the potentially stigmatising dynamics that underpin its classification.

Second, it would seem beneficial for there to be more overt acknowledgement at the policy level that 'vulnerability' and 'transgression' are not mutually exclusive states. Indeed, they are inextricably connected. Such an approach might help to moderate some of the tensions and contradictions in the wider social systems and processes that underpin the governance of vulnerable people's lives, and may subvert some of the behavioural conditionalities that accompany vulnerability. Although links between vulnerability and transgression appear in research and campaigning work, this is usually a device used to demonstrate that people's vulnerability is a causal factor in transgressions. While this is a useful strategy in bringing into view structural aspects of crime and deviance, it also plays into binary understandings of behaviours that fall short of appreciating the more complicated relationships between vulnerability, transgression, agency and structural disadvantage that have been brought into focus through this research. Moving further beyond the dichotomy of vulnerable/deserving and transgressive/undeserving citizens to consider implications of people being *both transgressive and vulnerable* might be more useful as a starting point for policy arrangements and research agendas. It seems likely that such an approach could help policy and practice initiatives to have greater congruence with the realities of vulnerable people's lives.

Finally, how vulnerability connects with and is shaped by normative assumptions and practices related to various *aspects of difference and intersectionality* is an area that requires further investigation. Findings in earlier chapters of this book indicated that young men might find themselves less well served than women by notions of vulnerability, echoing other research in relation to gendered responses to housing need (see Passaro, 1996, reporting from New York; Cramer, 2005). Similarly, age was another aspect of difference that seemed to structure understandings of vulnerability in policy and practice. Vulnerability classifications may map on to other normative social constructions related to matters of difference such as ethnicity, sexuality and disability, in ways that are significant and which deserve further attention. One of the strengths of vulnerability rationales is that they offer multidimensional and dynamic ways of approaching inequality and social difficulty, making them suited to taking account of difference. However, vulnerability classifications necessarily involve 'an evaluative judgement' (Collins, 2013: 29), which inevitably invites certain prejudices and differentials. A more deliberated and reflexive approach to such judgements might offer mitigation against potentially discriminatory effects of vulnerability classifications.

Concluding reflections

The notion of vulnerability has come to fundamentally influence the ways in which welfare and criminal justice interventions are designed, delivered and received. Such developments can be seen as part of a broader and intensifying 're-moralisation' agenda in contemporary social policy, serving to discipline certain transgressions and further marginalise those who pursue socially unacceptable resistance strategies. Although often well intentioned, the popular deployment of vulnerability as a concept in social policy and practice is part of the tapestry of increasingly selective welfare and social control processes, which are reconfiguring and reworking citizens' entitlements. In many ways, vulnerability rationales offer a means of reconciling tensions between the somewhat contradictory approaches of fairness, targeted public services and stronger disciplinary mechanisms orientated at the less advantaged in society.

The malleability of vulnerability would also seem to enable localised translations of the broader policy moves and particular policy initiatives, offering spaces for flexible approaches to addressing social difficulties. Exceptions made on the basis of vulnerability can be deployed within broader moves to specialise provision, while retaining overtures of social justice. Indeed, the popularity of vulnerability as a concept in contemporary social policy seems connected to its ability to serve increasingly blurred and interwoven practices of care and control in welfare and disciplinary processes. The apparent compassion attached to the notion, along with its tacit regulatory implications, might go some way to explaining why enduring concerns about 'problem' behaviours of disadvantaged groups are now increasingly configured in terms of vulnerability. Given the potency of current debates about which groups are deemed deserving and undeserving in society, 'vulnerable' people seem set to be singled out, judged and gifted resources for some time to come.

Vulnerability can act as an important lever for claims-making, social acceptability and worthiness, serving to help galvanise vital sources of access to extra support and assistance for those who need them most. But in classifying particular people as 'vulnerable', a discursive mechanism is activated that helps to trigger patience and sympathy towards certain groups or individuals, rather than a more fundamental reorganisation of society or redistribution of resources. Too often, arguments about the 'most vulnerable' contribute towards processes that ration the limited resources available to those who are less well-off, rather than encouraging questions about the distribution of resources and opportunities across the whole of society. Due to its strong links with ethics and morality, targeting or prioritising supposedly vulnerable people for interventions or resources has a seductive veneer of fairness, deflecting attention from narrowing entitlement and wider social divisions of welfare and social control.

Alongside other ideas such as risk and resilience, vulnerability is a notion that in practice reinforces and reaffirms concerns about those who do not conform to standards of the self-regulating, active and responsibilised citizen at the heart of economic liberal political agendas. For a more socially just way of understanding and addressing the enduring and often severe experiences of disadvantage and difficulty in contemporary society, we might make a case for the use of conceptual tools that are less paternalistic than vulnerability. However, moves to alleviate the precariousness and adversity experienced by some citizens require more than discursive strategies. Alongside effective theoretical approaches and ideas, transforming lived experiences of vulnerability requires addressing the steady advancement of punitive and exclusive regulatory mechanisms that increasingly bear down on those who face hardship. It seems appropriate to end on John's advice:

> *Find out why you think they're vulnerable first instead of just telling them they're vulnerable, 'cos they're gonna put up a block and go like, 'well no I'm not'.... So don't just have a shot in the dark, with the word 'you're vulnerable'. You should try and figure it out first.*

Appendix: Pen portraits of vulnerable young people

All of the young people's names have been changed and pseudonyms were chosen by the interviewees.

Alicia, female, 16, White British

Alicia was adopted at the age of four. Her mother was a heroin user, her father was in prison and they could not look after her. She had lived with a number of foster carers and in different residential care homes. At 14, she became involved in selling sex and started using heroin with an older boyfriend. After being caught stealing tanning wipes from a chemist, she received a community youth justice intervention. There was a period around her 16th birthday when Alicia 'slept rough' (in a tent) for a month. At the time of the interview she had her own tenancy with an agency that supports young people leaving care. She had been clean from heroin for about a year and no longer sold sex, but still saw her drugs worker regularly. She said that she would like a job before she was 18, and wanted to work with children in care or in a prison. She would also like to get married, have children and pay to go on a holiday.

Anna, female, 12, White Eastern European

Anna was originally from Lithuania and moved to the UK aged nine. She was living in a hostel for homeless families at the time of the interview. Before that, she lived in houses shared with other families and also lived at another hostel. Her parents separated when she was small. Her mother has told Anna that her father was physically abusive and used alcohol heavily. Anna's mother had another boyfriend who was also violent, and Anna had witnessed this abuse, but they are now separated. Anna's mother had spent some time working in prostitution, which Anna felt angry and upset about. Anna said that when she got older she would like to be a singer and to write a book. She also wanted to have a house and for her grandmother and brother to live with her.

Brook, female, 16, White British

At the time of the interview, Brook was homeless and living in a hostel, having left her mother's house the previous year as she did not get on with her mother's new partner. When she lived with her mother she was on the Child Protection Register; social services considered her mother's new partner to be a risk. The previous year she was served with a three-month Youth Offending Service order, which she breached, and was given a further three months. Brook was excluded for the most part of her final year at school. She attended an off-site alternative education provision. A keen football player, Brook had played in football teams for several years. She planned to teach sport as a job, after studying at university. She hoped to secure permanent accommodation, have her own house, a car, a husband and two children.

Charlie, female, 16, White British

Charlie had been in care for over three years. During that time she had around 15 foster placements and lived at several children's homes. Her mother was employed and had schizophrenia, her father used alcohol heavily. Her grandparents were a very important source of support to her. She had recently been charged with criminal damage for an incident that took place at the children's home. She was due to complete a health and beauty course the following year. Shortly after the interview she expected to secure a tenancy on a house that she would share with her sister. In later life, Charlie would like to run a hairdressing salon and eventually move to America.

Chris, male, 17, British Pakistani

At the age of 10, Chris was taken by his parents to Pakistan. He lived there for six years with his uncle, who beat him on a daily basis. He did not attend school. He was moved back to England the year before the interview to live with his parents and two younger siblings. He continued to be physically abused by his family. His father told him that if he told anyone they would kill him. Earlier in the year before the interview, Chris explained the situation at home to a teacher. The police and social services got involved, and Chris lived in hostels for a period. Several days before the interview he had secured his own property. Chris wanted to finish his education and to join the army at 18. He also hoped to get married and have a family during his late twenties.

Elle, female, 14, Black African

Elle's family moved to the UK from Eritrea when she was around eight years old. She lived in a hostel with her four siblings (one of whom was Sam who was also interviewed) and her mother, but when they had a house her mother and the family would live with her father again, as he lived nearby. She found it intimidating when she first started school because she hardly spoke English, but she now enjoyed school. In the future Elle wanted to be a pharmacist or a doctor and to get married. She felt that watching too much television and not working hard enough might get in the way of this.

Hayley, female, 16, White British

Technically homeless, Hayley was staying at her grandmother's house waiting for her own tenancy. Her mother had left the family home the year before the interview, and at the same time her father 'disowned' her. She had had caring responsibilities for her 11-year-old brother for several years. The separation of her parents followed years of domestic violence. During childhood, Hayley lived periodically in hostels and refuges due to her mother fleeing the violence. Hayley had herself been in a violent relationship, which was now over. Hayley had self-harmed since the age of 11, by cutting herself. She had been excluded from school around 10 times. She had received a final warning from the police for assaulting a police officer during an incident between her family and her ex-boyfriend. Having secured a place at college for the following year, her ambition was to work with primary school children.

Jade A, female, 17, White British

Jade had learning difficulties and dyslexia. She had been severely bullied, including an occasion three years prior to the interview where she was physically assaulted by another young person while with her mother. Since this incident she had suffered with post-traumatic stress disorder and had received support from the child and adolescent mental health service (CAMHS). She also had caring responsibilities for her father, who was physically disabled and suffered from depression and other mental health problems. At the time of the interview, Jade was receiving support from a local youth project. She planned to study childcare at college, undertake voluntary work with a view to working with disabled children, and also wanted to work as an 'extra' on television programmes. In the future she also saw herself losing weight, getting fit, becoming more confident and going into town on her own.

Jade B, female, 16, White British

In care since the age of seven, Jade B lived with her foster carer, her foster carer's husband and two other young people who were fostered. She had recently been on holiday to Turkey with them. Her older sister was an important person in her life. She stayed with her sister every weekend, but no longer had contact with her parents, who used alcohol very heavily. Her father was violent towards her mother and the children. Jade had received support in school to improve her behaviour, which she said had at times been challenging in terms of her 'attitude'. After sitting her GCSE [General Certificate of Secondary Education] examinations she would be starting a cookery course at college and planned to work in catering when she was 18.

Jay Jay, male, 17, White British

When Jay Jay was smaller, his father was violent and physically abused him. He moved house regularly, with periods spent out of school. When he was 13 he began running away. Around this time he was also excluded from school for fighting. When he was 15 he was sexually abused by a male friend of his mother's. He reported the abuse to the police, but the perpetrator was not prosecuted. He also had many problems with bullying. On one occasion he was hospitalised after being assaulted by two young men on his estate. He described himself as having a problem with anger. Six months previously, Jay Jay had received a community sentence with the Youth Offending Service, for criminal damage during an incident with his girlfriend. At the time of the interview he lived between his mother's house, his father's house and an older couple's house. He had befriended the couple and helped them with shopping and household chores. In the future he wanted to get a trade such as plumbing, or be a famous singer, get married to a nice wife and have some money to travel. He was awaiting the outcome of an interview for a cleaning job.

'Jeremy Clarkson', male, 15, British Bangladeshi

'Jeremy Clarkson' lived in a homeless hostel with his mother and seven brothers and sisters. The family moved there because they had some problems with neighbours where they lived before, and his father felt that the house was too small. His father lived separately from the family, but the family would move back in with him when they were in a house again. His father worked in 'management and security'. Both his parents were Bangladeshi. Jeremy was very focused on getting good GCSE examination grades so he could get a 'suitable' job. He had recently applied to go on a motor vehicle maintenance course. He also wanted to go to university locally, but was not sure whether he could afford this. As well as a job, in his future he wanted to have a house and for his family to live there with him.

Jess, female, 15, White British

Jess was taken into care the year before the interview after being sexually abused by her father from the age of 13. She regularly ran away, sold sex on the street and used drugs and alcohol. Excluded from school at 14 for violence towards staff and other pupils, Jess had spent time in a residential mental health unit. After three miscarriages since the age of 13, she very much wanted to get pregnant. At the time of the interview she was on a final warning at her care home; if she absconded again she would be taken into a secure unit for her own safety. Jess would like to work as a care worker in the future, and wanted to have a child by the age of 16.

John, male, 16, White British

John was sectioned under the Mental Health Act two months prior to the interview for a period of four weeks, for reasons related to drug use. In the previous three years he had used a mix of substances on a regular basis and described himself as being addicted to the stimulant mephedrone ('MCAT'). At around the same time he got involved in drug use, three family members/friends he was close to died. After he began using mephedrone he started stealing things to pay for drugs and was caught, receiving a one-year order with the Youth Offending Service. John went to a public school until around the age of 14, when he stopped attending. His father worked as a university lecturer and his mother was a doctor. He had a difficult relationship with his parents, and now lived independently in a council tenancy. The future was difficult for John to imagine. He was due to start a college course in youth work within the next few weeks.

Keith, male, 16, White British

The year before the interview, Keith had spent four months in a youth offending secure unit, after a period of offending related to cocaine and alcohol use. He used to steal money from his grandmother (who he lived with) in order to pay for his drugs. His mother and father used to 'argue' and split up when he was eight or nine. He lived with his mother until the age of 11, with his grandmother for a short period, and then at his father's for around a year. His father used alcohol heavily and Keith was beaten by him nearly every day. Aged 14 he began using cocaine and alcohol most days, and eventually stopped attending school. At the time of the interview he regularly attended a private sector-run specialist education provision and was due to sit his GCSE examinations the week after the interview. Since being released from the secure unit he had not used cocaine and had used alcohol only twice. He now used cannabis regularly. He was currently living at his grandmother's and enjoyed some contact with his mother. His father was in prison for domestic violence offences. Keith's ambition was to own a unisex hairdressing salon.

Kotaa, female, 12, Romany Gypsy

Kotaa's father died when she was 10. Following this, her behaviour changed and she started running away from home. One of her older brothers regularly spent periods of time in prison. Kotaa had been on the Child Protection Register in the past due to 'arguments' between her mother and father, and allegations of sexual abuse during a period when she was living with a family friend. She was also on the register at the time of the interview. Kotaa had moved several times, including once to a different country, and reported that she might be moving to live in mainland Spain in the following few months. When she was older she wanted to be a singer and a model and had already done some modelling for catalogue companies. She also wanted her mother to be alive when she got married.

Laura, female, 16, White British

Laura experienced some bullying at school when she moved schools at the age of 14 after a falling out with some of her friends. Her parents helped her to deal with this. Tutors at her school were also helpful. Laura was apprehensive about going up to high school from primary school at the age of 11, as she was afraid of meeting new people, but she managed the transition, met new people and made friends. Later in her education, Laura attended an off-site education programme for certain days in each week after her school teachers felt that she was involved in 'gangs', although Laura never indicated that this was an issue for her. After sitting her GCSE examinations, Laura planned to study childcare and wanted to work with children. She also saw herself getting married, having children and owning a house.

Mackenzie, male, 16, White British

Mackenzie had spent substantial periods of time out of school. Having moved from Ireland during primary school, he spent three years out of education waiting for a place in a Catholic school. At 14 he was diagnosed with diabetes. He was absent from school for around three months at that time, and had had other periods of absence subsequently. During the first year of study for his GCSE examinations he usually stayed at home for three days a week, partly due to his health and partly because of negative attitudes towards school. Mackenzie lived with his mother and his younger sister. His father was in prison until he was three years old, and now lived with a new partner and their children. The year after the interview, Mackenzie planned to study fabrication and welding at college, although this was a 'back-up' strategy; he hoped to work as a mentor for older children when he reached the age of 18. Later in life he wanted a family and he thought he would live in a rented house.

Mercedez, female, 15, White British

Mercedez lived with her mother and her younger brother. She had a difficult relationship with her parents; both her mother and her father used alcohol heavily and Mercedez had substantial caring responsibilities for her brother. After some problems with school attendance and being assessed by social services, Mercedez was placed on the Child Protection Register. She also had a worker from a support service for young people with parents who used drugs/alcohol. She wanted to live independently as soon as possible, and her other ambitions were to be a hairdresser and to be able to afford to go on holiday to places with a warm climate. She saw herself settling down and having children with her current partner, who was an important source of support for her.

Naz, female, 14, British Pakistani

Naz ran away from home regularly. Her mother tried to control her movements, which Naz felt was restrictive. When she was away from home she was usually with older men, who drove her and her friends around in cars and gave them drugs and alcohol. She regularly absconded from school, and had been excluded in the past. Naz had a large family, with nine (step) sisters and brothers, some of whom grew up in care. When she was five, Naz's father raped her. At the time of the interview she was on the Child Protection Register due to her 'risk-taking behaviour' and might soon be placed in a secure unit for her own safety. She planned to move into a hostel as soon as she was 16. She would like to study health and social care at college and go to university, stay single and live in a flat with her best friend.

'Peter Schmeichel', male, 16, dual heritage (African Caribbean/White)

Having been in care since around the age of 12, 'Peter Schmeichel' now lived with foster carers. He was taken into care because people thought that his father was not looking after him properly, but his mother and father were an important source of support in his life. He described having behavioural difficulties and being 'disruptive' in school, and had moved secondary schools several times, spending a period of eight months not attending school at all. At the time of the interview he attended a private sector specialist education provision for three days a week. He aspired to be a football coach in the future, and had just been accepted onto a course for this. He wanted to be rich, by marrying someone with a large income such as a teacher or a doctor.

Sam, male, 14, Black African

Sam was Elle's brother (see above). He moved to the UK from Eritrea at the age of around 11. He lived in a hostel with his mother and four siblings. Sam planned to attend university when he left school, as he wanted to be a civil engineer. However, he had some concerns that forthcoming changes in university fees may mean that he needed to be a mechanic instead.

Scott, male, 18, White British

Scott had been in prison twice for robbery and violent crime, and also had an Anti-Social Behaviour Order (ASBO). He started selling heroin at the age of nine and had also used a variety of drugs regularly in the past. He was permanently excluded from school for violence at the age of 13. Scott's mother used heroin and alcohol for most of Scott's early life. The family lived mainly in bedsits where they would all share a bed. His stepfather regularly spent time in prison, supporting the family by stealing things. Scott was beaten as a child and was taken into care at 14 after his mother attacked him with a knife. He had lived in many different care homes and was sexually abused at one by a member of staff. While in care he often ran away, living with a group of men who gave him food, and who offered him work in a takeaway restaurant, drugs and a place to stay. From the age of 16 he had lived in various adult homeless hostels but was now staying with his girlfriend. His plans for the future were to control his anger, live a life with no crime in it, gain qualifications and a secure job, and also live well with his girlfriend and have children with her.

Stephanie, female, 16, White British

Stephanie had moved out of living with her mother twice, and at the time of the interview was living with her aunt. She had a difficult relationship with her mother and there had been periods where they did not speak to each other. Stephanie had caring responsibilities for her six-year-old brother and two-year-old sister, which she found difficult to manage, and which affected her behaviour. Social services were involved with her briefly after a period where her mother experienced domestic violence. At age 13 she started self-harming, but was not self-harming around the time of the interview after support from a youth service in her local area where she did a lot of sport. Stephanie planned to work supporting disabled children. She was about to start a college course in childcare, and did voluntary work with children every Saturday.

Wadren, male, 17, White British

Wadren lived with his mother, who suffered from depression and who had experienced several breakdowns, in the property she owned with her husband. Describing himself as 'spoilt', Wadren said that his mother bought him many things. Two years previously, Wadren became the father of a child with an ex-girlfriend, with whom he had a difficult relationship. At the time of the interview he had a new girlfriend. Having suffered with depression, Wadren attempted suicide the previous year. He tried to hang himself, and also took a large dose of tablets. He found his anger difficult to manage and had been excluded from school periodically since primary school. He attended a local youth centre regularly, for sports and education sessions as well as other support. Wadren had been involved with the police on several occasions. He was a keen footballer and played regularly, but felt he was not good enough to play professionally. He would like to be a paramedic, and wanted to move to Holland, as his girlfriend would like to study there to be a child psychologist. They wanted to have two children, and two houses (one abroad).

'2Pac', male, 14, White British

'2Pac' had lived with his mother for most of his life except for a period of three years spent living with his father. At the time of the interview he lived with his mother, her partner and his baby sister in their private rented house, which he said was not on an estate. His mother had multiple sclerosis. Since her diagnosis two years prior to the interview there had been periods where he had looked after her and his baby sister. He described having had a brief period of 'gang life' when he lived in another town. He was now slim but used to be overweight and was bullied because of this. He played basketball, practised a martial art and also attended a church youth group several times a week. He had been on holiday abroad and in the UK and had a girlfriend. At school, he received support from someone who helped him to control his anger and was also involved in participation work with a local youth project. He planned to go to university and study physiotherapy.

References

Adger, N. (2006) 'Vulnerability', *Global Environmental Change*, 16 (3): 268-281.

ADSS (Association of Directors of Social Services) (2005) *Safeguarding Adults: A National Framework of Standards for Good Practice and Outcomes in Adult Protection Work*, London: ADSS.

Alaszewski, A., Alaszewski, H., Manthorpe, J. and Ayer, S. (1998) *Assessing and Managing Risk in Nursing Education and Practice: Supporting Vulnerable People in the Community*, London: English National Board for Nursing, Midwifery and Health Visiting.

Allen, K. and Mendick, H. (2013) 'Keeping it real? Social class, young people and authenticity in reality TV', *Sociology*, 47 (3): 460-476.

Anderson, J. and Honneth, A. (2009) 'Autonomy, vulnerability, recognition, and justice', in Christman, J. and Anderson, A. (eds) *Autonomy and the Challenges to Liberalism*, Cambridge: Cambridge University Press.

Appleton, J. V. (1999) 'Assessing vulnerability in families', in McIntosh, J. (ed) *Research Issues in the Community*, Basingstoke: Macmillan.

Archer Copp, L. (1986) 'The nurse as an advocate for vulnerable persons', *Journal of Advanced Nursing*, 11: 255-263.

Bagguley, P. and Mann, K. (1992) 'Idle thieving bastards? Scholarly representations of the "underclass"', *Work, Employment & Society*, 6 (1): 113-126.

Bagnoli, A. (2009) 'Beyond the standard interview: the use of graphic elicitation and art-based methods', *Qualitative Research*, 9: 547-570.

Bankoff, G., Frerks, G. and Hilhorst, T. (eds) (2004) *Mapping Vulnerability: Disasters, Development and People*, London: Earthscan.

Barnes, C. and Mercer, G. (1996) *Exploring the Divide: Illness and Disability*, Leeds: The Disability Press.

Barnes, M. and Prior, D. (eds) (2009) *Subversive Citizens: Power, Agency and Resistance in Public Services*, Bristol: Policy Press.

Barnes, M., Green, R. and Ross, A. (2011) *Understanding Vulnerable Young People: Analysis from the Longitudinal Study of Young People in England*, London: NatCen and Department for Education.

Barry, M. (2001) *Challenging Transitions: Young People's Views and Experiences of Growing Up*, London: Save the Children.

Bateman, T. (2011) '"We now breach more kids in a week than we used to in a whole year": the punitive turn, enforcement and custody', *Youth Justice*, 11 (2): 115-133.

Bateman, T. (2012a) 'Who pulled the plug? Towards an explanation of the fall in child imprisonment in England and Wales', *Youth Justice*, 12 (1): 36-51.

Bateman, T. (2012b) 'Youth justice news', *Youth Justice*, 12 (3): 144-155.

Batty, E. and Flint, J. (2013) 'Talking 'bout poor folks (thinking 'bout my folks): perspectives on comparative poverty in working class households', *International Journal of Housing Policy*, 13 (1): 1-16.

Bauman, Z. (2000) *Liquid Modernity*, Cambridge: Polity Press.

BBC (2010) *The Ander Marr Show*, 2 May, transcript accessed at http://news.bbc.co.uk/1/hi/programmes/andrew_marr_show/8656998.stm

Beard, R.L., Knauss, J. and Moyer, D. (2009) 'Managing disability and enjoying life: how we reframe dimentia through personal narratives', *Journal of Aging Studies*, 23: 227-36.

Beck, U. (1992) *Risk Society: Towards a New Modernity*, London: Sage Publications.

Beck, U. (2009) *World at Risk*, Cambridge: Polity Press.

Beckett, A. (2006) *Citizenship and Vulnerability: Disability and Issues of Social and Political Engagement*, Basingstoke: Palgrave Macmillan.

Beddoe, C. (2006) *The End of the Line for Child Exploitation: Safeguarding the Most Vulnerable Children*, London: ECPAT UK.

Bell, C. C. and Jenkins, E. J. (1993) 'Community violence and children on Chicago's southside', *Psychiatry*, 56: 46-54.

Bell, E. (2011) *Criminal Justice and Neoliberalism*, Basingstoke: Palgrave Macmillan.

Benard, B. (1991) *Fostering Resiliency in Kids: Protective Factors in the Family, School, and Community*, Portland, OR: Northwest Regional Educational Laboratory.

Bhavnani, K.-K. and Phoenix, A. (1994) 'Shifting identities, shifting racisms', *Feminism & Psychology*, 4 (1): 5-18.

BIBIC (British Institute for Brain Injured Children) (2005) 'Young people with learning and communication difficulties and anti-social behaviour', www.bibic.org.uk

Bichard, M. (2004) *The Bichard Inquiry Report*, London: The Stationery Office.

Birch, M. and Miller, T. (2000) 'Inviting intimacy: the interview as therapeutic opportunity', *International Journal of Social Research Methodology*, 3 (3): 189-202.

Blackie, P., Cannon, T., Davis, I. and Wisner, B. (1994) *At Risk: Natural Hazards, People's Vulnerability and Disasters*, London: Routledge.

Bolin, R. and Stanford, L. (1998) *The Northridge Earthquake: Vulnerability and Disaster*, New York, NY: Routledge.

Bottoms, A. and Roberts, J. V. (2010) *Hearing the Victim: Adversarial Justice, Crime Victims and the State*, Cullompton: Willan.

Bottrell, C. (2007) 'Resistance, resilience and social identities: reframing "problem youth" and the problem of schooling', *Journal of Youth Studies*, 10 (5): 597-616.

Bourdieu, P. (1977) *Outline of a Theory of Practice*, Cambridge: Cambridge University Press.

Bourdieu, P. (1984) *Distinction: A Social Critique on the Judgement of Taste*, London: Routledge.

Bowlby, J. (1969) *Attachment and Loss (Vol 1.): Attachment*, London: Hogarth Press.

Bradshaw, S. (2013) *Gender, Development and Disasters*, Cheltenham: Edward Elgar.

Brannen, J. and Nilsen, A. (2002) 'Young people's time perspectives: from youth to adulthood', *Sociology*, 36 (3): 513-537.

Brotherton, G. and Cronin, M. (2013) *Working with Vulnerable Children, Young People and Families*, Abingdon: Routledge.

Brown, B. (2012) *Daring Greatly: How the Courage to Be Vulnerable Transforms the Way We Live, Love, Parent and Lead*, London: Penguin.

Brown, G. (2011) 'Emotional geographies of young people's aspirations for adult life', *Children's Geographies*, 9 (1): 7-22.

Brown, K. (2004) *Paying the Price: A Consultation Paper on Prostitution: Consultation Response from the National Youth Campaign on Sexual Exploitation*, London: The Children's Society and ECPAT UK.

Brown, K. (2006) 'Participation and young people involved in prostitution', *Child Abuse Review*, 15 (2): 294-312.

Brown, K. (2011a) 'Beyond badges of honour: young people's perceptions of their Anti-Social Behaviour Orders', *People, Place and Policy Online*, 5 (1): 12-24.

Brown, K. (2011b) '"Vulnerability": handle with care', *Journal of Ethics and Social Welfare*, 5 (3): 313-321.

Brown, K. (2012) 'Re-moralising "vulnerability"', *People, Place and Policy Online*, 6 (1): 41-53.

Brown, K. (2013) 'The concept of vulnerability and its use in the care and control of young people', PhD thesis, University of Leeds.

Brown, K. (2014a) 'Questioning the vulnerability zeitgeist: care and control practices with "vulnerable" young people', *Social Policy and Society*, 13 (3): 371-387.

Brown, K. (2014b) 'Beyond protection: "the vulnerable" in the age of austerity', in Harrison, M. and Sanders, T. (eds) *Social Policies and Social Control: New Perspectives on the Not-so-Big Society*, Bristol: Policy Press, pp 39-52.

Brown, S. (2005) *Understanding Youth and Crime*, Buckingham: Open University Press.

Burney, E. (2005) *Making People Behave: Anti-Social Behaviour, Politics and Policy*, Cullompton: Willan

Burton, I., Kates, R. W. and While, G. F. (1978) *The Environment as Hazard*, New York, NY: Oxford University Press.

Butler, J. (1990) *Gender Trouble: Feminism and the Subversion of Identity*, London: Routledge.

Butler, J. (2004) *Precarious Life: The Powers of Mourning and Violence*, London: Verso.

Butler, J. (2009) 'Performativity, precarity and sexual politics', lecture given at Complutense University of Madrid, 8 June, *AIBR Revista de Anthropologia Iberomericana*, 4 (3): i-xiii.

Bynner, J. (2001) 'Childhood risks and protective factors in social exclusion', *Children and Society*, 15: 285-301.

Callender, C. and Jackson, J. (2005) 'Does the fear of debt deter students from higher education?', *Journal of Social Policy*, 34 (4): 509-540.

Cameron, D. (2011) Speech on the Welfare Reform Bill, 17 February, https://www.gov.uk/government/speeches/pms-speech-on-welfare-reform-bill

Campbell, A. (1991) 'Dependency revisited: the limits of autonomy in medical ethics', in Brazier, M. and Lobjoit, M. (eds) *Protecting the Vulnerable: Autonomy and Consent in Healthcare*, London: Routledge, pp 101-113.

Campbell, R. (2014) 'Not getting away with it: linking sex work and hate crime in Merseyside', in Chakraborti, N. and Garland, J. (eds) *Responding to Hate Crime: The Case for Connecting Policy and Research*, Bristol: Policy Press, pp 57-72.

Carline, A. (2009) 'Ethics and vulnerability in street prostitution: an argument in favour of managed zones', *Crimes and Misdemeanours*, 3 (1): 20-53.

Carline, A. (2011) 'Criminal justice, extreme pornography and prostitution: protecting women or promoting morality?', *Sexualities*, 14 (3): 312-333.

Carr, H. (2013) 'Housing the vulnerable subject: The English context', in M. Fineman and A. Grear (eds) *Vulnerability: Reflections on a New Ethical Foundation for Law and Politics*, Farnham: Ashgate, pp 107-24.

Carr, H. and Hunter, C. (2008) 'Managing vulnerability: homelessness law and the interplay of the social, the political and the technical', *Journal of Social Welfare and Family Law*, 30 (4): 293-307.

Casey, L. (2015) *Report of Inspection of Rotherham Metropolitan Borough Council*, London: The Stationery Office.

Castro, A. P., Taylor, D. and Brokensha, D. (2012) *Climate Change and Threatened Communities: Vulnerability, Capacity and Action*, Rugby: Practical Action Publishing.

Centre for Social Justice (2010) *Green Paper on the Family*, London: Centre for Social Justice.

Chambers, R. (1989) 'Vulnerability, coping and policy', *Institute of Development Studies (IDS) Bulletin*, 37, 4: 33-40.

Chandler, R. (2014) *Resilience: The Governance of Complexity*, London: Routledge.

Christie, N. (1986) 'The ideal victim', in Fattah, E. (ed) *From Crime Policy to Victim Policy: Reorienting the Justice System*, Basingstoke: Macmillan, pp 17-32.

Clark, N. (2007) 'Living through the tsunami: vulnerability and generosity on a volatile earth', *Geoforum*, 38 (6): 1127-1139.

Clarke, J. (2005) 'New Labour's citizens: activated, responsibilised, abandoned?', *Critical Social Policy*, 25: 447-463.

Cleaver, H., Nicholson, D., Tarr, S. and Cleaver, D. (2007) *Child Protection, Domestic Violence and Parental Substance Misuse: Family Experiences and Effective Practice*, London: Jessica Kingsley Publishers.

Cleaver, H., Unell, I. and Aldgate, J. (2011) *Children's Needs – Parenting Capacity. Child Abuse: Parental Mental Illness, Learning Disability, Substance Misuse, and Domestic Violence*, London: The Stationery Office.

Cohen, S. (1972) *Folk Devils and Moral Panics*, London: Routledge.

Cohen, S. (1979) 'The punitive city: notes on the dispersion of social control', *Contemporary Crises*, 2 (4): 341-363.

Cole, T., Visser, J. and Upton, G. (2001) *Effective Schooling for Pupils with Emotional and Behavioural Difficulties*, London: David Fulton.

Collins, J. (2013) 'The contours of vulnerability', in Wallbank, J. and Herring, J. (eds) *Vulnerabilities, Care and Family Law*, London: Routledge, pp 22-43.

Connell, R. W. (1987) *Gender and Power*, Cambridge: Polity Press.

Connell, R. W. and Messerschmidt, J. W. (2005) 'Hegemonic masculinity: rethinking the concept', *Gender & Society*, 19 (6): 829-859.

Connolly, P. (2003) *Ethical Principles for Researching Vulnerable Groups*, Ulster: Office of the First Minister and Deputy First Minister.

Connor, H., Dawson, S., Tyers, C., Eccles, J., Regan, J. and Aston, J. (2001) *Social Class and Higher Education: Issues Affecting Decisions on Participation by Lower Social Class Groups*, Research Report RR 267, London: Department for Education and Employment.

Conolly, A. (2008) 'Challenges of generating qualitative data with socially excluded young people', *International Journal of Social Research Methodology*, 11 (3): 201-214.

Cooper, P. (1993) *Effective Schools for Disaffected Students: Integration and Segregation*, London: Routledge.

Coppock, V. and McGovern, M. (2014) '"Dangerous minds"? Deconstructing counter-terrorism discourse, radicalisation and the "psychological vulnerability" of Muslim children and young people in Britain', *Children & Society*, 28: 242-256.

Corby, B. (2001) *Child Abuse: Towards Knowledge Base* (2nd edition), Buckingham: Open University Press.

Corr, C. A. and Balk, D. E. (eds) (1996) *Handbook of Adolescent Death and Bereavement*, New York, NY: Springer.

Corston, J. (2007) *The Corston Report: A Review of Women with Particular Vulnerabilities in the Criminal Justice System*, London: Home Office.

Cramer, H. (2005) 'Informal and gendered practices in a homeless person's unit', *Housing Studies*, 20 (5): 737-751.

Crawford, A. (2003) '"Contractual governance" of deviant behaviour', *Journal of Law and Society*, 30 (4): 479-505.

Croll, P., Attwood, G. and Fuller, C. (2010) *Children's Lives, Children's Futures: A Study of Children Starting Secondary School*, London: Continuum.

Culpitt, I. (1999) *Social Policy and Risk*, London: Sage Publications.

Cutter, S. L. (1996) 'Vulnerability to environmental hazards', *Progress in Human Geography*, (20): 529-539.

Daniel, B. (2010) 'Concepts of adversity, risk, vulnerability and resilience: a discussion in the context of the "child protection system"', *Social Policy and Society*, 9 (2): 231-241.

DCLG (Department for Communities and Local Government) (2011) Website information on troubled families, www.communities.gov. uk/communities/troubledfamilies/

DCSF (Department for Children, Schools and Families) (2009) *Safeguarding Children and Young People from Sexual Exploitation*, London: HM Government.

Deacon, A. and Patrick, R. (2011) 'A new welfare settlement? The coalition government and welfare-to-work', in Bochel, H. (ed) *The Conservative Party and Social Policy*, Bristol: Policy Press, pp 161-179.

Dean, H. with Melrose, M. (1999) *Poverty, Riches and Social Citizenship*, London: Macmillan.

Dench, G., Ogg, J. and Thomson, K. (2000) 'The role of grandparents', in Jowell, R., Curtice, J., Park, A. and Thompson, K. (eds) *British Social Attitudes Survey 16th Report*, Aldershot: Aldgate.

Denzin, L. and Lincoln, Y. S. (eds) (2005) *The Sage Handbook of Qualitative Research* (3rd edition), London: Sage Publications.

Deuchar, R. (2010) '"It's just pure harassment... as if it's a crime to walk in the street": anti-social behaviour, youth justice and citizenship – the reality for young men in the east end of Glasgow', *Youth Justice*, 10 (3): 258-274.

Devadason, R. (2008) 'To plan or not to plan? Young adult future orientations in two European cities', *Sociology*, 42 (6): 1127-1145.

DfE (Department for Education) (2011) *Tackling Child Sexual Exploitation Action Plan*, London: DfE.

DfE, Department of Health and Home Office (2011) *Vetting & Barring Scheme Remodelling Review: Report and Recommendations*, London: Home Office.

DfES (Department for Education and Skills) (2003) *Every Child Matters*, London: Cabinet Office.

DfES (2007) *Targeted Youth Support: A Guide*, London: Cabinet Office.

DH (Department of Health) (2000) *No Secrets: Guidance on Developing and Implementing Multi-Agency Policies and Procedures to Protect Vulnerable Adults from Abuse*, London: Cabinet Office.

DH and Home Office (2000) *Safeguarding Children Involved in Prostitution: Supplementary Guidance to Working Together to Safeguard Children*, London: DH.

Dodd, V. (2014) 'Police want right to see medical records without consent', *The Guardian*, 10 August.

Dodds, S. (2007) 'Depending on care: recognition of vulnerability and the social construction of care provision', *Bioethics*, 21 (9): 500-510.

Donnelly, D. and Kenyon, S. (1996) '"Honey, we don't do men": gender stereotypes and the provision of services to sexually assaulted males', *Journal of Interpersonal Violence*, 11 (3): 441-448.

Dorling, D. (2010) *Injustice*, Bristol: Policy Press.

Downing, T. E. (1991) 'Vulnerability to hunger and coping with climate change in Africa', *Global Environmental Change*, 1: 365-80.

Dunn, M., Clare, I. and Holland, A. (2008) 'To empower or protect? Constructing the "vulnerable adult" in English law and public policy', *Legal Studies*, 28 (2): 234-253.

Dwyer, P. (2004) 'Creeping conditionality in the UK: from welfare rights to conditional entitlements?', *Canadian Journal of Sociology*, 29 (2): 265-287.

Dwyer, P. (2008) 'The conditional welfare state', in Powell, M. (ed) *Modernising the Welfare State: The Blair Legacy*, Bristol: The Policy Press.

Dwyer, P. (2010) *Understanding Social Citizenship: Themes and Perspectives for Policy and Practice* (2nd edition), Bristol: Policy Press.

Ebert, A., Kerle, N. and Stein, A. (2009) 'Urban social vulnerability assessment with physical proxies and spatial metrics derived from air- and spaceborne imagery and GIS data', *Natural Hazards*, 48 (2): 275-294.

Ecclestone, K. and Goodley, D. (2014) 'Political and educational springboard or straightjacket? Theorizing post/humanist subjects in an age of vulnerability', *Discourse: Studies in the Cultural Politics of Education*, doi: 10.1080/01596306.2014.927112.

Ecclestone, K. and Lewis, L. (2014) 'Interventions for resilience in educational settings: challenging policy discourses of risk and vulnerability', *Journal of Education Policy*, 29 (2): 195-216.

Egeland, B., Sroufe, L. and Erikson, M. (1983) 'Developmental consequences of different patterns of child maltreatment', *Child Abuse and Neglect*, 7: 459-69.

Elgar, F. J., Craig, W., Boyce, W., Morgan, A. and Vella-Zarb, R. (2009) 'Income inequality and school bullying: multi-level study of adolescents in 37 countries', *Journal of Adolescent Health*, 45: 351-359.

Emmel, N. and Hughes, K. (2014) 'Vulnerability, inter-generational exchange, and the conscience of generations', in Holland, J. and Edwards, R. (eds) *Understanding Families over Time: Research and Policy*, Basingstoke: Palgrave, pp 161-175.

Emmel, N., Davies, L. and Hughes, K. (2011) *The Aspirations of vulnerable Grandparents and the life Chances of their Grandchildren*, Timescapes Policy Briefing Paper Series, Leeds: Leeds Social Sciences Institute, www.lssi.leeds.ac.uk/special-reports/timescapes/

Emmel, N. D. and Hughes, K. (2010) 'Recession, it's all the same to us son? The longitudinal experience (1999-2010) of deprivation', *Journal of the Academy of Social Sciences. 21st Century Society*, 5 (2): 171-181.

Emmel, N. D., Hughes, K., Greenhalgh, J. and Sales, A. (2007) 'Accessing socially excluded people: trust and the gatekeeper in the researcher–participant relationship', *Sociological Research Online*, 12 (2): 171-191.

Erikson, E. (1968) *Identity: Youth and Crisis*, New York, NY: Norton.

Erikson, M., Egeland, B. and Pianta, R. (1989) 'Effects of maltreatment on the development of young children', in Cicchetti, D. and Carlson, V. (eds) *Child Maltreatment: Theory and Research on the Causes and Consequences of Child Abuse and Neglect*, Cambridge: Cambridge University Press.

Fairclough, N. (2001) 'Critical discourse analysis as a method in social scientific research', in Wodak, R. and Meyer, M. (eds) *Methods of Critical Discourse Analysis*, London: Sage Publications.

Fairclough, N. (2003) *Analysing Discourse*, London: Routledge.

Farrell, A. D. and Bruce, S. (1997) 'The impact of exposure to community violence on violence and emotional distress among urban adolescents', *Journal of Clinical Child Psychology*, 26: 2-14.

Fawcett, B. (2009) 'Vulnerability: questioning the certainties in social work and health', *International Journal of Social Work*, 52: 473-484.

Feeley, M. and Simon, J. (1992) 'The new penology: notes on the emerging strategy of corrections and its implications', *Criminology*, 30 (4): 452-474.

Feinstein, L. and Sabates, R. (2006) *The Prevalence of Multiple Deprivation for Children in the UK: Analysis of the Millennium Cohort and Longitudinal Survey of Young People in England*, London: Centre for Research on the Wider Benefits of Learning, Institute of Education.

Fineman, M. (2008) 'The vulnerable subject: anchoring equality in the human condition', *Yale Journal of Law and Feminism*, 20 (1): 1-23.

Fineman, M. (2013) 'Equality, autonomy and the vulnerable subject in law and politics', in Fineman, M. and Grear, A. (eds) *Vulnerability: Reflections on a New Ethical Foundation for Law and Politics*, Farnham: Ashgate, pp 13-29.

Fineman, M. and Grear, A. (eds) (2013) *Vulnerability: Reflections on a New Ethical Foundation for Law and Politics*, Farnham: Ashgate.

Fionda, J. (1998) 'Case commentary: the age of innocence? The concept of childhood in the punishment of young offenders (R v Secretary of State for the Home Department ex parte Venables and Thompson)', *Child and Family Law Quarterly*, 10 (1): 77-87.

Fionda, J. (2005) *Devils and Angels: Youth Policy and Crime*, Oxford: Hart.

Fitzpatrick, S. (2000) *Young Homeless People*, Basingstoke: Macmillan.

Fitzpatrick, S. and Jones, A. (2005) 'Pursuing social justice or social cohesion? Coercion in street homelessness policies in England', *Journal of Social Policy*, 34 (3): 389-406.

Flint, J. (2006a) 'Housing and the new governance of conduct', in Flint, J. (ed) *Housing, Urban Governance and Anti-Social Behaviour: Perspectives, Policy, Practice*, Bristol: Policy Press, pp 19-36.

Flint, J. (2006b) 'Maintaining an arm's length? Housing, community governance and the management of "problematic" populations', *Housing Studies*, 21 (2): 171-186.

Flint, J. (2009) 'Governing marginalised populations: the role of coercion, support and agency', *European Journal of Homelessness*, 3: 247-260.

Flint, J. (2012) 'The inspection house and neglected dynamics of governance: the case of domestic visits in family intervention projects', *Housing Studies*, 27 (6): 822-835.

Flint, J. and Nixon, J. (2006) 'Governing neighbours: Anti-Social Behaviour Orders and new forms of regulating conduct in the UK', *Urban Studies*, 33 (5/6): 939-955.

Flint, J. and Powell, R. (2012) 'The English city riots of 2011, "Broken Britain" and the retreat into the present', *Sociological Research Online*, 17 (3): 20.

Forsyth, A. and Furlong, A. (2003) *Losing Out? Socioeconomic Disadvantage and Experience in Further and Higher Education*, Bristol and York: Policy Press and Joseph Rowntree Foundation.

Foucault, M. (1972) *The Archaeology of Knowledge*, New York, NY: Pantheon.

Foucault, M. (1980) *Power/Knowledge: Selected Interviews and Other Writings 1972-1977*, London: Harvester Press.

Foucault, M. (1984) 'The order of discourse', in Shapiro, M. (ed) *The Language of Politics*, Oxford: Blackwell.

Foxley, B. (trans) (1974) *Emile*, London: Guernsey Press.

France, A. (2007) *Understanding Youth in Late Modernity*, Maidenhead: Open University Press.

Francis, B. (1996) 'Doctor/nurse, teacher/caretaker: children's gendered choice of adult occupation in interviews and role plays', *British Journal of Education and Work*, 9 (3): 47–58.

Francis, B. (2001) 'Is the future really female? The impact and implications of gender for 14–16 year olds' career choices', *Journal of Education and Work*, 15 (1): 75-88.

Fraser, S., Lewis, V., Ding, S., Kellet, M. and Robinson, C. (2004) *Doing Research with Children and Young People*, London: Sage Publications.

Frost, L. and Hoggett, P. (2008) 'Human agency and social suffering', *Critical Social Policy*, 28 (4): 438-460.

Fryson, R. and Yates, J. (2011) 'Anti-Social Behaviour Orders and young people with learning disabilities', *Critical Social Policy*, 31 (1): 102-125.

Fuller, C. (2009) *Sociology, Gender and Educational Aspirations: Girls and their Ambitions*, London: Continuum.

Furedi, F. (2003) *A Culture of Fear Revisited: Risk Taking and the Morality of Low Expectation* (4th edition), London: Continuum Books.

Furedi, F. (2007) *Invitation to Terror: The Expanding Empire of the Unknown*, London: Continuum.

Furedi, F. (2008) 'Fear and security: a vulnerability-led policy response', *Social Policy and Administration*, 42 (6): 645-661.

Furlong, A. and Cartmel, F. (1997) *Young People and Social Change: Individualisation and Risk in Late Modernity*, Buckingham: Open University Press.

Gallagher, J. J. (1976) 'The sacred and profane uses of labels', *Exceptional Children*, 45: 3-7.

Garland, D. (2001) *The Culture of Control*, Oxford: Oxford University Press.

Garmezy, N. (1991) 'Resiliency and vulnerability to adverse developmental outcomes associated with poverty', *American Behavioural Scientist*, 34 (4): 416-430.

Giddens, A. (1991) *Modernity and Self Identity: Self and Society in the Late Modern Age*, Cambridge: Polity Press.

Gill, T. (2007) *No Fear: Growing Up in a Risk Averse Society*, London: Calouste Gulbenkian Foundation.

Gilligan, R. (2000) 'Adversity, resilience and young people: the protective value of positive school and spare time experiences', *Children & Society*, 14: 37-47.

Glendening, N. and Carter, S. (2013) 'Psychological perspectives of vulnerability', in Heaslip, V. and Ryden, J. (eds) *Understanding Vulnerability: A Nursing and Healthcare Approach*, Chichester: Wiley-Blackman.

Goffman, E. (1959) *The Presentation of the Self in Everyday Life*, New York, NY: Anchor.

Goffman, E. (1963) *Stigma: Notes on the Management of Spoiled Identity*, Englewood-Cliffs, NJ: Prentice Hall.

Goldsmith, C. (2012) '"It just feels like it's always us": young people, peer bereavement and community safety', *Journal of Youth Studies*, 15 (5): 657-675.

Goldson, B. (2000) '"Children in need" or "young offenders"? Hardening ideology, organisational change and new challenges for social work with children in trouble', *Child and Family Social Work*, 5 (3): 255-265.

Goldson, B. (2002a) 'New Labour, social justice and children: political calculation and the deserving–undeserving schism', *British Journal of Social Work*, 32: 683-695.

Goldson, B. (2002b) 'New punitiveness: the politics of child incarceration', in Muncie, J., Hughes, G. and McLaughlin, E. (eds) *Youth Justice: Critical Readings*, London: Sage Publications.

Goldson, B. (2002c) *Vulnerable Inside: Children in Secure and Penal Settings*, London: The Children's Society.

Goldson, B. (2004) 'Victims or threats: children, care and control', in Fink, J. (ed) *Personal Lives and Social Policy*, Bristol: Policy Press, pp 78-107.

Goldson, B. (2009) 'Counterblast "difficult to understand or defend": a reasoned case for raising the age of criminal responsibility', *The Howard Journal*, 48 (5): 514–521.

Goldson, B. and Muncie, J. (2006) *Youth Crime and Justice*, London: Sage Publications.

Goodin, R. (1985) *Protecting the Vulnerable: A Re-analysis of our Social Responsibilities*, London: University of Chicago Press.

Gorman-Smith, D. and Tolan, P. H. (1998) 'The role of exposure to community violence and development problems amongst inner city youth', *Development and Psychopathology*, 10: 101–116.

Gorman-Smith, D. and Tolan, P. H. (2003) 'Positive adaptation among youth exposed to community violence', in Luthar, S. (ed) *Resilience and Vulnerability: Adaptation in the Context of Childhood Adversities*, Cambridge: Cambridge University Press, pp 392–413.

Gove, M. (2011) Statement to the House of Commons, 28 March, from *Hansard* House of Commons Debates.

Gruman, D., Tracy, W., Harachi, T., Abbott, R., Catalano, R. and Fleming, C. (2008) 'Longitudinal effects of student mobility on three dimensions of elementary school engagement', *Child Development*, 79 (6): 1833–1852.

Hagan, J. (1991) 'Destiny and drift: the risks and rewards of youth', *American Sociological Review*, 56: 567–82.

Hall, M. (2009) *Victims of Crime: Policy and Practice in Criminal Justice*, Cullompton: Willan.

Hall, S. (1996) 'Introduction: who needs identity?', in Hall, S. and du Gay, P. (eds) *Questions of Cultural Identity*, London: Sage Publications, pp 1–17.

Hammersley, M. (1992) 'What's wrong with ethnography? The myth of theoretical description', *Sociology*, 24 (4): 597–615.

Harden, J., Scott, S., Backett-Milburn, K. and Jackson, S. (2000) 'Can't talk, won't talk? Methodological issues in researching children', *Sociological Research Online*, 5 (2), www.socresonline.org.uk/5/2/harden.html

Hargreaves, D. H. (1976) 'Reactions to labelling', in Hammersely, M. and Wood, P. (eds) *The Process of Schooling*, London: Open University Press.

Harrison, E. (2013) 'Bouncing back? Recession, resilience and everyday lives', *Critical Social Policy*, 33 (1): 97–113.

Harrison, M. (2010) 'The new behaviourism, the "real third way", and housing futures: some ideas under development', paper for the HSA Conference, York, April.

Harrison, M. and Sanders, T. (2006) 'Vulnerable people and the development of "regulatory therapy"', in Dearling, A., Newburn, T. and Somerville, P. (eds) *Supporting Safer Communities: Housing, Crime and Neighborhoods*, Coventry: Chartered Institute of Housing, pp 155-168.

Harrison, M. and Sanders, T. (2014) *Social Policies and Social Control: New Perspectives on the Not-so-Big Society*, Bristol: Policy Press.

Harrison, M. with Davis, C. (2001) *Housing, Social Policy and Difference*, Bristol: Policy Press.

Harrison, M. with Hemingway, L. (2014) 'Social policy and the new behaviourism: towards a more excluding society', in Harrison, M. and Sanders, T. (eds) *Social Policies and Social Control: New Perspectives on the Not-so-Big Society*, Bristol: Policy Press.

Harrison, P. (2008) 'Corporeal remains: vulnerability, proximity, and living on after the end of the world', *Environment and Planning A*, 40: 423-445.

Harvey, D. (2005) *A Brief History of Neoliberalism*, Oxford: Oxford University Press.

Hasler, F. (2004) 'Disability, care and controlling services', in Swain, J., French, S., Barnes, C. and Thomas, C. (eds) *Disabling Barriers: Enabling Environments*, London: Sage Publications.

Haveman, R., Wolfe, B. and Spaulding, J. (1991) 'Childhood events and circumstances influencing high school completion', *Demography*, 28: 133-157.

Hayward, K. (2002) 'The vilification and pleasures of youthful transgression', in Muncie, J., Hughes, G. and McLaughlin, E. (eds) *Youth Justice: Critical Readings*, London: Sage Publications.

Heaslip, V. and Ryden, J. (eds) (2013) *Understanding Vulnerability: A Nursing and Healthcare Approach*, Chichester: Wiley-Blackman.

Heath, S., Brooks, R., Cleaver, E. and Ireland, E. (2009) *Researching Young People's Lives*, London: Sage Publications.

Henderson, J. (1994) 'Masculinity and crime: the implications of a gender conscious way of working with young men involved in "joyriding"', *Social Action*, 2 (2): 19-25.

Henderson, S., Holland, J., McGrellis, S., Sharpe, S. and Thomson, R. (2007) *Inventing Adulthoods: A Biographical Approach to Youth Transitions*, London: Sage Publications.

Hendrick, H. (2006) 'Histories of youth crime and justice', in Goldson, B. and Muncie, J. (eds) *Youth Crime and Justice*, London: Sage Publications, pp 3-17.

Hester, M., Pearson, C. and Harwin, N. (2007) *Making an Impact: Children and Domestic Violence: A Reader* (2nd edition), London: Jessica Kingsley Publishers.

Hewitt, K. (1997) *Regions of Risk: A Geographical Introduction to Disasters,* Harlow: Longman.

Hildyard, C. and Wolfe, D. (2002) 'Child neglect: developmental issues and outcomes', *Child Abuse and Neglect,* 26: 679-695.

HM Government (2009) *Pursue, Prevent, Protect, Prepare: The United Kingdom's Strategy for Countering International Terrorism,* London: The Stationery Office.

Hoggett, P. (2001) 'Agency, rationality and social policy', *Journal of Social Policy,* 30: 37-56.

Hollander, J. (2001) 'Vulnerability and dangerousness: the construction of gender through conversation about violence', *Gender & Society,* 15: 83-109.

Hollomotz, A. (2009) 'Beyond "vulnerability": an ecological model approach to conceptualizing risk of sexual violence against people with learning difficulties', *British Journal of Social Work,* 39: 99-112.

Hollomotz, A. (2011) *Learning Difficulties and Sexual Vulnerability: A Social Approach,* London: Jessica Kingsley Publishers.

Holstein, J. and Gubrium, J. (1995) *The Active Interview,* London: Sage Publications.

Holt, S., Bucklay, H. and Whelen, S. (2008) 'The impact of exposure to domestic violence on children and young people: a review of the literature', *Child Abuse and Neglect,* 32 (8): 797-810.

Home Office (1997) *No More Excuses: A New Approach To Tackling Youth Crime in England and Wales,* London: Home Office.

Home Office (2002) *Vulnerable Witnesses: A Police Service Guide,* London: Home Office.

Home Office (2011) *More Effective Responses to Anti-Social Behaviour,* London: Home Office.

Honneth, A. (1995) *The Struggle for Recognition: The Moral Grammar of Social Conflicts,* Cambridge: Polity Press.

Hooper, C.-A. (2005) 'Child maltreatment', in Bradshaw, J. and Mayhew, E. (eds) *The Well-Being of Children in the UK 2005* (vol 2), London: Save the Children/University of York.

Hopkins Burke, R. (2008) *Young People, Crime and Justice,* Cullompton: Willan.

Horwath, J. (2007) *Child Neglect: Identification and Assessment,* Basingstoke: Palgrave Macmillan.

House of Commons Education Committee (2012) *Children First: The Child Protection System in England: Fourth Report of Session 2012-13*, London: The Stationery Office.

Howe, D. (2005) *Child Abuse and Neglect: Attachment, Development and Intervention*, Basingstoke: Palgrave Macmillan.

Hudson, A. (1989) 'Troublesome girls: towards alternative definitions and policies', in Cain, M. (ed) *Growing up Good: Policing the Behaviour of Girls in Europe*, London: Sage Publications.

Hudson, A. (2002) 'Troublesome girls: towards alternative definitions and policies', in Muncie, J., Hughes, G. and McLaughlin, E. (eds) *Youth Justice: Critical Readings*, London: Sage Publications, pp 296-311.

Hughes, K. and Emmel, N. (2011) *Inter-Generational Exchange: Grandparents, their Grandchildren, and the Texture of Poverty*, Timescapes Policy Briefing Paper Series, Leeds: Leeds Social Sciences Institute, www.lssi.leeds.ac.uk/special-reports/timescapes/

Hunter, S. (2003) 'A critical analysis of approaches to the concept of social identity in social policy', *Critical Social Policy*, 23 (3): 322-344.

Hurst, S. A. (2008) 'Vulnerability in research and health care; describing the elephant in the room', *Bioethics*, 22 (4): 191-202.

Independent Police Complaints Commission (2011) *Report into the Contact between Fiona Pilkington and Leicestershire Constabulary 2004-2007*, London: Independent Police Complaints Commission.

Irwin, S. (1995) *Rights of Passage: Social Change and the Transition from Youth to Adulthood*, London: UCL Press.

Jackson, S. and Thomas, N. (1999) *On the Move Again? What Works in Creating Stability for Looked After Children*, Ilford: Barnardo's.

Jacobson, J., Bhardwa, B., Gyateng, T., Hunter, G. and Hough, M. (2010) *Punishing Disadvantage: A Profile of Children in Custody*, London: Prison Reform Trust.

James, A. and James, A. (2008) *Key Concepts in Childhood Studies*, London: Sage Publications.

James, A. and Prout, A. (1997) *Constructing and Reconstructing Childhood: Contemporary Issues in the Sociological Study of Childhood* (2nd edition), London: Falmer.

Jenks, C. (ed) (1982) *The Sociology of Childhood: Essential Readings*, London: Batsford.

Jenks, C. (2004) 'Constructing childhood sociologically', in Kehily, M. (ed) *An Introduction to Childhood Studies*, Maidenhead: McGraw-Hill.

Jessor, R., John, D. and Frances, C. (1993) *Beyond Adolescence: Problem Behavior and Young Adult Development*, New York, NY: Cambridge University Press.

Johnston, L., MacDonald, R., Mason, P., Ridley, L. and Webster, C. (2000) *Snakes and Ladders: Young People, Transitions and Social Exclusion*, Bristol: Policy Press.

Jones, O. (2011) *Chavs: The Demonization of the Working Class*, London: Verso Press.

Jones, R., Pykett, J. and Whitehead, M. (2013) 'Psychological governance and behaviour change', *Policy & Politics*, 41 (2): 159-82.

Karner, T. X. (1998) 'Engendering violent men: oral histories of military masculinity', in Bowker, L. H. (ed) *Masculinities and Violence*, London: Sage Publications, pp 197-232.

Kelly, P. (2003) 'Growing up as risky business? Risks, surveillance and the institutionalised mistrust of youth', *Journal of Youth Studies*, 3 (3): 301-315.

Kemshall, H. (2002) 'Key organising principles of social welfare and the new risk-based welfare', in Kemshall, H. (ed) *Risk, Social Policy and Welfare*, Buckingham: Open University Press.

Kendall, S., Johnson, A., Gulliver, C., Martin, K. and Kinder, K. (2004a) *Evaluation of the Vulnerable Children Grant Part I*, Slough: National Foundation for Educational Research.

Kendall, S., Johnson, A., Gulliver, C., Martin, K. and Kinder, K. (2004b) *Evaluation of the Vulnerable Children Grant Part II*, Slough: National Foundation for Educational Research.

Kintrea, K., St Clair, R. and Houston, M. (2011) *The Influence of Parents, Places and Poverty on Educational Attitudes and Aspirations*, York: Joseph Rowntree Foundation.

Kittay, E. (1999) *Love's Labor: Essays on Women, Equality and Dependency*, New York, NY: Routledge.

Lansdown, G. (1994) 'Children's rights', in Mayall, B. (ed) *Children's Childhoods: Observed and Experienced*, London: The Falmer Press, pp 33-45.

Leathers, S. J. (2002) 'Foster children's behavioural disturbance and detachment from caregivers and community institutions', *Children and Youth Services Review*, 24 (4): 239-268.

Lee, N. (2001) *Childhood and Society: Growing Up in an Age of Uncertainty*, Maidenhead: Open University Press.

Lein, H. (2009) 'The poorest and most vulnerable? On hazards, livelihoods and labelling of riverine communities in Bangladesh', *Singapore Journal of Tropical Geography*, 30 (1): 98-113.

Lemert, C. (1994) 'Dark thoughts about the self', in Calhoun, C. (ed) *Social Theory and the Politics of Identity*, Oxford: Blackwell.

Levine, C., Faden, R., Grady, C., Hammerschmidt, D., Eckenwiler, L. and Sugarman, J. (2004) 'The limitations of "vulnerability" as a protection for human research participants', *The American Journal of Bioethics*, 4 (3): 44-49.

Levitas, R. (1998) *The Inclusive Society? Social Exclusion and New Labour*, London: Macmillan.

Levitas, R. (2012) *There May Be Trouble Ahead: What we Know about those 120 00 'Troubled' Families*, Working Paper No 3, London: Poverty and Social Exclusion UK.

Lévy-Vroelant, C. (2010) 'Housing vulnerable groups: the development of a new public action sector', *International Journal of Housing Policy*, 10 (4): 443-456.

Lidstone, P. (1994) 'Rationing housing to the homeless applicant', *Housing Studies*, 9 (4): 459-472.

Lindley, S., O'Neill, J., Kandeh, J., Lawson, N., Christian, R. and O'Neill, M. (2011) *Climate Change, Justice and Vulnerability*, York: Joseph Rowntree Foundation.

Lipsky, M. (1980) *Street-Level Bureaucracy: The Dilemmas of the Individual in Public Service*, New York, NY: Russell Sage Foundation.

Lister, R. (2004) *Poverty*, Chichester: Wiley.

Lloyd, E. (2008) 'The interface between childcare, family support and child poverty strategies under New Labour: tensions and contradictions', *Social Policy and Society*, 7 (4): 479-494.

Lord Chancellor's Department (1997) *Who Decides? Making Decisions on Behalf of Mentally Incapacitated Adults*, London: Lord Chancellor's Department.

Loveland, I. (1995) *Housing Homeless Persons: Administrative Law and Process*, Oxford: Clarendon Press.

Lowe, S. (1997) 'Homelessness and the law', in Burrows, R., Pleace, N. and Quilgars, D. (eds) *Homelessness and Social Policy*, London: Routledge, pp 19-35.

Lupton, D. (1999) *Risk*, London: Routledge.

Luthar, S. (2006) 'Resilience in development: a synthesis of research across five decades', in Cicchetti, D. and Cohen, D. J. (eds) *Development Psychopathy: Risk, Disorder and Adaption*, New York, NY: Wiley.

MacDonald, R., Shildrick, T., Webster, C. and Simpson, D. (2005) 'Growing up in poor neighbourhoods: the significance of class and place in the extended transitions of "socially excluded" young adults', *Sociology*, 39: 873-891.

MacGregor, S. (2003) 'Social exclusion', in Ellison, N. and Pierson, C. (eds) *Developments in British Social Policy 2*, Basingstoke: Palgrave Macmillan.

Mackenzie, C. (2009) 'What is vulnerability', paper for the Vulnerability, Agency and Justice Conference, Sydney, August.

Mackenzie, C., Rogers, W. and Dodds, S. (2014) *Vulnerability: New Essays in Ethics and Feminist Philosophy*, Oxford: Oxford University Press.

Malin, N., Wilmot, S. and Manthorpe, J. (2002) *Key Concepts and Debates in Health and Social Policy*, Maidenhead: Open University Press.

Matthews, R. (2005) 'The myth of punitiveness', *Theoretical Criminology*, 9 (2): 175-201.

Mayall, B. (1994) *Children's Childhoods: Observed and Experienced*, London: Falmer Press.

Mayall, B. (2002) *Towards a Sociology of Childhood: Thinking from Children's Lives*, Buckingham: Open University Press.

McCarthy, J. R. (2006) *Young People's Experiences of Loss and Bereavement: Towards an Interdisciplinary Approach*, Maidenhead: Open University Press.

McDonald, P., Pini, B., Bailey, J. and Price, R. (2011) 'Young people's aspirations for education, work, family and leisure', *Work, Employment & Society*, 25 (1): 68-84.

McLaughlin, E. and Muncie, J. (2013) *The Sage Dictionary of Criminology*, London: Sage Publications.

McLaughlin, K. (2012) *Surviving Identity: Vulnerability and the Psychology of Recognition*, London: Routledge.

McLeod, J. (2012) 'Vulnerability and the neoliberal youth citizen: a view from Australia', *Comparative Education*, 48 (1): 11-26.

McNaughton, C. (2006) 'Agency, structure and biography: charting transitions through homelessness in late modernity', *Auto Biography*, 14 (2): 134-152.

McRobbie, A. (2007) 'Illegible rage: reflections on young women's post-feminist disorders', Gender Institute, Sociology and ESRC New Femininities Series, www2.lse.ac.uk/publicevents/pdf/20070125_ McRobbie.pdf .

Meers, J. (2012) 'What is meant by the term "vulnerable" in the Housing Act 1996, s.189? Is the discretion given to local housing authorities in deciding who is vulnerable too wide?', *The Student Journal of Law*, 3.

Meers, J. (2014) 'The downward drag of Pereira: ongoing disputes with vulnerability', *Critical Urbanists*, blog: https://criticalurbanists. wordpress.com/category/housing-law/

Meers, J. (2015: forthcoming) 'The downward drag of Pereira: the assessment of vulnerability under s.189 Housing Act 1996', *Journal of Social Welfare and Family Law*, 37 (2).

Melrose, M. (2013) 'Young people and sexual exploitation: a critical discourse analysis', in Melrose, M. and Pearce, J. (eds) *Critical Perspectives on Sexual Exploitation and Related Trafficking*, Basingstoke: Palgrave Macmillan, pp 9-23.

Miller, T. and Bell, L. (2002) 'Consenting to what? Issues of access, gatekeeping and "informed" consent', in Mauthner, M., Birch, M., Jessop, J. and Miller, T. (eds) *Ethics in Qualitative Research*, London: Sage Publications.

Ministry of Justice (2010) *Breaking the Cycle: Effective Punishment, Rehabilitation and Sentencing of Offenders*, London: The Stationery Office.

Ministry of Justice (2011) *Vulnerable and Intimidated Witnesses: A Police Service Guide*, London: The Stationery Office.

Misztal, B. A. (2011) *The Challenges of Vulnerability: In Search of Strategies for a Less Vulnerable Social Life*, Houndmills: Palgrave Macmillan.

Mitchell, J. K., Devine, N. and Jagger, K. (1989) 'A contextual model of natural hazards', *Geographical Review*, 79, 391-409.

Mitchell, W. and Glendinning, C. (2007) 'Risk and adult social care: what does UK research evidence tell us?', paper presented at the 'Risk and Rationalities Conference' organised by the ESRC Social Contexts and Responses Risk Network, March.

Monaghan, M. (2011) 'The recent evolution of UK drug strategies: from maintenance to behaviour change?', *People, Place and Policy Online*, 6 (1): 29-40.

Monfort, J. (2009) *Family Life: The Significance of Family Life to Homeless Young People*, London: Centrepoint.

Moon, G. (2000) 'Risk and protection: the discourse of confinement in contemporary mental health policy', *Health and Place*, 6: 239-250.

Moran-Ellis, J. (2010) 'Reflections on the sociology of childhood in the UK', *Current Sociology*, 58 (2): 186-205.

Morris, K. (2013) 'Troubled families: vulnerable families' experiences of multiple service use', *Child & Family Social Work*, 18 (2): 198-206.

Morrison Gutman, L. and Akerman, R. (2008) *Determinants of Aspirations*, London: Centre for Research on the Wider Benefits of Learning.

Mulcahy, H. (2004) '"Vulnerable family" as understood by public health nurses', *Community Practitioner*, 77 (7): 257-260.

Muncie, J. (1999) *Youth and Crime*, London: Sage Publications.

Muncie, J. (2006) 'Governing young people: coherence and contradiction in contemporary youth justice', *Critical Social Policy*, 26 (4): 770-793.

Muncie, J., Hughes, G. and McLaughlin, E. (eds) (2002) *Youth Justice: Critical Readings*, London: Sage Publications

Munro, E. and Hardy, A. (2006) *Placement Stability: A Review of the Literature*, Loughborough: Centre for Child and Family Research.

Murray, C. (1984) *Losing Ground*, New York: Basic Books.

Mythen, G. (2004) *Ulrich Beck: A Critical Introduction to the Risk Society*, London: Pluto.

National Institute for Health Research (2001) *Involving Marginalised and Vulnerable People in Research*, accessed online at www.invo.org.uk

Newman, T. and Blackburn, S. (2002) *Transitions of Young People: Resilience Factors*, Edinburgh: Scottish Executive Education Department.

NICE (National Institute for Clinical Excellence) (2007) *Community-Based Interventions to Reduce Substance Use Among the Most Vulnerable and Disadvantaged Children and Young People*, London: NICE.

Nilsen, A. (1999) 'Where is the future? Time and space as categories in the analysis of young people's images of the future', *Innovation: European Journal of the Social Sciences*, 12 (2): 175-194.

Niner, P. (1989) *Homelessness in Nine Local Authorities: Case Studies of Policy and Practice*, London: HMSO.

Nygard, M. (2009) 'Competent actors or vulnerable objects? Constructions of children and state interventions among Finnish politicians in relation to the Child Protections Act 1983 and 2006', *Social Policy & Administration*, 43 (5): 464-482.

O'Connell Davidson, J. (2011) 'Moving children? Child trafficking, child migration and child rights', *Critical Social Policy*, 31 (3): 454-477.

O'Malley, P. (2000) *Crime and Risk*, London: Sage Publications.

O'Neill, T. (2001) *Children in Secure Accommodation: A Gendered Exploration of Locked Institutional Care for Children in Trouble*, London: Jessica Kingsley Publishers.

OECD (Organisation for Economic Co-operation and Development) (2013) *Report on Integrated Service Delivery for Vulnerable Groups*, Paris: OECD.

Ofsted (2012) *After Care: Young People's Views on Leaving Care, Reported by the Children's Rights Director for England*, Manchester: Ofsted.

Palmer, J. L., Smeeding, T. M. and Boyle Torrey, B. (1988) *The Vulnerable*, Washington, DC: Urban Institute Press.

Parley, F. (2011) 'What does vulnerability mean?', *British Journal of Learning Disabilities*, 39: 266-276.

Parton, N. (2006) *Safeguarding Childhood: Early Intervention and Surveillance in Late Modern Society*, Basingstoke: Palgrave Macmillan.

Parton, N. (2007) 'Safeguarding children: a socio-historic analysis', in Wilson, K. and James, A. (eds) *The Child Protection Handbook*, Philadelphia, PA: Baillière Tindall, pp 9-30.

Passaro, J. (1996) *The Unequal Homeless: Men on the Streets, Women in their Place*, London: Routledge.

Patrick, R. (2011) 'Disabling or enabling: the extension of work-related conditionality to disabled people', *Social Policy and Society*, 10 (3): 309-320.

Patrick, R. (2014) 'Working on welfare: findings from a qualitative longitudinal study into the lived experiences of welfare reform in the UK', *Journal of Social Policy*, 43: 705-725.

Pearson, G. (1983) *Hooligan: A History of Respectable Fears*, Basingstoke: Macmillan.

Pearson, G. (2009) '"A Jekyll in the classroom, a Hyde in the street": Queen Victoria's hooligans', in Mille, A. (ed) *Securing Respect: Behavioural Expectations and Anti-Social Behaviour in the UK*, Bristol: Policy Press, pp 23-40.

Peroni, L. and Timmer, A. (2013) 'Vulnerable groups: the promise of an emergent concept in European Human Rights Convention law', *International Journal of Constitutional Law*, 11 (4): 1056-1085.

Peterson, A. and Wilkinson, I. (eds) (2008) *Health, Risk and Vulnerability*, Abingdon: Routledge.

Phoenix, J. (2002) 'In the name of protection: youth prostitution policy reforms in England and Wales', *Critical Social Policy*, 22 (2): 353-375.

Phoenix, J. (2008) 'ASBOs and working women: a new revolving door?', in Squires, P. (ed) *ASBO Nation: The Criminalisation of Nuisance*, Bristol: Policy Press, pp 289-303.

Phoenix, J. (2012a) 'Sex work, sexual exploitations and consumerism', in Carrington, K., Ball, M., O'Brien, E. and Tauri, J. (eds) *Crime, Justice and Social Democracy: International Perspectives*, Basingstoke: Palgrave Macmillan, pp 149-161.

Phoenix, J. (2012b) *Out of Place: The Policing and Criminalisation of Sexually Exploited Girls and Young Women*, London: The Howard League for Penal Reform.

Phoenix, J. (2013) 'Vulnerability', in Goldson, B. (ed) *Dictionary of Youth Justice*, London: Routledge.

Phoenix, J. and Oerton, S. (2005) *Illicit and Illegal: Sex, Regulation and Social Control*, Cullumpton: Willan.

Pinsker, D. M., McFarland, K. and Pachana, N. A. (2010) 'Exploitation in older adults: social vulnerability and personal competence factors', *Journal of Applied Gerontology*, 29: 740-761.

Piper, C. (2008) *Investing in Children: Policy, Law and Practice in Context*, Cullompton: Willan.

Pitts, J. (2000) 'The new youth justice and the politics of electoral anxiety', in Goldson, B. (ed) *The New Youth Justice*, Lyme Regis: Russell House Publishing.

Potter, T. and Brotherton, G. (2013) 'What do we mean when we talk about vulnerability?', in Brotherton, G. and Cronin, M. (eds) *Working with Vulnerable Children, Young People and Families*, London: Routledge, pp 1-15.

Pugh, J. (2014) 'Resilience, complexity and post-liberalism', *Area*, 46 (3): 313-319.

Punch, S. (2002) 'Research with children: the same or different from research with adults', *Childhood*, 9: 321-340.

Quicke, J. and Winter, C. (1994) 'Labelling and learning: an interactionist perspective', *Support for Learning*, 9: 16-21.

Raco, M. (2009) 'From expectations to aspirations: state modernisation, urban policy, and the existential politics of welfare in the UK', *Political Geography*, 28: 436-444.

Ramsay, P. (2008) *The Theory of Vulnerable Autonomy and the Legitimacy of the Civil Preventative Order*, LSE Working Papers 1/2008, London: London School of Economics and Political Science.

Ranci, C. (2009) *Social Vulnerability in Europe: The New Configuration of Social Risks*, Basingstoke: Palgrave Macmillan.

Randall, G. and Brown, S. (2001) *Trouble at Home: Family Conflict, Young People and Homelessness*, London: Crisis.

Rashed, T. and Weeks, J. (2003) 'Assessing vulnerability to earthquake hazards through spatial multicriteria analysis of urban areas', *International Journal of Geographical Information Science*, 17 (6): 547-576.

Reece, H. (2009) 'Feminist anti-violence discourse as regulation', in Sclater, S. D. (ed) *Regulating Autonomy: Sex, Reproduction and Family*, Oxford: Hart, pp 37-55.

Ribbens McCarthy, J., Hooper, C.-A. and Gilles, V. (eds) (2013) *Family Troubles? Exploring Changes and Challenges in the Family Lives of Children and Young People*, Bristol: Policy Press.

Richards, A. (2011) 'The problem with "radicalisation": the remit of "Prevent" and the need to refocus on terrorism in the UK', *International Affairs*, 87 (1): 143-152.

Riddick, B. (2000) 'An examination of the relationship between labelling and stigmatisation with special reference to dyslexia', *Disability & Society*, 15 (4): 653-667.

Robson, P. and Watchman, P. (1981) 'The homeless person's obstacle race', *Journal of Social Welfare Law*, 3 (1): 1-15.

Rochdale Borough Safeguarding Children Board (2012) *Review of Multi-Agency Responses to the Sexual Exploitation of Children*, Rochdale: Rochdale Borough Safeguarding Children Board.

Rock, P. (2002) 'On becoming a victim', in Hoyle, C. and Young, R. (ed) *New Visions of Crime and Victims*, Oxford: Hart Publishing, pp 1-22.

Rodger, J. (2008) *Criminalising Social Policy: Anti-Social Behaviour and Welfare in a De- Civilised Society*, Cullompton: Willan.

Room, G. (ed) (1995) *Beyond the Threshold: the Measurement and Analysis of Social Exclusion*, Bristol: Policy Press.

Rose, N. (1999) *Powers of Freedom: Reframing Political Thought*, Cambridge: Cambridge University Press.

Rossman, B. B. (2001) 'Time heals all: how much and for whom?', *Journal of Emotional Abuse*, 2 (1): 31-50.

Roulstone, A. and Sadique, K. (2013) '"Vulnerability" and the fight for legal recognition', in Roulstone, A. and Mason-Bish, H. (eds) *Disability, Hate Crime and Violence*, Abingdon: Routledge.

Roulstone, A., Thomas, P. and Balderson, S. (2011) 'Between hate and vulnerability: unpacking the British criminal justice system's construction of disablist hate crime', *Disability & Society*, 26 (3): 351-364.

Rousseau, J. J. (1792) *Emile*, translated by Foxley, B. (1974), London: Guernsey Press.

Runswick-Cole, K. and Goodley, D. (2014) 'You don't have to be a super-crip: reclaiming resilience in the lives of disabled people', in Cameron, C. (ed) *Disability Studies: A Student's Guide*, London: Sage Publications.

Rutherford, A. (1992) *Growing Out of Crime* (2nd edition), Winchester: Waterside Press.

Rutter, J. (2003) *Working with Refugee Children*, York: Joseph Rowntree Foundation.

Rutter, J. and Evans, B. (2011) *Listening to Grandparents*, London: Daycare Trust.

Rutter, M. (1990) 'Psychosocial resilience and protective mechanisms', in Rolf, J., Masten, A. S., Cicchenuchterkein, K. H. and Weintrab, S. (eds) *Risk and Protective Factors in the Development of Psychopathology*, Cambridge: Cambridge University Press, pp 181-215.

Sanders, T. and Campbell, R. (2007) 'Designing out vulnerability, building in respect: violence, safety and sex work policy', *British Journal of Sociology*, 58 (1): 1-19.

Sarewitz, D., Pielke, R. Jr. and Keykhah, M. (2003) 'Vulnerability and risk: some thoughts from a political and policy perspective', *Risk Analysis*, 23 (4): 805-810.

Schiller, A., de Sherbinin, A., Hsieh, W.-H. and Pulsipher, A. (2001) 'The vulnerability of global cities to climate hazards', paper presented at the Open Meeting of the Human Dimensions of Global Environmental Change Research Community, Rio de Janeiro, October.

Scoular, J. and O'Neill, M. (2007) 'Regulating prostitution: social inclusion, responsibilization and the politics of prostitution reform', *British Journal of Criminology*, 47: 764-778.

Sen, A. K. (1981) *Poverty and Famines: An Essay on Entitlement and Deprivation*, Oxford: Clarendon Press.

Sheppard, M. (2006) *Social Work and Social Exclusion: The Idea of Practice*, Aldershot: Ashgate.

Shildrick, T. and MacDonald, R. (2013) 'Poverty talk: how people experiencing poverty deny their poverty and why they blame "the poor"', *The Sociological Review*, 61: 285-303.

Shore, H. (2002) 'Reforming the juvenile: gender, justice and the child criminal in nineteenth century England', in Muncie, J., Hughes, G. and McLaughlin E. (eds) *Youth Justice: Critical Readings*, London: Sage Publications, pp 159-173.

Sinfield, A. (1978) 'Analyses in the social division of welfare', *Journal of Social Policy*, 7 (2): 129-156.

Sirriyeh, A. (2008) 'Young asylum seekers' conceptions of "home" at a time of transition to adulthood', *International Journal of Migration, Health and Social Care*, 4 (1): 12-27.

Slater, T. (2014) 'The resilience of neoliberal urbanism', published online at: www.opendemocracy.net/opensecurity/tom-slater/resilience-of-neoliberal-urbanism

Smith, R. (2003) *Youth Justice: Ideas, Policy, Practice*, Cullompton: Willan.

Social Exclusion Task Force (2007) *Reaching Out: Think Family*, London: Cabinet Office.

Social Exclusion Task Force (2008) *Think Research: Using Research Evidence to Inform Service Developments for Vulnerable Groups*, London: Cabinet Office.

Squires, P. (1990) *Anti-Social Policy: Welfare, Ideology and the Disciplinary State*, Hemel Hempstead: Harvester-Wheatsheaf.

Squires, P. (2008a) 'The politics of anti-social behaviour', *British Politics*, 3: 300-323.

Squires, P. (ed) (2008b) *ASBO Nation: The Criminalisation of Nuisance*, Bristol: Policy Press.

Squires, P. and Stephen, D. (2005) *Rougher Justice*, Cullompton: Willan.

Stainton Rogers, W., Hevey, D. and Ashe, E. (eds) (1992) *Child Abuse and Neglect: Facing the Challenge* (2nd edition), London: Batsford.

Standing, G. (2011) *The Precariat: The New Dangerous Class*, London: Bloomsbury Academic.

Strand, S. (2007) *Minority Ethnic Pupils in the Longitudinal Study of Young People in England (LSYPE)*, Research Report 002, London: Department for Children, Schools and Families.

Such, E. and Walker, R. (2005) 'Young citizens or policy objects? Children in the "rights and responsibilities" debate', *Journal of Social Policy*, 34 (1): 39-57.

Taylor-Gooby, P. (ed) (2000) *Risk, Trust and Welfare*, Basingstoke: Macmillan.

Thomson, R. and Holland, J. (2002) 'Imagined adulthood: resources, plans and contradictions', *Gender and Education*, 14 (4): 337-350.

Thomson, R., Henderson, S. and Holland, J. (2002) 'Critical moments: choice, chance and opportunity in young people's narratives of transition', *Sociology*, 36 (2): 335-354.

Timmer, A. (2013) 'A quiet revolution: vulnerability in the European Court of Human Rights', in Fineman, M. and Grear, A. (eds) *Vulnerability: Reflections on a New Ethical Foundation for Law and Politics*, Farnham: Ashgate, pp 147-171.

Titmuss, R. M. (1958) 'The social division of welfare: some reflections on the search for equity', in Titmuss, R. (ed) *Essays on the Welfare State* (2nd edition), London: Allen & Unwin, pp 34-55.

Turner, B. (2006) *Vulnerability and Human Rights*, University Park, PA: Pennsylvania State University Press.

Tyler, I. (2013) *Revolting Subjects: Social Abjection and Resistance in Neoliberal Britain*, London: Zed Books.

UNDP (United Nations Development Programme) (2014) *Human Development Report 2014: Sustaining Human Progress: Reducing Vulnerabilities and Building Resilience*, New York, NY: UNDP

Van Loon, J. (2008) 'Governmentality and the subpolitics of teenage sexual risk behaviour', in Peterson, A. and Wilkinson, I. (eds) *Health, Risk and Vulnerability*, Abingdon: Routledge.

Vonk, G. (2014) 'Homelessness and the law: challenges from the European Union', paper presented at the 21st International Conference of Europeanists, Washington, DC, 14-16 March.

Wacquant, L. (2009) *Punishing the Poor: The Neoliberal Government of Social Insecurity*, London: Duke University Press.

Waiton, S. (2001) *Scared of the Kids? Curfews, crime and the regulation of young people*, Sheffield: Sheffield Hallam University Press.

Waiton, S. (2008) *The Politics of Anti-Social Behaviour: Amoral Panics*, Abingdon: Routledge.

Walker, A. (1962) 'Special problems of delinquents and maladjusted girls', *Howard Journal of Penology and Crime Prevention*, 11: 26-36.

Walker, J. and Donaldson, C. (2011) *Intervening to Improve Outcomes for Vulnerable Young People: A Review of the Evidence*, London: Department for Education.

Wallbank, J. and Herring, J. (eds) (2013) *Vulnerabilities, Care and Family Law*, London: Routledge.

Warner, J. (2008) 'Community care, risk and the shifting locus of danger and vulnerability in mental health', in Peterson, A. and Wilkinson, I. (eds) *Health, Risk and Vulnerability*, London: Routledge, pp 30-48.

Watts, M. J. and Bohle, H. G. (1993) 'The space of vulnerability: the causal structure of hunger and famine', *Progress in Human Geography*, 17 (1): 43-67.

Waugh, F. (2008) 'Violence against children within the family', in Fawcett, B. and Waugh, F. (eds) *Addressing Violence, Abuse and Oppression: Debates and Challenges*, London: Routledge, pp 109-121.

Welsh, M. (2013) 'Resilience and responsibility: governing uncertainty in a complex world', *The Geographical Journal*, 180 (1): 15-26.

Welshman, J. (2013) *Underclass: A History of the Excluded since 1880* (2nd edition), London: Bloomsbury.

Wiles, J. (2011) 'Reflections on being a recipient of care: vexing the concept of vulnerability', *Social and Cultural Geography*, 12 (6): 573-588.

Willoughby, R. (2013) 'Notes of psychologies of vulnerability', in Brotherton, G. and Cronin, M. (eds) *Working with Vulnerable Children, Young People and Families*, Abingdon: Routledge, pp 16-35.

Winterton, M., Crown, G. and Morgan-Brett, B. (2011) *Young Lives and Imagined Futures: Insights from Archived Data*, Timescapes Working Paper Series No. 6, accessed online at www.timescapes.leeds.ac.uk/resources/publications

Wishart, G. (2003) 'The sexual abuse of people with learning difficulties: do we need a social approach model approach to vulnerability?', *The Journal of Adult Protection*, 5 (3): 14-27.

Wolfenden, J. (1957) *Report of the Committee on Homosexual Offences and Prostitution*, London: HMSO, accessed online via House of Commons parliamentary papers.

Wright, S. (2009) 'Welfare to work', in Millar, J. (ed) *Understanding Social Security: Issues for Policy and Practice* (2nd edition), Bristol: Policy Press, pp 193-212.

Young, J. (1999) *The Exclusive Society: Social Exclusion, Crime and Difference in Late Modernity*, London: Sage Publications.

Youth Justice Board (2006) *Asset*, London: Youth Justice Board.

Youth Justice Board (2014) *AssetPlus Model Document*, London: Youth Justice Board.

Zedner, L. (2006) 'Policing before and after the police: the historical antecedents of contemporary crime control', *British Journal of Criminology*, 46 (1): 78-96.

Index

Note: Page numbers in *italics* indicate tables and figures. Page numbers in **bold** indicate the young people's pen portraits.

witnesses 55
Wolfenden Report 9
women 55
see also gender; young women
work 118–119

Y

young men 92–93, 94–95, 118,
127–129, 166–169, 181
young offenders 59, 77, 132, 137–138
see also youth justice policy; Youth
Offending Service (YOS)
young people 83
perception of vulnerability 134–139
public perception of 8–9
receptiveness to vulnerability
classifications 141–144
resistance to vulnerability
classifications 139–141
as a social problem 6–7
understandings of vulnerability
127–134
vulnerable groups as cited by key
informants 75
young people's services 56–59
young women 92, 94–95, 118,
127–129, 166–169, 181
youth 29
see also childhood; young people
Youth Justice Board screening tool 59,
84
youth justice policy 13–15, 59
youth justice service 164
Youth Offending Service (YOS) 59,
79, 84, 84–85, 86, 137–138